Elementary Algebra

HARPERCOLLINS COLLEGE OUTLINE

Elementary Algebra

Joan Dykes, Ph.D.
Edison Community Collegte

 HarperPerennial
A Division of HarperCollins*Publishers*

An American BookWorks Corporation Production
Project Manager: William R. Hamill
Editor: Robert A. Weinstein

Library of Congress Catalog Card Number 90-56204
ISBN 0-06-467118-6

91 92 93 94 95 ABW/RRD 10 9 8 7 6 5 4 3 2 1

Contents

1

Number Systems and the Basics

1.1 LANGUAGE—FROM ARITHMETIC TO ALGEBRA

The four basic operations used in arithmetic—addition, subtraction, multiplication, and division—are also used in algebra. This section reviews some language and symbols from arithmetic and describes the uses of some of these familiar symbols in algebra. You may want to highlight words that are unfamiliar and refer back to this section as necessary. Variables (letters like x and y) will be used in some of the examples to represent numbers.

The basic operations

The following table reviews some of the language and symbols associated with addition, subtraction, multiplication, and division.

Operation	Symbol	Example	English Phrases
Addition	+	4 + 6	The sum of 4 and 6
			4 plus 6
			4 added to 6
Subtraction	−	5 − 2	The difference of 5 and 2
			5 minus 2
			5 less 2
			2 subtracted from 5
Multiplication	•	3 • 2	The product of 3 and 2
			3 times 2
Division	÷	6 ÷ 2	The quotient of 6 and 2
			6 divided by 2
			2 into 6

We avoid the use of x for multiplication in algebra to prevent confusion between the variable x and x to imply multiplication. Other ways to show multiplication in algebra may involve the use of parentheses.

Multiplication with Numbers	Multiplication with Variables
3(4)	$a(b)$
(3)4	$(a)b$
3)(4)	$(a)\,(b)$
No numerical equivalent	ab

When there is *no* symbol between two variables, between a variable and a number, or between a variable and a parenthesis, multiplication is implied. You *cannot* use this convention when multiplying two numbers. 34 means thirty-four, *never* 3 times 4!

There are several ways to imply division.

Division with Numbers	Division with Variables
$6 \div 2$	$a \div b$
$\dfrac{6}{2}$	$\dfrac{a}{b}$
$2\overline{)6}$	$b\overline{)a}$
$6 / 2$	a / b

Simplifying

In arithmetic, many problems contain only one of the four basic operations of addition, subtraction, multiplication, and division. In algebra, there will often be more than one operation involved. Thus, you will often see directions that say "Simplify," meaning perform any indicated operations.

Grouping symbols

The following symbols are used to group numbers together:

Symbols	Name of the Symbols
( )	Parentheses
[ ]	Brackets
{ }	Braces
| |	Absolute Value Bars
_____	Fraction Bar

When simplifying, perform operations inside parentheses, brackets, braces, and absolute value bars first. The fraction bar as a grouping symbol means to simplify above and below the bar separately.

Example 1 Simplify.

a) $(4 + 8)$
b) $[10 - 5]$
c) $\dfrac{4 + 5}{6 - 3}$

Solution 1

a) $(4 + 8) = (12) = 12$ Add inside the parentheses.
b) $[10 - 5] = [5] = 5$ Subtract inside the brackets.

c) $\dfrac{4+5}{6-3} = \dfrac{9}{3}$

$= 3$

Simplify above the bar.
Simplify below the bar.
Reduce the fraction.

Language

The numbers and/or variables involved in the four basic operations have names as given in the following table.

Example	Terms
$5 + 8 = 13$	5 and 8 are called **addends**. 13 is called the **sum**.
$10 - 1 = 9$	10 is called the **minuend**. 1 is called the **subtrhend**. 9 is called the **difference**.
$2(7) = 14$	2 and 7 are called **factors**. 14 is called the **product**.
$\dfrac{48}{4} = 12$	48 is called the **numerator**. 4 is called the **denominator**. 12 is called the **quotient**.
$6\overline{)19}$ $\dfrac{18}{1}$	19 is called the **dividend**. 6 is called the **divisor**. 3 is called the **quotient**. 1 is called the **remainder**.

1.2 SYMBOLS AND NUMBER SYSTEMS

Numbers

Although the word "algebra" usually brings to mind working with letters like x and y, a strong background in working with numbers is also essential to success. There are several number systems with which you should be familiar.

The **natural numbers** (or counting numbers) are probably the first numbers you encountered in arithmetic and consist of the numbers 1, 2, 3, 4, . . . (the three dots mean to continue the pattern).

The **whole numbers** include all of the natural numbers as well as the number 0.

The **integers** are made up of positive integers, negative integers, and 0. Thus, the whole numbers are included in the integers.

The **rational numbers** include all of the integers, as well as the fractions you encountered in arithmetic. Remember that repeating decimals and terminating decimals can be written as fractions and are therefore part of the rational numbers.

The **irrational numbers** include numbers such as π, nonrepeating, nonterminating decimals, and square roots such as $\sqrt{2}$ and $\sqrt{26}$.

The **real numbers** include both the rational numbers and irrational numbers.

Number Systems	Examples
Natural Numbers	1, 2, 3, 4, . . .
Whole Numbers	0, 1, 2, 3, . . .
Integers	. . . -3, -2, -1, 0, 1, 2, 3 . . .
Rational Numbers	$0.4, -1.33 \ldots, \frac{1}{2}, -\frac{2}{5}, 1\frac{2}{3}, -4$
Irrational Numbers	$\sqrt{2}, , \sqrt{3}$
Real Numbers	$\frac{1}{2}, \sqrt{2}, -\frac{2}{5}, 6, 3\frac{1}{3} -3$

The table below contains some examples of each type of number system.

Example 2   List the numbers in the set

$$\{\sqrt{5}, 10, -\frac{1}{4}, 0, -5, 2.75, -\sqrt{7}\}$$

that belong to each of the following number systems.

a) Natural numbers
b) Whole numbers
c) Integers
d) Rational numbers
e) Irrational numbers
f) Real numbers

Solution 2

a) 10 is the only natural number in the list.
b) Whole numbers are 10 and 0.
c) Integers are 10, 0, -5.
d) Rational numbers are $10, -\frac{1}{4}, 0, -5, 2.75$.
e) Irrational numbers are $\sqrt{5}$ and $-\sqrt{7}$.
f) Real numbers — all the numbers listed are real numbers!

Number lines and signed numbers

We often use a **number line** to picture the real numbers. We begin by drawing a line and labeling a convenient point as 0. Mark a point to the right of 0 and label it as 1. The distance between 0 and 1 gives us a way to measure and label other numbers on the number line.

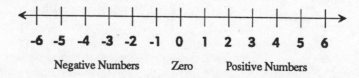

Notice that the positive numbers are located to the right of zero on the number line, and the negative numbers are located to the left of zero. Numbers increase in value from the left to the right of the number line. Note also that a negative number *must* have a negative sign preceding it, while a positive number can be written either with a positive sign preceding it or with no sign preceding it. Since fractions and decimals are real numbers, they also can be pictured (or graphed) on the number line.

Example 3   Graph the following numbers on a number line.

$2, 5, -1, -4, \frac{1}{2}, 3.8$

Solution 3   Use a point on the number line to locate each point:

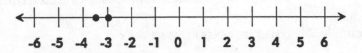

Equality and inequality symbols

We can use a number line to decide the order relationship between numbers. You will need to use the following symbols:

Symbol	English Translation	Example
<	less than	$2 < 4$
>	greater than	$5 > -1$
≤	less than or equal to	$8 \le 10$
≥	greater than or equal to	$4 \ge 4$
=	equal to	$-2 = -2$
≠	not equal to	$5 \ne 3$

When a number a is to the left of a number b on the number line, a is less than b. If c is to the right of b on the number line, c is greater than b. Consider the following number line and the inequalities it represents

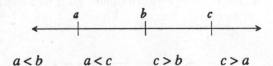

You may change the order in which an inequality is written as long as you keep the symbol "pointing" at the same number. Thus, the inequality stated above as $a < b$ can be written as $b > a$.

Although it is usually easy to compare two positive numbers, you may want to draw a number line to help you compare negative numbers.

Example 4 Insert $<$ or $>$ to make each statement true. Use a number line if you need help.

a) -1 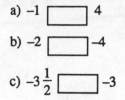 4

b) -2 $\boxed{}$ -4

c) $-3\frac{1}{2}$ $\boxed{}$ -3

Solution 4

a) $-1 < 4$ since -1 is to the left of 4.
b) $-2 > -4$ since -2 is to the right of -4.
c) You may want to draw a number line to help with this one

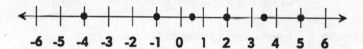

Notice that $-3\frac{1}{2}$ is to the left of -3 and, therefore,

$$-3\frac{1}{2} < -3.$$

Example 5 Write an equivalent sentence in English for each mathematical expression.

a) $0 > -2$
b) $-6 \leq 1$
c) $5 \neq 2$

Solution 5

a) 0 is greater than -2.
b) -6 is less than or equal to 1.
c) 5 is not equal to 2.

Remember that the inequality symbol points at the smaller quantity!

Absolute value

We also use a number line to define absolute value. The distance of a number *a* from zero is its **absolute value**, written $|a|$.

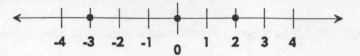

Example 6   Find the absolute value of
a) 2
b) −3
c) 0

Solution 6

You can use the number line to note that
a) $|2| = 2$ because 2 is 2 units away from 0.
b) $|-3| = 3$ because −3 is 3 units away from 0.
c) $|0| = 0$ because 0 is 0 units away from 0.

Example 7   Insert < or > to make each statement true.

a) $|4|$ ☐ $|-2|$

b) $|3|$ ☐ $|7|$

c) $|-6|$ ☐ $|9|$

d) $|-5|$ ☐ $|3|$

Solution 7   The absolute value of a number is *never* negative, so first rewrite each number using the definition of absolute value:

a) 4 ☐ 2

b) 3 ☐ 7

c) 6 ☐ 9

d) 5 ☐ 3

Now compare, picturing a number line in your head if you need to

a) 4 > 2, which means $|4| > |-2|$.
b) 3 < 7 which means $|3| < |7|$.
c) 6 < 9 which means $|-6| < |9|$.
d) 5 > 3 which means $|-5| > |3|$.

Additive inverse

We also use a number line to describe the additive inverse or **opposite** of a number. The **additive inverse** of a number *a* is the number that is the same distance from 0 as *a*, but on the opposite side of 0.

Example 8 Find the additive inverse of
a) 3
b) −2
c) 0

Solution 8

a) Using a number line, you can see that −3 is the additive inverse of 3

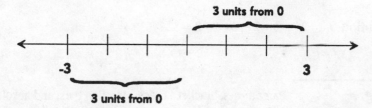

b) 2 is the additive inverse of −2.
c) 0 is the only number that is its own additive inverse.

Another way to write the additive inverse of a number is to use the symbol −. For example, the additive inverse of 3 is written −3. The additive inverse of −2 is written −(−2). Notice from Example 8 that −(−2) = 2.

1.3 EXPONENTS AND ORDER OF OPERATIONS

Exponents

We use exponents to write repeated multiplications.

Exponent or power
$$5^2 = 5 \cdot 5 = 25$$
Base

The exponent or power tells you how many times to use the base as a factor.

Exponent Form	How to Read It	Meaning
3^2	3 squared or 3 to the second power	$3 \cdot 3 = 9$
4^3	4 cubed or 4 to the third power	$4 \cdot 4 \cdot 4 = 64$
2^4	2 to the fourth power	$2 \cdot 2 \cdot 2 \cdot 2 = 16$

Example 9   Find the value of 25.

Solution 9 $2^5 = 2 \cdot 2 \cdot 2 \cdot 2 \cdot 2 = 32$

Grouping symbols

Parentheses, brackets, braces, fraction bars, and absolute value bars are all grouping symbols. Grouping symbols are used to help you decide which operation to do first.

Example 10   Simplify $(7 - 3) + | \, 6 - 4 \, |$.

Solution 10

$(7 - 3) + | \, 6 - 4 \, | = (4) + | \, 2 \, |$ Simplify within the parentheses.
                                                   Simplify within the absolute value bars.

                     $= 4 + 2$ $| \, 2 \, | = 2$.
                     $= 6$ Simplify by adding.

Order of operations

Often there will be more than one operation or one set of grouping symbols in a problem. Mathematicians have agreed upon the order of operations to be followed in solving problems.

Order of Operations
1. Simplify inside grouping symbols, starting with the innermost pair and working out.
2. Simplify exponents.
3. Perform multiplication and division steps in order from left to right.
4. Perform addition and subtraction steps in order from left to right.

You may find it helpful in remembering the order of operations to memorize the expression: **P E M D A S**, or Please Excuse My Dear Aunt Sally, which stands for Parentheses, Exponents, Multiplication, Division, Addition, Subtraction.

Example 11   Simplify $\{5 + [8 - (3-1)]\}$.

Solution 11

$$
\begin{aligned}
\{5 + [8 - (3-1)]\} &= \{5 + [8 - (2)]\} \\
&= \{5 + [6]\} \\
&= \{11\} \\
&= 11
\end{aligned}
$$

Work inside parentheses.
Work inside brackets.
Work inside braces.
Answer.

Example 12   Simplify $4 + 6 \div 2 + 3 \cdot 5 - 4$.

Solution 12

$$
\begin{aligned}
4 + 6 \div 2 + 3 \cdot 5 &= 4 + 3 + 3 \cdot 5 - 4 \\
&= 4 + 3 + 15 - 4 \\
&= 18
\end{aligned}
$$

Multiply and divide in order from left to right: $6 \div 2 = 3$.
Multiplication is next: $3 \cdot 5 = 15$.
Add and subtract in order from left to right.

Example 13   Simplify $2^3 \div 2 + 4(9 - 2^2)$.

Solution 13

$$
\begin{aligned}
2^3 \div 2 + 4(9 - 2^2) &= 2^3 \div 2 + 4(9 - 4) \\
&= 2^3 \div 2 + 4(5) \\
&= 8 \div 2 + 4(5) \\
&= 4 + 4(5) \\
&= 4 + 20 \\
&= 24
\end{aligned}
$$

Work inside parentheses. Simplify exponents.
Work inside parentheses.
Simplify exponents: $2^3 = 8$.
Divide: $8 \div 2 = 4$.
Multiply: $4(5) = 20$.
Add.

Example 14   Simplify $\dfrac{2(6-3)+8}{4(2)-6}$

Solution 14   Remember, a fraction bar is a grouping symbol! Simplify above the fraction bar and below the fraction bar separately.

$$
\frac{2(6-3)+8}{4(2)-6} = \frac{2(3)+8}{4(2)-6}
$$

Work inside parentheses.

$$
= \frac{6+8}{8-6}
$$

Multiply.

$$
= \frac{14}{2}
$$

Add in the numerator, subtract in the denominator.

$$
= 7
$$

Simplify.

1.4 ADDING REAL NUMBERS

Adding like-signed numbers

Addition of two signed numbers can be demonstrated using a number line. For example, 2 + 4 would be shown by starting at 0, drawing an arrow 2 units to the right, then drawing an arrow 4 more units to the right. Where this second arrow ends, 6 is the sum

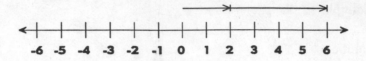

Similarly, to add (–3) + (–2), start at 0 and draw an arrow 2 units to the left to represent –2. Then draw an arrow 3 more units to the left to represent –3. This second arrow ends at –5, which is the sum

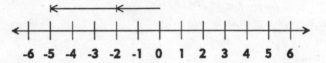

These two examples lead to the following rule:

> **Adding Numbers with Like Signs**
> 1. Add the absolute values of the numbers.
> 2. Write the common sign.

Example 15 Find the sums.
  a) 5 + 2
  b) –4 + (– 7)

Solution 15

  a) 5 + 2 = 7   Like signs of +.
  b) –4 + (–7)
     4 + 7 $|-4| = 4, |-7| = 7$
     11   Add absolute values.
     –4 + (–7) = –11   Write the common sign –.

Adding unlike-signed numbers

A number line can also be used to demonstrate adding unlike-signed numbers. For example, add 5 + (–3) by beginning with an arrow drawn from 0 to the right 5 units. Then draw an arrow from the end of that arrow 3 units to the left. The second arrow ends at the sum, which is 2:

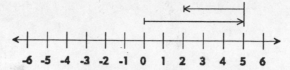

We can also show –6 + 2 on a number line. Begin at 0 and draw an arrow 6 units to the left. Then draw an arrow from the end of that arrow 2 units to the right. The second arrow ends at the sum, –4

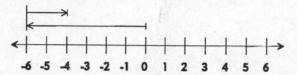

You may need to work several more examples to convince yourself that the following rules work.

Adding Signed Numbers with Unlike Signs
1. Find the absolute value of each number.
2. Subtract the number with the smaller absolute value from the number with the larger absolute value.
3. Write the sign of the number with the larger absolute value in front of the sum. (Remember that positive signs do not have to be written, but negative signs must be written.)

Example 16   Find the sums.

    a) 4 + (–2)
    b) 3 + (–7)
    c) (–6) + 9
    d) (–5) + 3

Solution 16

a) 4 + (–2)

$|4| = 4$ Larger absolute value.
$|-2| = 2$

$4 - 2 = 2$ Subtract absolute values.
$4 + (-2) = 2$ Use sign of number with larger absolute value for sign of sum.

b) 3 + (–7)

$|3| = 3$
$|-7| = 7$ Larger absolute value.

$7 - 3 = 4$ Subtract absolute values.
$3 + (-7) = -4$ Use sign of number wit[h] absolute value.

c) $(-6) + 9$
$\quad |-6| = 6$
$\quad |9| = 9$ — Larger absolute value.

$9 - 6 = 3$ — Subtract.
$(-6) + 9 = 3$ — Use sign of number with larger absolute value.

d) $(-5) + 3$
$\quad |-5| = 5$
$\quad |3| = 3$ — Larger absolute value.

$5 - 3 = 2$ — Subtract.

$(-5) + 3 = -2$ — Use sign of number with larger absolute value.

Signed numbers and grouping symbols

Example 17   Find the sums.
a) $-6 + 4 + (-8)$
b) $(-7 + 12) + [(-2) + (-6)]$
c) $-8 + 2(-4 + 7) + 6$

Solution17

a) $-6 + 4 + (-8) =$
$\quad -2 + (-8) =$ — Add from left to right.
$\quad -10$ — Like signs: add, keep sign.

b) $(-7 + 12) + [(-2) + (-6)] =$
$\quad (5) + [-8] =$ — Work inside parentheses. Work inside brackets.
$\quad -3$ — Unlike signs: use sign of number with larger absolute value.

c) $-8 + 2(-4 + 7) + 6 =$
$\quad -8 + 2(3) + 6 =$ — Work inside parentheses first.
$\quad -8 + 6 + 6 =$ — Multiply.
$\quad -2 + 6 =$ — Add from left to right.
$\quad 4$ — Unlike signs, use sign of number with larger absolute value.

1.5 SUBTRACTING REAL NUMBERS

Subtraction is actually defined in terms of addition. For example, $5 - 3$ is defined to be $5 + (-3)$, where -3 represents the additive inverse of 3. This definition leads to the following rules

---

Rules for Subtracting
1. Change the subtraction symbol to addition.
2. Write the additive inverse of the number being subtracted.
3. Use the rules for adding signed numbers.

Subtracting two numbers

Example 18 Find the differences.
a) $6 - 11$
b) $-3 - 7$
c) $8 - (-3)$
d) $-12 - (-5)$

Solution18

a) $6 - 11 = 6 + (-11)$

Change subtraction symbol to +; additive inverse of 11 is -11.

$= -5$

Unlike signs: subtract, use sign of -11.

b) $3 - 7 = -3 + (-7)$

Change subtraction symbol to +; additive inverse of 7 is $-$.

$= -10$

Like signs: add, use common sign.

c) $8 - (-3) = 8 + (+3)$

Change subtraction symbol to + additive inverse of -3 is 3.

$= 11$

Like signs, add, use common sign.

d) $-12 - (-5) = -12 + (+5)$

Change subtraction symbol to +; additive inverse of -5 is $+5$.

$= 7$

Unlike signs: subtract, use sign of -12.

Subtracting with more than two numbers

Some exercises will involve grouping symbols and order of operation rules. Remember to work inside grouping symbols first.

Example 19   Simplify each of the following
a) $2 - 6 - 5$
b) $2 - (6 - 5)$
c) $7 - (-4 + 2)$
d) $(-5 - 4) - (-7 - 1)$

Solution19

a) $2 - 6 - 5 = 2 + (-6) + (-5)$ Change subtraction symbol to +; additive inverse of 6 is –6; additive inverse of 5 is –5.

$\quad\quad\quad = -4 + (-5)$ Add from left to right.

$\quad\quad\quad = -9$ Like signs: add, use common sign.

b) $2 - (6 - 5) = 2 - (6 + (-5))$ Work inside parentheses first.

$\quad\quad\quad = 2 - (1)$ Unlike signs: subtract, use sign of 6.

$\quad\quad\quad = 2 + (-1)$ Change subtraction symbol to +; additive inverse of 1 is –1.

$\quad\quad\quad = 1$ Unlike signs: subtract, use sign of 2.

Note that examples a and b differ by a set of parentheses, which leads to different answers. If there are no grouping symbols, you must work in order from left to right. If there are grouping symbols, you must work inside them first.

c) $7 - (-4 + 2) = 7 - (-2)$ Work inside parentheses first.

$\quad\quad\quad = 7 + (2)$ Change subtraction symbol to +; additive inverse of –2 is 2.

$\quad\quad\quad = 9$ Like signs: add, use common sign.

d) $(-5 - 4) - (-7 - 1)$

$\quad\quad\quad = (-5 + (-4)) - (-7 + (-1))$ Change subtraction symbol to +; additive inverse of 4 is –4; additive inverse of 1 is –1.

$\quad\quad\quad = (-9) - (-8)$ Work inside parentheses.

$\quad\quad\quad = (-9) + (8)$ Change subtraction symbol to +; additive inverse of –8 is 8.

$\quad\quad\quad = -1$ Unlike signs: subtract, use sign of –9.

1.6 MULTIPLYING REAL NUMBERS

Multiplying two signed numbers

There are four cases to consider when multiplying two signed numbers:

1. Positive number times positive number = positive number
2. Negative number times negative number = positive number
3. Positive number times negative number = negative number
4. Negative number times positive number = negative number

> Many students remember only these two rules when multiplying two numbers:
> same signs = positive product
> different signs = negative product

Example 20 Find each product.

a) 4 (6)
b) (–2) (–5)
c) 3 (–6)
d) (–2) (8)

Solution 20

a) 4 (6) = 24   Same signs: positive product.
b) (–2) (–5) = 10   Same signs: positive product.
c) 3 (–6) = –18   Different signs: negative product.
d) (–2) (8) = –16   Different signs: negative product.

Multiplying more than two numbers

When two or more factors are involved in the multiplication, you may find the following shortcuts useful

> **Even and Odd Number of Factors**
> If there are an even number of negative factors, the product is positive.
> If there are an odd number of negative factors, the product is negative.

> **Zero as a Factor**
> If *any* factor is 0, the product is 0.

Example 21 Find each product.

a) (–6) (2) (–3) (1)
b) (–4) (–3) (–1) (2)
c) 256 (–48) (13) (0)

Solution 21

a) $(-6)(2)(-3)(1) = 36$ Two negative factors: positive product.

b) $(-4)(-3)(-1)(2) = -24$ Three negative factors: negative product.

c) $256(-48)(13)(0) = 0$ 0 as a factor makes the product 0.

Multiplying and order of operations

The following example involves order of operations and multiplication of signed numbers. Remember to work inside parentheses first, perform multiplications and divisions in order from left to right, and then perform additions and subtractions in order from left to right.

Example 22   Simplify:
a) $-8 + 2(-2)(-1)$
b) $(5 - 7)(6 - 10)$
c) $(-2)(-3)(-1) - 6[5 - (-3)]$

Solution 22

a) $-8 + 2(-2)(-1) =$
    $-8 + 4 =$ Multiply before adding, two negative factors: positive product.

    -4 Add: unlike signs.

b) $(5 - 7)(6 - 10) =$
    $(5 + (-7))(6 + (-10)) =$ Work inside parentheses first.
    $(-2)(-4) =$ Unlike signs: use sign of number with larger absolute value.

    8 Two negative factors: positive product.

c) $(-2)(-3)(-1) - 6[5 - (-3)] =$
    $(-2)(-3)(-1) - 6[5 + 3] =$ Work inside brackets first.
    $(-2)(-3)(-1) - 6[8] =$
    $-6 - 6[8] =$ Multiply from left to right.
    $-6 - 48 =$ Subtract.
    $-6 + (-48) =$
    -54 Like signs: use the common sign.

1.7 DIVIDING REAL NUMBERS

Dividing two signed numbers

There are four cases to consider when dividing two signed numbers:

1. Positive number divided by positive number = positive number
2. Negative number divided by negative number = positive number
3. Positive number divided by negative number = negative number
4. Negative number divided by positive number = negative number

---

Many students remember only these two rules when dividing two numbers:
same signs = positive quotient
different signs = negative quotient

Example 23   Divide.

a) $\dfrac{8}{2}$

b) $-6 \div -3$

c) $-5\overline{)10}$

d) $\dfrac{-12}{4}$

Solution 23

a) $\dfrac{8}{2} = 4$ Same signs: positive quotient.

b) $-6 \div -3 = 2$ Same signs: positive quotient.

c) $-5\overline{)10}^{\,-2}$ Different signs: negative quotient.

d) $\dfrac{-12}{4} = -3$ Different signs: negative quotient.

Division and zero

Division is defined in terms of multiplication.

Definition of Division
a divided by b, where b does not equal 0, is defined to be
$$\frac{a}{b} = a \cdot \frac{1}{b}, b \neq 0$$

Thus, each division problem can be rewritten as a multiplication problem.

Example 24 Rewrite each division problem as a multiplication problem.

a) $\dfrac{8}{2}$

b) $-10 \div 2$

c) $\dfrac{0}{9}$

Solution 24

a) $\dfrac{8}{4} = 8 \cdot \dfrac{1}{4}$

b) $-10 \div 2 = -10 \cdot \dfrac{1}{2}$

c) $\dfrac{0}{9} = 0 \cdot \dfrac{1}{9}$

Note in example c that 0 divided by a nonzero number equals 0 times a nonzero number, which equals 0!

Rule: 0 divided by a nonzero number equals 0
   or
   $\dfrac{0}{a} = 0$, where $a \neq 0$.

Dividing by zero

Notice in the definition of division that b, the divisor (or denominator), cannot equal 0. This leads to the following rule:

Rule: Any number divided by zero is not defined

or

$\dfrac{a}{0}$ is not defined, for any number a.

In particular, $\dfrac{0}{0}$ is *not* defined!

Example 25   Divide, if possible.

a) $\dfrac{0}{4}$

b) $\dfrac{6}{0}$

c) $\dfrac{0\,(-6)}{2}$

d) $\dfrac{0}{0}$

Solution 25

a) $\dfrac{0}{4} = 0$

b) $\dfrac{6}{0}$ is not defined.   Division by 0 is not defined.

c) $\dfrac{0\,(-6)}{2} = \dfrac{0}{2} = 0$

d) $\dfrac{0}{0}$ is not defined.   Division by 0 is not defined.

Division and order of operations

Remember that a fraction bar, which is actually a division symbol, is a grouping symbol. It separates the entire numerator from the entire denominator. Thus, you must simplify the numerator and denominator separately.

Example 26   Find each quotient.

a) $\dfrac{-10}{4-(-6)}$

b) $\dfrac{-6\,(-2)-8}{-10+6-(-3)}$

c) $\dfrac{6^2 - 3^2}{-3\,(4-5)}$

Solution 26

a) $\dfrac{-10}{4-(-6)} = \dfrac{-10}{4+6}$

Change subtraction symbol to +; additive inverse of –6 is 6.

$= \dfrac{-10}{10}$

$= -1$

Different signs: negative quotient.

b) $\dfrac{-6\,(-2)-8}{-10+6-(-3)} =$

$\dfrac{12-8}{-10+6-(3)} =$

Multiplying: same signs: positive product .

Change subtraction to adding the additive inverse.

$\dfrac{12+(-8)}{-4+3} =$

Change subtraction to adding the additive inverse.

Add from left to right.

$\dfrac{4}{-1} = -4$

Different signs: negative quotient.

c) $\dfrac{6^2-3^2}{-3\,(4-5)} =$

$\dfrac{36-9}{-3\,(4+(-5))} =$

Exponents first.

Work inside parentheses first.

$\dfrac{27}{-3\,(-1)} =$

Simplify numerator and denominator.

$\dfrac{27}{3} =$

Same signs: positive product in denominator.

9

Same signs: positive quotient.

1.8 PROPERTIES OF REAL NUMBERS

The properties of real numbers are rules that hold true for *all* real numbers (including rational and irrational numbers). The following is a list of these properties using variables, along with an example of each.

For real numbers a, b, and c:

Name	Property	Example	Look For
Commutative Property of Addition	$a + b = b + a$	$3 + 4 = 4 + 3$	Change in the order
Commutative Property of Multiplication	$a \bullet b = b \bullet a$	$4 \bullet 6 = 6 \bullet 4$	Change in the order
Associative Property of Addition	$(a+b)\,c = a + (b+c)$	$(2 + 3) + 5 = 2 + (3 + 5)$	Grouping symbols around a different pair of numbers
Associative Property of Multiplication	$(a \bullet b)\,c = a\,(b \bullet c)$	$(2 \bullet 3) \bullet 6 = 2 \bullet (3 \bullet 6)$	Grouping symbols around a different pair of numbers
Additive Identity Property	$a + 0 = a$ and $0 + a = a$	$5 + 0 = 5$ and $0 + 5 = 5$	Adding 0 to a number
Multiplicative Identity Property	$a(1) = a$ and $1(a) = a$	$6(1) = 6$ and $1(6) = 6$	Multiplying 1 times a number
Additive Inverse Property	$a + (-a) = 0$	$3 + (-3) = 0$	Adding a number and its additive inverse
Multiplicative Inverse Property	$a\left\{\dfrac{1}{a}\right\} = 1$	$6\,\dfrac{1}{6} = 1$	Multiplying a number times 1 over the number
Distributive Property	$a(b + c) = a(b) + a(c)$ and $(b + c)a = b(a) + c(a)$	$2(3 + x) = 2(3) + 2(x)$	Multiplying across parentheses

Commutative and associative properties

Example 27 State the property or properties that justify each statement.

a) $-5 + 8 = 8 + (-5)$

b) $x2 = 2x$

c) $5 + (7 + 10) = (5 + 7) + 10$

d) $6(5y) = (6 \cdot 5)y$
e) $4 + (5 + a) = (5 + a) + 4$

Solution 27

a) $-5 + 8 = 8 + (-5)$

Commutative Property of Addition. The order of the numbers changed, and addition was the operation.

b) $x2 = 2x$

Commutative Property of Multiplication. The order of the variable and number changed, and multiplication was the implied operation.

c) $5 + (7 + 10) = (5 + 7) + 10$

Associative Property of Addition. The order of the numbers 5, 7, 10 stayed the same on both sides of the equal sign. The numbers within the parentheses changed from 7 and 10 on one side, to 5 and 7 on the other side.

d) $6(5y) = (6 \cdot 5)y$

Associative Property of Multiplication. The order of the terms 6, 5, y stayed the same on both sides of the equal sign. The parentheses first grouped 5 and y, then 6 and 5.

e) $4 + (5 + a) = (5 + a) + 4$

Commutative Property of Addition. Notice only the order changed, *not* the number and variable in the parentheses.

Identity and inverse properties

0 is called the **additive identity**; 1 is called the **multiplicative identity**. The numbers a and $-a$ are called **additive inverses**. The numbers a and $\frac{1}{a}$, where $a \neq 0$ are called multiplicative inverses.

Example 28 State the property or properties that justify each statement.

a) $6 + 0 = 6$
b) $1(p) = p$
c) $x + (-x) = 0$
d) $10\left(\frac{1}{10}\right) = 1$

Solution 28

a) $6 + 0 = 6$

Additive Identity Property. Zero added to any number equals the original number.

b) $1(p) = p$

Multiplicative Identity Property. One multiplied times any number equals the original number.

c) $x + (-x) = 0$

Additive Inverse Property. x and $-x$ are called additive inverses, and they sum to 0.

d) $10 \left(\frac{1}{10} \right) = 1$

Multiplicative Inverse Property. 10 and $\frac{1}{10}$ are called multiplicative inverses, and their product is 1.

Distributive property

Example 29   Apply the Distributive Property to rewrite each of the following

a) $5(2 + 6)$
b) $4(x + y)$
c) $-2(2a + 3b)$

Solution 29

a) $5(2 + 6) = 5 \cdot 2 + 5 \cdot 6$
$= 10 + 30$

$= 40$

Apply the Distributive Property. Perform multiplications before addition.

b) $4(x + y) = 4x + 4y$

c) $-2(2a + 3b) = (-2)2a + (-2)3b$
$= -4a + (-6b)$

You can use the Associative Property here:
$(-2)(2a) = (-2 \cdot 2)a = -4a$.

Before we introduced the Distributive Property, we told you to work inside parentheses first. Note from part a in Example 29 that

$$5(2 + 6) = 5(8) = 40$$

and

$$5 \cdot 2 + 5 \cdot 6 = 10 + 30 = 40.$$

The Distributive Property guarantees that you will get the same answer whether you simplify inside the parentheses first or distribute first. We will use this property extensively when solving equations in Chapter 2.

The Distributive Property also allows you to simplify expressions such as -(5 + 8) and $-(4c - 2d)$, where the negative symbol directly preceding the parentheses means to multiply the expression in parentheses by -1.

Example 30 Simplify each of the following using the Distributive Property

    a) $-(5 + 8)$

    b) $-(4c - 2d)$

Solution 30

a) $-(5 + 8) = -1(5 + 8)$

    $= -1(5) + -1(8)$ Apply the Distributive Property.

    $= -5 + -8$ Perform multiplications before addition.

    $= -13$

b) $-(4c - 2d) = -1(4c - 2d)$ A negative symbol directly preceding the parentheses means multiply by -1.

    $= -1(4c + (-2d))$ Use rules for subtraction.

    $= -1(4c) + -1(-2d)$ Use the Distributive Property.

    $= -4c + 2d$ Use Rules for Multiplying Signed Numbers.

Combining two or more properties

Some problems will require the use of two or more properties. Refer back to the table at the beginning of this section to help you decide which ones to look for in these examples.

Example 31 State the property or properties that justify each statement.

    a) $2 + (8 + 5) = (8 + 2) + 5$

    b) $x(6y) = 6(xy)$

Solution 31

a) $2 + (8 + 5) = (2 + 8) + 5$ Associative Property of Addition.

    $= (8 + 2) + 5$ Commutative Property of Addition.

Note that first the parentheses were changed to contain 2 and 8. Then the order of the 2 and 8 was changed to $8 + 2$.

b) $x(6y) = (x6)y$ Associative Property of Multiplication.

$$= (6xy) \qquad\qquad \text{Commutative Property of}$$
Multiplication.

$$= 6(xy) \qquad\qquad \text{Associative Property of}$$
Multiplication.

Note that first the parentheses were changed to contain x and 6. Then the order of the x and 6 was changed to $6x$. Finally, the parentheses were changed to contain x and y.

1.9 OPERATIONS USING RATIONAL NUMBERS

Review of language

You have worked in the past with rational numbers and called them fractions. This section blends your past work with fractions with the signed number rules and properties of real numbers. Some language you will need is reviewed below.

Example	Language
$4 \cdot 5 = 20$	4 and 5 are **factors** of 20.
$2, 3, 5, 7, 11, \ldots$	These are a few of the **prime numbers**. A **prime number** is a number greater than 1 whose *only* factors are 1 and the number itself.
$2 \cdot 2 \cdot 5 = 20$	20 is written here as a **product of prime factors**.
$\dfrac{14}{21} = \dfrac{2 \cdot 7}{3 \cdot 7} = \dfrac{2}{3}$	$\dfrac{14}{21}$ is written in **lowest terms** as $\dfrac{2}{3}$.
$\dfrac{2}{7}$ and $\dfrac{5}{7}$	Fractions with equal denominators are called **like fractions**.

Reducing a Fraction to Lowest Terms
1. Write numerator and denominator as a product of prime factors.
2. Divide the numerator and denominator by any common factors.

Example 32   Reduce $\dfrac{30}{105}$ to lowest terms.

Solution 32

$$30 = 2 \cdot 3 \cdot 5$$
$$105 = 3 \cdot 5 \cdot 7$$

so $\dfrac{30}{105} = \dfrac{2 \cdot 3 \cdot 5}{3 \cdot 5 \cdot 7}$ Write numerator and denominator as a product of prime factors.

$= \dfrac{3 \cdot 5 \cdot 2}{3 \cdot 5 \cdot 7}$ Use Commutative Property of Multiplication to change the order in the numerator.

$= \dfrac{2}{7}$ Divide by common factors of 3 and 5.

Basic operations with fractions

Recall these basic rules for adding, subtracting, multiplying, and dividing fractions

$\dfrac{a}{b} \cdot \dfrac{c}{d} = \dfrac{ac}{bd}$	Multiplying fractions
$\dfrac{a}{b} \cdot \dfrac{c}{d} = \dfrac{a}{b} \cdot \dfrac{d}{c} = \dfrac{ad}{bc}$	Dividing fractions
$\dfrac{a}{b} + \dfrac{c}{b} = \dfrac{a+c}{b}$	Adding like fractions
$\dfrac{a}{b} - \dfrac{c}{b} = \dfrac{a-c}{b}$	Subtracting like fractions

Example 33   Perform the indicated operations. Write your answers in lowest terms.

a) $\dfrac{1}{4} \cdot \dfrac{3}{8}$

b) $\dfrac{2}{5} \div \dfrac{4}{25}$

c) $\dfrac{2}{7} + \dfrac{3}{7}$

d) $\dfrac{4}{6} - \dfrac{1}{6}$

Solution 33

a) $\dfrac{1}{4} \cdot \dfrac{3}{8} = \dfrac{3}{32}$

To multiply fractions, multiply numerators, multiply denominators.

b) $\dfrac{2}{5} \div \dfrac{4}{25} = \dfrac{2}{5} \cdot \dfrac{25}{4}$

To divide fractions, invert divisor and then multiply.

$= \dfrac{50}{20}$

Multiply the numerators, multiply the denominators.

$= \dfrac{5}{2}$

Reduce the fraction to lowest terms.

c) $\dfrac{2}{7} + \dfrac{3}{7} = \dfrac{5}{7}$

To add fractions with the same denominator, add the numerators and keep the common denominator.

d) $\dfrac{4}{6} - \dfrac{1}{6} = \dfrac{3}{6} = \dfrac{1}{2}$

To subtract fractions with the same denominator, subtract the numerators and keep the common denominator. Then reduce fraction to lowest terms.

Least common denominator

The rules in the previous section for adding and subtracting fractions are for fractions with equal denominators. If the given fractions do not have equal denominators, you will first have to rewrite them with a common denominator. There are two popular methods for finding common denominators.

Method 1 for Finding the Least Common Denominator
1. Write a list containing multiples of each denominator. Multiples are found by multiplying by 1, 2, 3, 4, etc.
2. Find the smallest number common to each list. This will be the least common denominator.

Example 34 Find the least common denominator for $\dfrac{5}{6}$ and $\dfrac{2}{9}$.

Solution 34 Multiples of 6 are 6, 12, 18, 24, 30, **36**, 42, 48, 54, 60, . . .
Multiples of 9 are 9, 18, 27, **36**, 45, 54, 63, 72, . . .

36 is the smallest number common to both lists and so is the least common denominator. Note that 54 is also common to both lists and may be used for the common denominator, but it is not the *least* common denominator.

> **Method 2 for Finding the Least Common Denominator**
> 1. Write each denominator as a product of prime factors, using exponents as necessary.
> 2. The least common denominator is the product of each factor, raised to its highest power, that appears in *any* denominator.
> 3. Simplify your answer.

Example 35 Find the least common denominator for $\frac{7}{8}$ and $\frac{1}{12}$.

Solution 35

$8 = 2 \cdot 2 \cdot 2 = 2^3$ Write each denominator as a product of prime factors.

$12 = 2 \cdot 2 \cdot 3 = 2^2 \cdot 3$

Least Common Denominator $= 2^3 \cdot 3$ Use each factor raised to its highest power, so use 2^3 and 3.

$\qquad\qquad\qquad = 8 \cdot 3$

$\qquad\qquad\qquad = 24$

Just as fractions can be reduced by dividing the numerator and denominator by any common factors, fractions can be "built up" by multiplying the numerator and denominator by a common factor.

Example 36 Write each fraction with the indicated denominator.

a) $\frac{5}{6} = \frac{}{36}$

b) $\frac{2}{9} = \frac{}{36}$

c) $\frac{7}{8} = \frac{}{24}$

d) $\frac{1}{12} = \frac{}{24}$

Solution 36

a) $\dfrac{5}{6} = \dfrac{5 \cdot 6}{6 \cdot 6}$

Since $6 \cdot 6 = 36$, multiply the numerator and denominator by 6.

$= \dfrac{30}{36}$

b) $\dfrac{2}{9} = \dfrac{2 \cdot 4}{9 \cdot 4}$

Since $9 \cdot 4 = 36$, multiply the numerator and denominator by 4.

$= \dfrac{8}{36}$

c) $\dfrac{7}{8} = \dfrac{7 \cdot 3}{8 \cdot 3}$

Since $8 \cdot 3 = 24$, multiply the numerator and denominator by 3.

$= \dfrac{21}{24}$

d) $\dfrac{1}{12} = \dfrac{1 \cdot 2}{12 \cdot 2}$

Since $12 \cdot 2 = 24$, multiply the numerator and denominator by 2.

$= \dfrac{2}{24}$

Adding and subtracting fractions— finding the common denominator

You *must* have a common denominator to use the basic rules for adding and subtracting fractions. The following rules outline the procedure.

> **Adding and Subtracting Fractions with Unlike Denominators**
> 1. Find the least common denominator by Method 1 or Method 2.
> 2. Build up each fraction to have the least common denominator by multiplying the numerator and denominator by a common factor.
> 3. Use the basic rules for adding and subtracting fractions.

Example 37 Perform the indicated operations. Write your answers in lowest terms.

a) $\dfrac{5}{6} + \dfrac{2}{9}$

b) $\dfrac{7}{8} - \dfrac{1}{12}$

Solution 37

a) $\dfrac{5}{6} + \dfrac{2}{9} = \dfrac{5}{6} \cdot \dfrac{3}{3} + \dfrac{2}{9} \cdot \dfrac{2}{2}$

The least common denominator for 6 and 9 is 18. Build up each fraction to get the least common denominator.

$= \dfrac{15}{18} = \dfrac{4}{18}$

Add numerators, keep common denominator.

$= \dfrac{19}{18}$

b) $\dfrac{7}{8} - \dfrac{1}{12} = \dfrac{7}{8} \cdot \dfrac{3}{3} - \dfrac{1}{12} \cdot \dfrac{2}{2}$

The least common denominator of 8 and 12 is 24. Build up each fraction to get the least common denominator.

$= \dfrac{21}{24} - \dfrac{2}{24}$

$= \dfrac{19}{24}$

Subtract numerators, keep common denominator

Now that you know the rules for signed numbers, you can also use these rules with fractions!

Example 38 Perform the indicated operations. Write your answers in lowest terms.

a) $\left(-\dfrac{8}{7}\right) + \left(-\dfrac{2}{3}\right)$

b) $\left(-\dfrac{3}{8}\right) + \left(-\dfrac{9}{16}\right)$

c) $\left(-\dfrac{3}{5}\right) + \left(-\dfrac{3}{10}\right)$

d) $-\dfrac{4}{7} - \left(-\dfrac{2}{3}\right)$

e) $\dfrac{7}{8} - \dfrac{11}{12}$

Solution 38

a) $\left(-\dfrac{8}{7}\right)\left(-\dfrac{2}{3}\right)=\dfrac{16}{21}$

Same signs: positive product.

b) $\left(-\dfrac{3}{8}\right)\div\left(\dfrac{9}{16}\right)=\left(-\dfrac{3}{8}\right)\left(\dfrac{16}{9}\right)$

Invert divisor and multiply.

$=-\dfrac{48}{72}$

Different signs: negative product.

$=\left(-\dfrac{2}{3}\right)$

Reduce.

c) $\left(-\dfrac{3}{5}\right)+\left(-\dfrac{3}{10}\right)=\left(-\dfrac{3}{5}\right)\cdot\dfrac{2}{2}+\left(-\dfrac{3}{10}\right)$

Build up first fraction to get the least common denominator

$=\left(-\dfrac{6}{10}\right)+\left(-\dfrac{3}{10}\right)$

$=\left(\dfrac{-6+(-3)}{10}\right)$

Add numerators, keep common denominator

$=\dfrac{-9}{10}$ or $-\dfrac{9}{10}$

d) $-\dfrac{4}{7}-\left(-\dfrac{2}{3}\right)=-\dfrac{4}{7}+\dfrac{2}{3}$

Subtract.

$=-\dfrac{4}{7}\cdot\dfrac{3}{3}+\dfrac{2}{3}\cdot\dfrac{7}{7}$

Build up each fraction to get the least common denominator.

$=\dfrac{-12}{21}+\dfrac{14}{21}$

$=\dfrac{-12+14}{21}$

Add numerators, keep common denominators.

$=\dfrac{2}{21}$

e) $\dfrac{7}{8}-\dfrac{11}{12}=\dfrac{7}{8}+\left(\dfrac{-11}{12}\right)$

Subtract.

$$= \frac{7}{8} \cdot \frac{3}{3} + \frac{-11}{12} \cdot \frac{2}{2}$$

Build up each fraction to get the least common denominator

$$= \frac{21}{24} + \frac{-22}{24}$$

$$= \frac{21 + (-22)}{24}$$

Add numerators, keep common denominator.

$$= \frac{-1}{24} \text{ or } -\frac{1}{24}$$

Practice Exercises

1. Simplify:
   (a) $(3 + 7)$
   (b) $[14 - 3]$
   (c) $6 \cdot 2$
   (d) $15 + 5$
   (e) $\dfrac{14 \cdot 2}{4 + 3}$

2. List the numbers in the set $\{-3.21, \sqrt{3}, \dfrac{1}{5}, 0, 6,$
   $-\sqrt{11}, -7$ that belong to each of the following:
   (a) Irrational numbers
   (b) Real numbers
   (c) Natural numbers
   (d) Rational numbers
   (e) Integers
   (f) Whole numbers

3. Graph the following numbers on a number line.
   $3, 6, -2, -5, \dfrac{1}{3}, 7.9, \dfrac{13}{3}, -4.1$

4. Insert $<$ or $>$ to make each statement true.
   (a) $0 \quad -2$
   (b) $3 \quad 6$
   (c) $4.6 \quad \dfrac{9}{2}$
   (d) $-2\dfrac{1}{4} \quad 2\dfrac{1}{4}$
   (e) $\sqrt{9} \quad 3.3$

5. Write an equivalent sentence in English for each of the following:
   (a) $5 \neq 3$
   (b) $2 > -4$
   (c) $1 \leq 31$
   (d) $0 \geq 0$
   (e) $-7 < -6$

6. Find the absolute value of
   (a) 8
   (b) $-4\dfrac{1}{3}$
   (c) 0
   (d) $-\sqrt{5}$
   (e) 119

7. Insert $<$ or $>$ to make each statement true.
   (a) $|3| \quad |-14|$
   (b) $|8| \quad |2|$
   (c) $|-4| \quad |7|$
   (d) $|-1| \quad |-9|$
   (e) $|0| \quad |10|$

8. Find the additive inverse.
   (a) 11
   (b) -11
   (c) 0
   (d) $-3\dfrac{1}{3}$
   (e) 2.6

9. Find the value of
   (a) 3^2
   (b) 1^7
   (c) -4^3
   (d) 2^5
   (e) -2^4

10. Simplify:
    (a) $(3 + 2) \div 5$
    (b) $|2 - 3| + 6$
    (c) $\{(9 - 3) \div |2 + 4|\}$
    (d) $7(8 \div 2) + 90$
    (e) $[|4 - 8| \bullet (6 + 3)] \bullet 5$

11. Simplify:
    (a) $\{4 + [7 - (2 - 1)]\}$
    (b) $(2 + 5^2 - 3 \div 3)$
    (c) $5 + 9 \div 3 + 2 \bullet 4$
    (d) $|-9|2 \div 3 + (4\dfrac{1}{2} - \dfrac{3}{2})$
    (e) $\{6 - (2 + 4^3) + (8 + 4^1)\}$

12. Find each sum.
    (a) $6 + 3$
    (b) $-2 + (-4)$
    (c) $-8 + (-9)$
    (d) $7 + 5$
    (e) $1 + 14$

13. Find each sum.
    (a) $5 + (-3)$
    (b) $4 + (-8)$
    (c) $(-7) + 10$
    (d) $(-6) + 4$
    (e) $0 + (-2)$

14. Find each sum.
    (a) $-5 + 3 + (-7)$
    (b) $(-6 + 13) + [(-1) + (-5)]$
    (c) $-7 + 3(-3 + 6) + 5$
    (d) $\{[2 + (-5)] + [(-3) + (-4)]\}$
    (e) $(10 + 11) + [(-10) + (-11)]$

15. Find each difference.
    (a) $3 - 6$
    (b) $-2 - 9$
    (c) $14 - (-12)$
    (d) $-8 - (-7)$
    (e) $16 - (-16)$

16. Simplify each of the following:
    (a) $1 - 5 - 4$
    (b) $1 - (5 - 4)$
    (c) $7 - (-2 + 4)$
    (d) $(-4 - 3) - (-8 - 6)$
    (e) $16 - (-16)$

17. Find each product.
    (a) $3(11)$
    (b) $(-7)(2)$
    (c) $(-6)(-4)$
    d) $5(-3)$
    (e) $(8)(1)$

18. Find each product.
    (a) $(13)(12)(11)(10)$
    (b) $(5)(-4)(0)(-9)$
    (c) $(-6)(8)(-1)(-2)$
    (d) $(-2)(-3)(-8)(0)$
    (e) $(-2)(-3)(-8)(0)$

19. Simplify.
    (a) $6 + (-3)(-4)$
    (b) $(7 + 3)(7 - 3)$
    (c) $(2)(0)(3) - 4[(2)(-1) + 7]$
    (d) $\{6[4 + (-30] - 2(4)\}$
    (e) $(-2)(-3)(-8)(0)$

20. Divide.
    (a) $\dfrac{9}{3}$
    (b) $-4 + -2$
    (c) $36 + 6$
    (d) $-\dfrac{15}{5}$
    (e) $(-7) + (-1)$

21. Rewrite each division problem as a multiplication problem.
    (a) $\dfrac{9}{3}$
    (b) $-4 + -2$
    (c) $36 + 6$
    (d) $-\dfrac{15}{5}$
    (e) $(-7) + (-1)$

22. Divide, if possible.
    (a) $\dfrac{0}{5}$
    (b) $\dfrac{3}{0}$
    (c) $\dfrac{0}{0}$
    (d) $\dfrac{0(-2)}{4}$
    (e) $\dfrac{4-4}{3}$

23. Find each quotient.
    (a) $\dfrac{2^5}{-8(1+3)}$
    (b) $\dfrac{6 + 2^2}{3 - (-7)}$
    (c) $\dfrac{2(0) + 5}{-14 + 7 - (-2)}$
    (d) $\dfrac{-14}{3 + 5 + (-1)}$
    (e) $\dfrac{6^2 - 3^2}{[3(-4) + 5]}$

24. State the property (or properties) that justifies each statement.
    (a) $-3 + 4 = 4 + (-3)$
    (b) $7 + 0 = 7$
    (c) $18(3 + x) = 18(3) + 18(x)$
    (d) $296(1) = 296$
    (e) $5(72) = 72(5)$

25. Apply the Distinctive Property to rewrite each of the following:
    (a) $3(7 + 9)$
    (b) $6(a + b)$
    (c) $-4(2x + 3y)$
    (d) $-(12s + 15t)$
    (e) $8(3 - 2)$

26. State the property (or properties) that justifies each statement.
    (a) $3 + (7 + 4) = (7 = 3) + 4$
    (b) $b(2a) = 2(ab)$

27. Perform the indicated operations. Write your answers in lowest terms.
    (a) $\dfrac{4}{2} \cdot \dfrac{2}{7}$
    (b) $\dfrac{1}{3} + \dfrac{4}{9}$
    (c) $\dfrac{4}{5} + \dfrac{7}{5}$
    (d) $\dfrac{8}{7} - \dfrac{6}{7}$
    (e) $\dfrac{0}{6} = \dfrac{7}{6}$

28. Find the least common denominator.
    (a) $\dfrac{3}{6}$ and $\dfrac{7}{9}$
    (b) $\dfrac{2}{5}$ and $\dfrac{1}{15}$
    (c) $\dfrac{7}{4}$ and $\dfrac{3}{7}$
    (d) $\dfrac{5}{2}$ and $\dfrac{4}{3}$
    (e) $\dfrac{0}{11}$ and $\dfrac{6}{13}$

29. Write each fraction with the indicated denominator.
    (a) $\dfrac{5}{7} = \dfrac{}{49}$
    (b) $\dfrac{3}{8} = \dfrac{}{24}$
    (c) $\dfrac{2}{9} = \dfrac{}{36}$
    (d) $\dfrac{1}{3} = \dfrac{}{12}$
    (e) $\dfrac{2}{3} = \dfrac{}{21}$

30. Perform the indicated operations.
    (a) $\dfrac{3}{4} - \dfrac{1}{3}$
    (b) $\dfrac{2}{7} + \dfrac{3}{14}$
    (c) $\dfrac{8}{2} + \dfrac{7}{2}$
    (d) $\dfrac{2}{9} + \dfrac{5}{6}$
    (e) $\dfrac{8}{5} - \dfrac{2}{3}$

31. Perform the indicated operations.
    (a) $\left(-\dfrac{7}{8}\right)\left(-\dfrac{2}{-3}\right)$
    (b) $\left(-\dfrac{5}{6}\right) \div \left\{\dfrac{15}{2}\right\}$
    (c) $\left(\dfrac{1}{6}\right) + \left(\dfrac{7}{2}\right)$
    (d) $\dfrac{2}{-3} - \left(\dfrac{4}{-7}\right)$
    (e) $\dfrac{7}{9} - \dfrac{5}{6}$

Answers

1. (a) 10
    (b) 11
    (c) 12
    (d) 3
    (e) 4

2. (a) $\sqrt{3}, -\sqrt{11}$

    (b) $-3.21, \sqrt{3}, \frac{1}{5}, 0, 6, -\sqrt{11}, -7$

    (c) 6

    (d) $-3.21, \frac{1}{5}, 0, 6, -7$

    (e) $0, 6, -7$
    (f) $0, 6$

3.

4. (a) >
    (b) <
    (c) >
    (d) <
    (e) <

5. (a) 5 is not equal to 3.
    (b) 2 is greater than negative 4.
    (c) 1 is less than or equal to 31.
    (d) 0 is greater than or equal to 0.
    (e) Negative 7 is less than negative 6.

6. (a) 8

    (b) $4\frac{1}{3}$

    (c) 0
    (d) $\sqrt{5}$
    (e) 119

7. (a) <
    (b) >
    (c) <
    (d) <
    (e) <

8. (a) −11
   (b) 11
   (c) 0
   (d) $3\frac{1}{3}$
   (e) −2.6

9. (a) 9
   (b) 1
   (c) −64
   (d) 32
   (e) 16

10. (a) 1
   (b) 7
   (c) 1
   (d) 118
   (e) 180

11. (a) 10
   (b) 26
   (c) 16
   (d) 30
   (e) −58

12. (a) 9
   (b) −6
   (c) −17
   (d) 12
   (e) 15

13. (a) 2
   (b) −4
   (c) 3
   (d) −2
   (e) −2

14. (a) −9
   (b) 1
   (c) 7
   (d) −10
   (e) 0

15. (a) −3
   (b) −11
   (c) 26
   (d) −1
   (e) 32

16. (a) −8
   (b) 0
   (c) 5
   (d) 7
   (e) 5

17. (a) 33
   (b) −14
   (c) 24
   (d) −15
   (e) 8

18. (a) 17,160
   (b) 0
   (c) −96
   (d) 0
   (e) 0

19. (a) 18
   (b) 40
   (c) −20
   (d) −2
   (e) 44

20. (a) 3
   (b) 2
   (c) 6
   (d) −3
   (e) 7

21. (a) $9 \cdot \frac{1}{3}$
   (b) $-4 \cdot -\frac{1}{2}$
   (c) $36 \cdot \frac{1}{6}$
   (d) $15 \cdot -\frac{1}{5}$
   (e) $-7 \cdot -1$

22. (a) 0
   (b) undefined
   (c) undefined
   (d) 0
   (e) 0

23. (a) −1
    (b) 1
    (c) −1
    (d) −2
    (e) 9

24. (a) Commutative Property of Addition
    (b) Additive Identity Property
    (c) Distributive Property
    (d) Multiplicative Identity Property
    (e) Commutative Property of Multiplication

25. (a) $3(7) + 3(9)$
    (b) $6(a) + 6(b)$
    (c) $(-4)(2x) + (-4)(3y)$
    (d) $(-1)12s + (-1)15t$
    (e) $8(3) - 8(2)$

26. (a) Commutative and Associative Properties of Addition
    (b) Commutative and Associative Properties of Multiplication

27. (a) $\dfrac{8}{21}$
    (b) $\dfrac{3}{4}$
    (c) $\dfrac{11}{5}$
    (d) $\dfrac{2}{7}$
    (e) $\dfrac{7}{6}$

28. (a) 18
    (b) 15
    (c) 28
    (d) 6
    (e) 143

29. (a) $\dfrac{35}{49}$
    (b) $\dfrac{9}{24}$
    (c) $\dfrac{8}{36}$
    (d) $\dfrac{4}{12}$
    (e) $\dfrac{14}{21}$

30. (a) $\dfrac{5}{12}$
    (b) $\dfrac{1}{2}$
    (c) $\dfrac{37}{6}$
    (d) $\dfrac{19}{18}$
    (e) $\dfrac{14}{15}$

31. (a) $\dfrac{7}{12}$
    (b) $-\dfrac{1}{9}$
    (c) $\dfrac{3}{4}$
    (d) $-\dfrac{2}{21}$
    (e) $-\dfrac{1}{18}$

2

Solving Linear Equations and Inequalities

2.1 SIMPLIFYING AND EVALUATING EXPRESSIONS

You need to be familiar with the following language:

Word	Meaning	Examples
Constant	A number	$5, -2$
Variable	A letter used to represent an unknown number	x, y, z, a, b, c
Term	A number or product of number and variable(s) raised to powers	$4, 2xy, -x^2, 5s^2r$
Numerical Coefficient	The number part of a term	In $2xy$, 2 is the numerical coefficient.
Similar or Like Terms	Terms with the same variables and exponents	$-6xy$ and $10xy$ $4x$ and $-3x$ x^2y and $5x^2y$

Note: The numerical coefficient of 1 does not need to be written. Thus, x means $1 \cdot x$, a means $1 \cdot a$, $-x$ means $-1 \cdot x$, $-a$ means $-1 \cdot a$.

Adding and subtracting similar terms

> **To Combine Similar Terms:**
> 1. Add or subtract the numerical coefficients.
> 2. Write the same variable part.

Only similar terms can be added or subtracted!

Example 1   Simplify by combining similar or like terms.

a) $-7xy - 9xy$

b) $x^2 - 5x^2$

c) $-4a + 7a + 2 - 5$

d) $2p^2 - 3p + 1 + 6p^2 - 8 + 4p$

e) $6x + 4x^2$

Solution 1

a) $-7xy - 9xy = (-7 - 9)xy$ Combine numerical coefficients.
  $= -16xy$ Write same variable part.

b) $x^2 - 5x^2 = 1x^2 - 5x^2$ x^2
  $= (1 - 5)x^2$ means $1x^2$.
       Combine numerical coefficients.
  $= -4x^2$ Write same variable part.

c) $-4a + 7a + 2 - 5$
  $= (-4 + 7)a + 2 - 5$ Combine numerical coefficients of similar terms.
  $= 3a + 2 - 5$ Write same variable part.
  $= 3a - 3$ Combine constants.

d) $2p^2 - 3p + 1 + 6p^2 - 8 + 4p$

  $= (2 + 6)p^2 + (-3 + 4)p + 1 - 8$ Combine numerical coefficients of similar terms.

  $= 8p^2 + 1p - 7$ Write same variable part, combine constants.

  $= 8p^2 + p - 7$ $1p$ is the same as p.

e) $6x + 4x^2 = 6x + 4x^2$ These are not similar terms and so cannot be added!

Simplifying expressions

An **algebraic expression** contains one or more of the four basic operations (addition, subtraction, multiplication, division), numbers, variables, and/or grouping symbols. For example,

$$5xy + 8x, \qquad 5(2x + y), \qquad \text{and} \qquad x^2 - 3x + 2$$

are algebraic expressions. To simplify expressions, we reduce the number of terms in the expression.

Simplifying Expressions
1. Follow order of operations (simplify inside grouping symbols, simplify exponents, multiply and divide in order from left to right, then add and subtract in order from left to right).
2. Remove parentheses, if necessary, using the Distributive Property.
3. Combine similar terms.

Example 2   Simplify.
a) $4(2x - 8)$
b) $-2(3m + 5)$
c) $-3(y - 2) + 4(2y + 5)$
d) $6 - 5(4a + 3)$

Solution 2

a) $4(2x - 8) = 4(2x) - 4(8)$ — Use the Distributive Property to remove parentheses.

$\quad = 8x - 32$ — Multiply. Stop here because $8x$ and 32 are not similar terms and cannot be combined further.

b) $-2(3m + 5) = -2(3m) + -2(5)$ — Use the Distributive Property.
$\quad = -6m + (-10)$ — Multiply.
$\quad = -6m - 10$ — We usually write $+ (-10)$ as $- 10$.

c) $-3(y - 2) + 4(2y + 5)$
$\quad = -3(y) - (-3)(2) + 4(2y) + 4(5)$ — Use the Distributive Property.
$\quad = -3y - (-6) + 8y + 20$ — Multiply.
$\quad = -3y + 6 + 8y + 20$ — $- (-6) = 6$.
$\quad = -3y + 8y + 6 + 20$ — Use Commutative Property to change order.

$\quad = (-3 + 8)y + (6 + 20)$ — Combine similar terms and combine constants.

$\quad = 5y + 26$

d) $6 - 5(4a + 3) = 6 + (-5)(4a) + (-5)(3)$

Follow order of operations. You *must* use the Distributive Property to multiply *before* subtracting $6 - 5$.

$$= 6 + (-20a) + (-15)$$
$$= -20a + 6 + (-15)$$

Multiply.
Use Commutative Property to change the order of 6 and -20a.

$$= -20a - 9$$

Combine constants. Stop here because -20a and 9 are not similar terms.

Evaluating expressions

We stated earlier that variables are used to represent unknown numbers. Once we know the value of a variable, we can replace that variable with its value. *Always replace a variable with a value by putting the value in parentheses.*

Example 3   Evaluate each expression using the given value of the variable(s).

a) $2x - 5; x = 3$

b) $4 - 6y; y = -2$

c) $(2p + 3q)(-2m); p = -1, q = 2, m = -3$

d) $x^2 - 3x + 2; x = 4$

Solution 3

a) $2x - 5 = 2(3) - 5$

$\quad = 6 - 5$

Replace variable using parentheses.
Multiply before adding or subtracting.

$\quad = 1$

b) $4 - 6y = 4 - 6(-2)$

$\quad = 4 - (-12)$

Replace variable using parentheses.
Multiply before adding or subtracting.

$\quad = 4 + 12$
$\quad = 16$

c) $(2p + 3q)(-2m) = [2(-1) + 3(2)][-2(-3)]$

Replace each variable using parentheses.

$\quad = [-2 + 6][6]$

Work inside parentheses first.

$\quad = [4][6]$
$\quad = 24$

d) $x^2 - 3x + 2 = (4)^2 - 3(4) + 2$

$\quad = 16 - 3(4) + 2$
$\quad = 16 - 12 + 2$

Replace variable using parentheses.
Simplify exponents first.
Multiply before adding or subtracting.

$\quad = 4 + 2$

Add and subtract in order from left to right.

$\quad = 6$

A variable may be replaced by a number, another variable, or another expression. Be careful to make replacements using parentheses.

Example 4

Simplify each expression using the given value of the variable.
a) $4x + 7; x = z$
b) $a + 5; a = 3 - c$
c) $3y; y = x + 2$
d) $4m + 8; m = n - 3$

Solution 4

a) $4x + 7 = 4(z) + 7$ Replace variable using parentheses.
  $= 4z + 7$

b) $a + 5 = (3 - c) + 5$ Replace variable using parentheses.
  $= 3 - c + 5$ $(3 - c) = 1(3 - c) = 3 - c$.
  $= 8 - c$ Combine similar terms: $3 + 5 = 8$.

c) $3y = 3(x + 2)$ Replace variable using parentheses.
  $= 3x + 3(2)$ Use Distributive Property.
  $= 3x + 6$

d) $4m + 8 = 4(n - 3) + 8$ Replace variable using parentheses.
  $= 4n - 4(3) + 8$ Use Distributive Property.
  $= 4n - 12 + 8$ Multiply before adding or subtracting.
  $= 4n - 4$ Combine similar terms.

Notice in part c that if you replace without parentheses, the expression becomes

$$3x + 2 \neq 3x + 6$$

and in part d if you replace without parentheses, the expression becomes

$$4n - 3 + 8 = 4n + 5 \neq 4n - 4.$$

2.2 ADDITION PROPERTY OF EQUALITY

An **equation** contains the following components

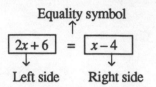

A **solution** to an equation is a number that replaces the variable and makes both sides equal. **Equivalent equations** are equations with the same solution(s). We use the Addition Property of Equality stated below to solve equations.

Addition property of equality

> **Addition Property of Equality**
> You may add the same quantity to both sides of an equation to produce equivalent equations.

Example 5   Solve and check each equation.

a) $x - 4 = 7$
b) $y - 8 = -6$
c) $m - 1 = -3$

Solution 5

a) $x - 4 + 4 = 7 + 4$ Add 4 to both sides of the equation.
   $x + 0 = 11$
   $x = 11$ 11 is the proposed solution to the given equation.

Check: We check a proposed solution to be sure it makes both sides of the equation equal. Later we will check to make sure the solution "makes sense."

$x - 4 = 7$ Original equation.

$(11) - 4 \stackrel{?}{=} 7$ Replace the variable with its proposed solution. The question mark means we are checking.

$7 = 7$ Both sides are equal, so the solution checks.

Since the proposed solution, 11, checks, $x = 11$ is the solution to the equation.

b) $y - 8 + \mathbf{8} = \text{-}6 + \mathbf{8}$

    $y + 0 = 2$

    $y = 2$

Add 8 to both sides of the equation.

2 is the proposed solution to the given equation.

Check:

    $y - 8 = \text{-}6$

    $(2) - 8 \overset{?}{=} \text{-}6$

    $\text{-}6 = \text{-}6$

Original equation.

Replace the variable with its proposed solution.

Both sides are equal, so the solution checks.

Since the proposed solution 2, checks, $y = 2$ is the solution to the equation.

c) $m - 1 + \mathbf{1} = \text{-}3 + \mathbf{1}$

    $m + 0 = \text{-}2$

    $m = \text{-}2$

Add 1 to both sides of the equation.

$\text{-}2$ is the proposed solution to the given equation.

Check:

    $m - 1 = \text{-}3$

    $(\text{-}2) - 1 \overset{?}{=} \text{-}3$

    $\text{-}3 = \text{-}3$

Original equation.

Replace the variable with its proposed solution.

Both sides are equal, so the solution checks.

Since the proposed solution, $\text{-}2$, checks, $m = \text{-}2$ is the solution to the equation.

Using the addition property of equality with subtraction

Your goal in solving these equations is to get the variable alone on one side of the equation, using the Addition Property of Equality. Because subtraction is defined as adding the additive inverse, this property also can bc used to *subtract* the same quantity from both sides of an equation.

Example 6   Solve and check each of the following.

a) $x + 5 = 8$

b) $7y = 6y - 3$

c) $2a - 4 = -6 + a$

d) $4k + 2k - 3 = -8k + 6 + 13k$

e) $3(2m - 1) - 5m = 4$

Solution 6

a) $x + 5 = 8$

$x + 5 - 5 = 8 - 5$ Subtract 5 from both sides of the equation.

$x + 0 = 3$

$x = 3$ x is alone on one side of the equation.

Check:

$x + 5 = 8$ Original equation.

$(3) + 5 \overset{?}{=} 8$ Replace the variable with its proposed solution.

$8 = 8$ Both sides are equal, so the solution checks.

$x = 3$ is the solution to the original equation.

b) $7y = 6y - 3$

$7y - \mathbf{6y} = 6y - 3 - \mathbf{6y}$ To get the variable on one side, subtract 6y from both sides of the equation.

$1y = -3$

$y = -3$ Remember that 1y is the same as y.

Check:

$7y = 6y - 3$ Original equation.

$7(-3) \overset{?}{=} 6(-3) - 3$ Replace the variable with its proposed solution.

$-21 \overset{?}{=} -18 - 3$

$-21 = -21$ Both sides are equal, so the solution checks.

$y = -3$ is the solution to the original equation.

c) $2a - 4 = -6 + a$

$2a - 4 - \mathbf{a} = -6 + a - \mathbf{a}$ To get the variable on one side, subtract a from both sides of the equation.

$a - 4 = -6$

$a - 4 + \mathbf{4} = -6 + \mathbf{4}$ To get constants on one side, add 4 to both sides of the equation.

$a = -2$

Check:

$2a - 4 = -6 + a$ Original equation.

$$2(-2) - 4 \overset{?}{=} -6 + (-2)$$

Replace the variable with its proposed solution.

$$-4 - 4 \overset{?}{=} -8$$
$$-8 = -8$$

Both sides are equal, so the solution checks.

$a = -2$ is the solution to the original equation.

d) $4k + 2k - 3 = -8k + 6 + 13k$
$\quad 6k - 3 = 5k + 6$

Begin by adding similar terms on each side.

$\quad 6k - 3 - 5k = 5k + 6 - 5k$

To get the variable on one side, subtract $5k$ from both sides of the equation.

$\quad k - 3 = 6$
$\quad k - 3 + 3 = 6 + 3$

To get constants on one side, add 3 to both sides of the equation.

$\quad k = 9$

Check: Try this check on your own. $k = 9$ is the solution.

e) $3(2m - 1) - 5m = 4$
$\quad 6m - 3 - 5m = 4$
$\quad m - 3 = 4$

Use the Distributive Property. Subtract similar terms on the left side.

$\quad m - 3 + 3 = 4 + 3$

To get constants on one side, add 3 to both sides of the equation.

$\quad m = 7$

Check: Try this check on your own. $m = 7$ is the solution.

2.3 MULTIPLICATION PROPERTY OF EQUALITY

We used the additive inverse in applying the Addition Property of Equality. We will need the reciprocal for the next step in solving equations.

Recall that the **reciprocal** or **multiplicative inverse** of a number a is $\frac{1}{a}$, $a \neq 0$.

Number	Reciprocal or Multiplicative Inverse
4	$\frac{1}{4}$
$\frac{1}{2}$	$\frac{2}{1} = 2$
-3	$-\frac{1}{3}$
$-\frac{2}{3}$	$-\frac{3}{2}$

Multiplication property of equality

An equation like $3x = 15$ cannot be solved with the Addition Property of Equality, but we have the Multiplication Property of Equality to help us:

> **The Multiplication Property of Equality**
> You may multiply both sides of an equation by the same nonzero quantity to produce equivalent equations.

Because division is defined in terms of multiplication, this property can also be used to divide both sides of an equation by the same quantity. Note that division by 0 is still not defined! Therefore, you cannot divide both sides by 0.

Example 7

Solve $\frac{1}{3}x = 6$.

Solution 7

$$3 \cdot \frac{1}{3}x = 3 \cdot 6$$ Multiply both sides of the equation by 3.

$$1x = 18$$ Multiply.
$$x = 18$$ Remember, $1x$ is the same as x.

You are probably asking, how did we decide to multiply by 3? *You multiply by the reciprocal of the numerical coefficient of the variable!*

Example 8 Solve and check.

a) $3x = 15$

b) $-4m = 8$

c) $\dfrac{a}{3} = 6$

d) $-\dfrac{2}{3}y = 12$

Solution 8

a) $3x = 15$

$$\frac{1}{3} \cdot 3x = \frac{1}{3} \cdot 15$$

Reciprocal of 3 is $\dfrac{1}{3}$. Multiply both sides by $\dfrac{1}{3}$.

$x = 5$ Proposed solution.

OR

$3x = 15$

$$\frac{3x}{3} = \frac{15}{3}$$

Divide both sides by 3.

$x = 5$

Proposed solution.

Check: $3x = 15$ Original equation.

$3(5) \overset{?}{=} 15$ Replace variable with its proposed solution.

$15 = 15$ Both sides are equal, so the solution checks.

x = 5 is the solution to the original equation.

It may be easier in some cases to divide, and in other cases to multiply, by the reciprocal of the coefficient.

b) $-4m = 8$

$$-\frac{1}{4} \cdot -4m = -\frac{1}{4} \cdot 8$$

Reciprocal of -4 is $-\dfrac{1}{4}$.

$m = -\dfrac{8}{4}$

$m = -2$

OR

$$-4m = 8$$

$$\frac{-4m}{-4} = \frac{8}{-4}$$

Divide both sides by –4.

$$m = -2$$

Check: $-4m = 8$ Original equation.

$$-4(-2) \stackrel{?}{=} 8$$ Replace the variable with its proposed solution.

$$8 = 8$$ Both sides are equal, so the solution checks.

$m = -2$ is the solution to the original equation.

c) $\frac{a}{3} = 6$

$$\frac{1}{3}a = 6$$

First rewrite $\frac{a}{3}$ as $\frac{1}{3}a$.

$$3 \cdot \frac{1}{3}a = 3 \cdot 6$$

Multiply both sides of equation by 3.

$$a = 18$$

Check: $\frac{a}{3} = 6$ Original equation.

$$\frac{(18)}{3} \stackrel{?}{=} 6$$ Replace the variable with its proposed solution.

$$6 = 6$$ Both sides are equal, so the solution checks.

$a = 6$ is the solution to the original equation.

d) $-\frac{2}{3}y = 12$

$$-\frac{3}{2} \cdot -\frac{2}{3}y = -\frac{3}{2} \cdot 12$$

Reciprocal of $-\frac{2}{3}$ is $-\frac{3}{2}$.

$$1y = -18$$

$$-\frac{3}{2} \cdot \frac{12}{1} = -\frac{3 \cdot 12}{2} = -\frac{36}{2} = -18$$

$$y = -18$$

Check: $-\frac{2}{3}y = 12$ Original equation.

$$-\frac{2}{3}(-18) \stackrel{?}{=} 12$$ Replace the variable with its proposed solution.

$$-\frac{2}{3} \cdot -\frac{18}{1} \overset{?}{=} 12$$

$$-18 = -\frac{18}{1}$$

$$\frac{-2}{3} \cdot \frac{18}{1} \overset{?}{=} 12$$

Multiply numerators, multiply denominators.

$$\frac{36}{3} \overset{?}{=} 12$$

Reduce $\frac{36}{3}$.

$$12 = 12$$

Both sides are equal, so the solution checks.

$$y = -18$$

is the solution to the original equation.

2.4 SOLVING LINEAR EQUATIONS

Let us now use the various properties together to solve linear equations.

Linear equations

A **linear equation** can be put in the form $ax + b = c$, where a, b, and c are real numbers. The following table gives examples of linear equations and of equations that are not linear.

Linear Equations	Not Linear Equations
$4x + 6 = 2$	$x^2 + 2x + 6 = 0$. Linear equations have only variables with exponents of 1.
$2x + 3 = 5x - 4$	$\sqrt{2x - 1} = 4$. Linear equations do not have variables under square root symbols.
$\frac{x}{4} = 8$	$x^3 - 8 = 0$ Linear equations have only variables with exponents of 1.
$2(x - 3) + 6 = -(x + 1) - 5$	

Solving linear equations

Solving a Linear Equation

1. Simplify the left side of the equation by removing parentheses and adding and subtracting similar terms.
2. Simplify the right side of the equation by removing parentheses and adding and subtracting similar terms.
3. Use the Addition Property of Equality to get the variable terms together on one side of the equation and the numbers on the other side of the equation.
4. Multiply both sides by the reciprocal of the numerical coefficient of the variable (or divide both sides by the numerical coefficient of the variable).

Example 9:   Solve and check each of the following:

a) $4x - 3 - 2x = 4 - x + 5$
b) $-2(x + 3) = 6(4 - 2x)$
c) $-2(4s - 6) + 8 = -3(s + 2) + 6$
d) $3(6 - 2n) - 2(3n + 4) = 16$
e) $4(p - 2) + 3p = -6 + 3p - 2$

Solution 9

a) $4x - 3 - 2x = 4 - x + 5$

$2x - 3 = -x + 9$ Combine similar terms.

$2x - 3 + x = -x + 9 + x$ Add x to both sides.

$3x - 3 = 9$

$3x - 3 + 3 = 9 + 3$ Add 3 to both sides.

$3x = 12$

$\dfrac{3x}{3} = \dfrac{12}{3}$ Divide both sides by numerical coefficient.

$x = 4$ Proposed solution.

Check: $4x - 3 - 2x = 4 - x + 5$ Original equation.

$4(4) - 3 - 2(4) \overset{?}{=} 4 - (4) + 5$ Replace the variable with its proposed solution.

$16 - 3 - 8 \overset{?}{=} 4 - 4 + 5$ Simplify each side. Be careful to follow the order of operations.

$5 = 5$ Both sides are equal, so the solution checks.

$x = 4$ is the solution to the original equation.

b) $-2(x + 3) = 6(4 - 2x)$

$-2x - 6 = 24 - 12x$ Use Distributive Property to remove parentheses.

$-2x - 6 + 12x = 24 - 12x + 12x$ Add $12x$ to both sides.

$10x - 6 = 24$

$10x - 6 + 6 = 24 + 6$

Add 6 to both sides.

$$10x = 30$$
$$\frac{10x}{10} = \frac{30}{10}$$

Divide both sides by 10.

$$x = 3$$

Check: Try the check on your own. $x = 3$ is the solution to the original equation.

c) $-2(4s - 6) + 8 = -3(s + 2) + 6$

$\quad -8s + 12 + 8 = -3s - 6 + 6$

Use Distributive Property to remove parentheses.

$\quad -8s + 20 = -3s$

Simplify left side; Simplify right side by combining similar terms.

$\quad -8s + 20 + 3s = -3s + 3s$

Add 3s to both sides of the equation.

$\quad -5s + 20 = 0$
$\quad -5s + 20 - 20 = 0 - 20$

Subtract 20 from both sides of the equation.

$\quad -5s = -20$
$\quad \dfrac{-5s}{-5} = \dfrac{-20}{-5}$

Divide both sides by –5.

$\quad s = 4$

Check: Try the check on your own. s = 4 is the solution to the original equation.

d) $3(6 - 2n) - 2(3n + 4) = 16$

$\quad 18 - 6n - 6n - 8 = 16$

Use Distributive Property to remove parentheses.

$\quad -12n + 10 = 16$

Simplify the left side by combining similar terms.

$\quad -12n + 10 - 10 = 16 - 10$

Subtract 10 from both sides.

$\quad -12n = 6$

$\quad -\dfrac{}{m} = -\dfrac{12n}{} = \dfrac{6}{-12}$

Divide both sides by –12.

$\quad n = \dfrac{1}{-2} = -\dfrac{1}{2}$

Negative in denominator is usually shown in front of fraction.

Check: Try the check on your own. $n = -\dfrac{1}{2}$ is the solution to the original equation.

e) $4(p - 2) + 3p = -6 + 3p - 2$

$\quad 4p - 8 + 3p = -6 + 3p - 2$

Remove parentheses.

$\quad 7p - 8 = -8 + 3p$

Simplify left side; simplify right side.

$\quad 7p - 8 - 3p = -8 + 3p - 3p$

Subtract 3p from both sides.

$\quad 4p - 8 = -8$

Combine similar terms.

$\quad 4p - 8 + 8 = -8 + 8$

Add 8 to both sides.

$\quad 4p = 0$

$$\frac{4p}{4} = \frac{0}{4}$$

$$p = 0$$

Divide both sides by 4.

$$\frac{0}{4} = 0.$$

Check: $4(p-2) + 3p = -6 + 3p - 2$ Original equation.

$$4((0) - 2) + 3(0) \overset{?}{=} -6 + 3(0) - 2$$

Replace the variable with the proposed solution.

$$4(-2) + 0 \overset{?}{=} -6 + 0 - 2$$

Simplify inside parentheses.

$$-8 + 0 \overset{?}{=} -6 + 0 - 2$$

Perform multiplication before addition and subtraction.

$$-8 = -8$$

Both sides are equal, so the solution checks.

$p = 0$ is the solution to the original equation.

2.5 SOLVING AND CHECKING WORD PROBLEMS

Translating words to symbols

We have already presented some words dealing with basic symbols and operations. Here are a few other translations:

Addition	Subtraction	Multiplication	Division
plus	difference	product	quotient
increased by	decreased by	times	divided by
sum	less than	double (2 times)	reciprocal
added to	minus	twice (2 times)	per
total		triple (3 times)	
more than		factor	

Memorizing these lists is *not* a substitute for reading and understanding the problem. "And" can mean to add, but Tom and Jerry does not mean Tom + Jerry!

Example 10 Translate each phrase into a mathematical expression using x as the variable.

a) 4 more than a number
b) A number increased by 6
c) 5 decreased by a number
d) 2 less than a number
e) Double a number
f) The reciprocal of a number

Solution 10

a) $4 + x$

b) $x + 6$

c) $5 - x$

d) $x - 2$ Be careful! "2 less than" means the 2 is subtracted from x.

e) $2x$

f) $\dfrac{1}{x}$

Many word problems can be translated into equations and then solved. When translating, the following words usually translate to = .

is

are

equals

was

other forms of "to be"

Number problems

Example 11 The sum of twice a number and 5 is 11. Find the number.

Solution 11 Begin by translating the English phrases into symbols. If we let x represent the number, then the problem translates to:

Twice a number	and	5	is	11
$2x$	$+$	5	$=$	11

Now solve the equation:

$2x + 5 - 5 = 11 - 5$ Subtract 5 from both sides.

$2x = 6$

$\dfrac{2x}{2} = \dfrac{6}{2}$ Divide both sides by 2.

$x = 3$ Proposed solution.

Check: With word problems, we must not only check the proposed solution in the original equation, but also check to be sure the answer makes sense.

$2x + 5 = 11$ Original equation.

$2(3) + 5 \overset{?}{=} 11$ Replace the variable with the proposed solution.

$6 + 5 \overset{?}{=} 11$ Multiply before adding.

$$11 = 11$$

Both sides are equal, so the solution checks.

The sum of twice 3 and 5 does equal 11, so the solution makes sense.

Example 12   If 4 is subtracted from the product of 5 and a number, the result is 26. Find the number.

Solution 12   product of 5 and a number   4 is subtracted from result is 26

$$5x \qquad\qquad\qquad -4 \qquad = \qquad 26$$

$$5x - 4 = 26$$
$$5x - 4 + 4 = 26 + 4 \qquad\qquad\qquad \text{Add 4 to both sides.}$$
$$5x = 30$$
$$\frac{5x}{5} = \frac{30}{5} \qquad\qquad\qquad\qquad \text{Divide both sides by 5.}$$
$$x = 6$$

Check: Try the check on your own.

Consecutive integers

Number problems may also deal with types of integers, such as consecutive integers, consecutive even integers, and consecutive odd integers. Study these examples.

Term	Using Numbers	Using Variables
Consecutive integers	4, 5, 6, 7	$x, x + 1, x + 2, x + 3$
Consecutive even integers	2, 4, 6, 8	$x, x + 2, x + 4, x + 6$
Consecutive odd integers	5, 7, 9, 11	$x, x + 2, x + 4, x + 6$

Example 13   Three times the larger of two consecutive odd integers is 17 more than the sum of the two integers. Find the integers.

Solution 13   Let x = smaller odd integer.

Then $x + 2$ = larger odd integer.

Three times the larger   is   17   more than   the sum   Translate.

$$3(x + 2) \qquad\qquad = \quad 17 \qquad + \qquad (x) + (x + 2)$$

$$3(x + 2) = 17 + (x) + (x + 2)$$
$$3x + 6 = 17 + x + x + 2 \qquad\qquad \text{Remove parentheses using Distributive Property.}$$

$$3x + 6 = 19 + 2x \qquad\qquad\qquad \text{Simplify each side of the equation.}$$
$$3x + 6 - 2x = 19 + 2x - 2x \qquad\qquad \text{Subtract } 2x \text{ from both sides.}$$
$$x + 6 = 19$$
$$x + 6 - 6 = 19 - 6 \qquad\qquad\qquad \text{Subtract 6 from both sides.}$$

$x = 13$ Proposed solution.
So $x + 2 = 15$

Check:

$3(x + 2) = 17 + (x) + (x + 2)$ Original equation.

$3((13) + 2) \stackrel{?}{=} 17 + (13) + ((13) + 2)$ Replace the variable with the
proposed solution.

$3(15) \stackrel{?}{=} 17 + 13 + (15)$ Simplify inside parentheses first.

$45 = 45$ Both sides are equal, so the
solution checks.

If the integers are 13 and 15, three times 15 is 17 more than their sum (28), so the solution makes sense.

Age problems

Consider this table for several different ages:

Age now	Age 3 years ago	Age 6 years from now
38	35	44
21	18	27
24	21	30
x	$x - 3$	$x + 6$

Now use the idea of this table to help you solve the following example.

Example 14   Joan is 16 years older than Lisa. In 5 years, the sum of their ages will be 70. Find the age of each now.

Solution 14   Let $x =$ Lisa's age now.
Then $x + 16 =$ Joan's age now.

A table may help you organize this data:

	Age Now	**Age 5 years from now**
Lisa	x	$x + 5$
Joan	$x + 16$	$x + 16 + 5$

The sum of their ages   will be   70
$(x + 5) + (x + 16 + 5)$ =   70   Translate.

$2x + 26 = 70$ Simplify the left side.
$2x + 26 - \mathbf{26} = 70 - \mathbf{26}$ Subtract 26 from both sides.

$$2x = 44$$

$$\frac{2x}{2} = \frac{44}{2}$$ Divide both sides by 2.

$$x = 22$$ Proposed solution.

So $x + 16 = 38$

The proposed solution checks in the original equation. In 5 years, Lisa will be 27 and Joan will be 43. Since $27 + 43 = 70$, the solution also makes sense. Therefore, Lisa is 22 and Joan is 38.

Example 15 Bill is twice as old as Emily. Five years ago, the sum of their ages was 32. How old are they now?

Solution 15 Let x = Emily's age now.

Then $2x$ = Bill's age now.

	Age Now	Age 5 years ago
Emily	x	$x - 5$
Bill	$2x$	$2x - 5$

the sum of their ages	was	32	Translate.
$(x - 5) + (2x - 5)$	=	32	

$$3x - 10 = 32$$ Simplify left side of equation.

$$3x - 10 + \mathbf{10} = 32 + \mathbf{10}$$ Add 10 to both sides.

$$3x = 42$$

$$\frac{3x}{3} = \frac{42}{3}$$ Divide both sides by 3.

$$x = 14$$ Proposed solution.

So $2x = 28$

Check: $(x - 5) + (2x - 5) = 32$ Original equation.

$((14) - 5) + (2(14) - 5) \overset{?}{=} 32$ Replace the variable with its proposed solution.

$(9) + (28 - 5) \overset{?}{=} 32$ Simplify inside parentheses first.

$9 + 23 \overset{?}{=} 32$

$32 = 32$ Both sides are equal, so the solution checks.

If Emily is 14 and Bill is 28, five years ago, Emily was 9 and Bill was 23. Since the sum of 9 and 23 is 32, the solution makes sense. Therefore, Emily is 14 and Bill is 28.

2.6 FORMULAS

Some formulas you may be familiar with are presented in the following table:

Formula	Formula Is Used For:	Description of the Formula
$A = LW$	Area of a rectangle	The Area of a rectangle equals the Length times the Width.
$A = \frac{1}{2}bh$	Area of a triangle	The Area of a triangle equals $\frac{1}{2}$ times the length of the base times the height.
$A = \pi r^2$	Area of a circle	The Area of a circle equals π times the radius squared.
$C = 2\pi r$	Circumference of a circle	The Circumference of a circle equals 2 times π times the radius.
$P = 4s$	Perimeter of a square	The Perimeter of a square equals 4 times the length of a side.

Notice that we often use the first letter of an important word as the variable in the formula (A for area, L for length, etc.). In the circle formulas above, π stands for the irrational number pi. You may be given a fraction or decimal approximation to replace π in some cases.

Using formulas to solve word problems

We can find the value of one of the variables if we know the values of the other variables in a formula.

Example 16 Find the length of a rectangle that has perimeter 20 feet and width 4 feet.

Solution 16 Let L = the length of the rectangle and W = the width of the rectangle. Then:

$P = 2L + 2W$	Write the formula.
$(20) = 2L + 2(4)$	Substitute the given values.
$20 = 2L + 8$	Simplify right side of equation.
$20 - 8 = 2L + 8 - 8$	Subtract 8 from both sides.
$12 = 2L$	
$\dfrac{12}{2} = \dfrac{2L}{2}$	Divide both sides by 2.

$6 = L$ Proposed solution.

Check:

$P = 2L + 2W$ Original equation.

$20 \overset{?}{=} 2(6) + 2(4)$ Replace L with the proposed solution and W with its given measurement.

$20 \overset{?}{=} 12 + 8$ Multiply before adding.

$20 = 20$ Both sides are equal, so the solution checks.

Thus, the length of a side of the rectangle is 6 feet.

Example 17   The volume of a circular cone is $V = \frac{1}{3}\pi r^2 h$, where r is the radius of the base and h is the height of the cone. If the volume is 352 cubic inches and the radius is 2 inches, find the height of the cone. Use $\frac{22}{7}$ for π.

Solution 17

$V = \frac{1}{3}\pi r^2 h$ Write the formula.

$(352) = \frac{1}{3}\left(\frac{22}{7}\right)(2)^2 h$ Substitute the given values.

$352 = \frac{1}{3}\left(\frac{22}{7}\right)4h$ Simplify exponents.

$352 = \left(\frac{88}{21}\right)h$ Simplify the right side.

$\frac{21}{88} \cdot 352 = \frac{21}{88} \cdot \left(\frac{88}{21}\right)h$ Multiply both sides by reciprocal of coefficient of h.

$84 = h$

Thus, the height of the cone is 84 inches.

Solving a formula for one of its variables   You may also need to solve a formula for one of the variables. Follow the rules for solving a linear equation to get the desired variable alone on one side of the equation.

Example 18   Solve $A = LW$ for L.

Solution 18

$$A = LW$$

Write the formula.

$$\frac{A}{W} = \frac{LW}{W}$$

The coefficient of L is W. Divide both sides by W.

$$\frac{A}{W} = L$$

$$L = \frac{A}{W}$$

Formula is now solved for L.

Example 19 Solve $y = mx + b$ for x.

Solution 19

$$y = mx + b$$

Write the formula.

$$y - b = mx + b - b$$

Subtract b from both sides of equation.

$$y - b = mx$$

$$\frac{y - b}{m} = \frac{mx}{m}$$

The coefficient of x is m. Divide both sides by m.

$$\frac{y - b}{m} = x$$

$$x = \frac{y - b}{m}$$

Formula is now solved for x.

Example 20 Solve $P = 2L + 2W$ for W.

Solution 20

$$P = 2L + 2W$$

Write the formula.

$$P - 2L = 2L + 2W - 2L$$

Subtract $2L$ from both sides.

$$P - 2L = 2W$$

$$\frac{P - 2L}{2} = \frac{2W}{2}$$

The coefficient of W is 2. Divide both sides by 2.

$$\frac{P - 2L}{2} = W$$

$$W = \frac{P - 2L}{2}$$

Formula is now solved for W.

2.7 SOLVING LINEAR INEQUALITIES

A linear inequality is similar to a linear equation, except that the equality symbol (=) is replaced by one of the four inequality symbols (<, >, ≤, ≥). The solution of a linear inequality is often graphed on a number line. We shall begin by graphing inequalities like $x < 4$ and $x > 2$.

Graphing
inequalities

> **To graph an inequality in the form $x < a$:**
> 1. Put an open circle on a.
> 2. Shade to the left of a, using an arrow to indicate that the shading continues.

> **To graph an inequality in the form $x > a$:**
> 1. Put an open circle on a.
> 2. Shade to the right of a, using an arrow to indicate that the shading continues.

If the inequality symbol is ≤ or ≥, use a closed (darkened) circle on a.

Example 21 Graph.
a) $x < 4$
b) $x \geq -1$

Solution 21

a) To graph $x < 4$, begin by putting an open circle on 4. Next, shade to the *left* of 4:

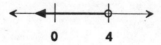

b) To graph $x \geq -1$, begin by putting a closed circle on -1. Next, shade to the *right* of -1:

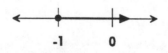

Example 22
Graph.
a) $2 < x$
b) $-3 \geq x$

Solution 22

a) First rewrite the inequality to get the variable on the left. $2 < x$ is equivalent to $x > 2$. Remember to keep the inequality symbol "pointing" at the 2. To graph $x > 2$, put on open circle on 2. Next, shade to the *right* of 2:

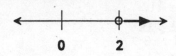

b) First rewrite the inequality to get the variable on the left. $-3 > x$ is equivalent to $x \leq -3$. Remember to keep the inequality symbol "pointing" at the x. To graph $x \leq -3$, put a closed circle on -3. Next, shade to the *left* of -3:

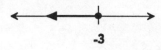

Solving linear inequalities

We solve linear inequalities almost the same way we solve linear equations. Here are the rules:

To Solve a Linear Inequality
1. Simplify the left side of the inequality by removing parentheses and adding and subtracting similar terms.
2. Simplify the right side of the inequality by removing parentheses and adding and subtracting similar terms.
3. Use addition to get the variable terms together on one side of the inequality and the numbers on the other side of the inequality.
4. Multiply both sides by the reciprocal of the numerical coefficient of the variable (or divide both sides by the numerical coefficient of the variable).
5. *If you multiply (or divide) by a negative number, you must reverse the inequality symbol.*

The exception to the rules for linear equations occurs in the last step. If you multiply or divide by a negative number, make one of the following changes:

Multiplying or Dividing by a Negative	
Change:	To:
>	<
<	>
≥	≤
≤	≥

Example 23 Solve and graph.

    a) $3x < 12$

    b) $-2x \leq 2$

Solution 23

a) $3x < 12$ Divide both sides by 3.

$\dfrac{3x}{3} < \dfrac{12}{3}$

                                        Solution.

$x < 4$

Put an open circle on 4.

Next, shade to the *left* of 4:

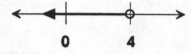

b) $-2x \leq 2$

$\dfrac{-2x}{-2} \geq \dfrac{2}{-2}$ Divide both sides by -2.

                                      Reverse the inequality symbol.

$x \geq -1$ Solution.

Put a closed circle on -1.

Next, shade to the *right* of -1:

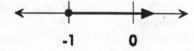

Example 24:

Solve and graph.

    a) $4(x-6) \leq -8$

    b) $4(x+1) - 7 + 2x > 5 + 2x$

Solution 24

a) $4(x-6) \leq -8$

   $4x - 24 \leq -8$ Remove parentheses using the

                                      Distributive Property.

   $4x - 24 + 24 \leq -8 + 24$ Add 24 to both sides.

   $4x \leq 16$

   $\dfrac{4x}{4} \leq \dfrac{16}{4}$ Divide both sides by 4.

   $x \leq 4$ Solution.

Put a closed circle on 4.
Next, shade to the *left* of 4:

b) $4(x + 1) - 7 + 2x > 5 + 2x$

$\quad 4x + 4 - 7 + 2x > 5 + 2x$ Remove parentheses by using the Distributive Property.

$\quad 6x - 3 > 5 + 2x$ Combine similar terms.

$\quad 6x - 3 - 2x > 5 + 2x - 2x$ Subtract $2x$ from both sides.

$\quad 4x - 3 > 5$

$\quad 4x - 3 + 3 > 5 + 3$ Add 3 to both sides.

$\quad 4x > 8$

$\quad \dfrac{4x}{4} > \dfrac{8}{4}$ Divide both sides by 4.

$\quad x > 2$ Solution.

Put an open circle on 2.
Next, shade to the *right* of 2:

Solving word problems with linear inequalities

You may need to solve word problems that involve inequalities. Some language translations are given below; x represents "the number."

The number is at most	$x \leq$
The number is at least	$x \geq$
The number is more than	$x >$
The number is less than	$x <$

Example 25   The sum of two consecutive odd integers is at most 32. What are the possibilities for the first of the two integers?

Solution 25   Let x = first odd integer.
Then $x + 2$ = next consecutive odd integer.

the sum	is at most	32	
$(x) + (x + 2)$	$\leq$	32	Translate.

$x + x + 2 \leq 32$

$2x + 2 \leq 32$ Combine similar terms.

$2x + 2 - 2 \leq 32 - 2$ Subtract 2 from both sides.

$2x \leq 30$

$\dfrac{2x}{2} \leq \dfrac{20}{2}$ Divide both sides by 2.

$x \leq 15$ Solution.

The first integer must be an odd integer less than or equal to 15, and the next consecutive odd integer must be less than or equal to 17. Then their sum must be **less than or equal to** 15 + 17 = 32. Thus, $x \leq 15$ checks.

Practice Exercises

1. Simplify by combining similar or like terms.
   (a) $2uv - 3uv$
   (b) $-7y^3 + y^3$
   (c) $11x + 5x - 6 + 4$
   (d) $6x^2 - 1 + 3x - 7x^2 - 9x + 8$
   (e) $p + 9p^2$

2. Simplify.
   (a) $7(3p + 2)$
   (b) $-4(6x - 8)$
   (c) $2(9t + 4s) - 3(2t - 8s)$
   (d) $6 + 2(4a - 3)$
   (e) $5(1 - 6a) + 7(2 - 3b)$

3. Evaluate each expression using the given value of the variablc(s).
   (a) $7y - 5; y = 2$
   (b) $4x + 6; x = -4$
   (c) $(6p - 3q)(4); p = 1, q = -3$
   (d) $t^2 - 3t + 9; t = 8$
   (e) $(4p - 3q)(p^2 - 4q + p); p = 2, q = -1$

4. Simplify each expression using the given value of the variable.
   (a) $3x + 4$ if $x = z$
   (b) $-2a + 5$ if $a = 9 - b$
   (c) $8y$ if $y = z - x + 2$
   (d) $4n - 3$ if $n = m - 1$
   (e) $-z - 2$ if $z = x + 3$

5. Solve and check each equation.
   (a) $2x + 6 = 4$
   (b) $x - 3 = 7$
   (c) $y + 9 = 12$
   (d) $8(y - 2) = 16$
   (e) $6m + 5 = 1$

6. Solve and check each equation.
   (a) $p + 4 = 7$
   (b) $6t = 5t - 2$
   (c) $a - 3 = -7 + 2a$
   (d) $8s + 3s - 9 = -16s + 3 + 3s$
   (e) $5m + 2(3m - 1) = 9$

7. Solve.
   (a) $\frac{1}{4}y = 8$
   (b) $-2x = 14$
   (c) $\frac{a}{7} = 21$
   (d) $-\frac{2}{3}t = 24$
   (e) $14b = 84$

8. Solve and check each equation.
   (a) $4(6 - n) - 3(8n + 9) = 12$
   (b) $2x - 5 + 4x = 3 - 7x + 9$
   (c) $3(p + 9) = 9(p + 3)$
   (d) $12y(2 - 8) - 12y = 0$
   (e) $11t - 2(t + 3) = 4 + t - 2t$

9. Translate each phrase into a mathematical expression using x.
   (a) The reciprocal of a number.
   (b) A number increased by 7.
   (c) Triple a number.
   (d) 4 more than twice a number.
   (e) 3 less than a number decreased by 2.

10. Find the numbers.
    (a) The difference of a number and 5 is 6.
    (b) If 8 is added to the product of 2 and a number, the result is 14.
    (c) A number is tripled and added to 9. The result is six times the number itself.
    (d) A number divided by 5 and added to 20 is the number itself.
    (e) The sum of 12 divided by a number and 7 is 10.

11. Solve.
    (a) Two times the smallest of three consecutive odd integers is one less than the largest integer. Find the integers.
    (b) 6 less than the middle integer of 3 consecutive even integers is 30 less than the sum of the other two integers. Find the integers.
    (c) Lisa is 11 years younger than James. In 12 years, James will be twice as old as Lisa is now. How old is James?
    (d) Bill is 4 years younger than Beth. In 10 years, the sum of their ages will be 72. Find their ages.

12. Solve.
    (a) Find the length of a rectangle that has perimeter 32 feet and width 6 feet.
    (b) The volume of a circular cone is $V = \frac{1}{3} \pi r^2 h$. If the volume is 352 cubic inches and the height is 84 inches, find the radius. Use $\pi = \frac{22}{7}$.
    (c) The perimeter of an equilateral triangle is 39 meters. Find the length of each side.
    (d) If one side of a square is 15 cm less than the perimeter, find the length of a side of the square.

13. Solve.
    (a) $A = \frac{1}{2} bh$ for b
    (b) $A = \pi r^2$ for r
    (c) $y = mx + b$ for m
    (d) $A = LW$ for W
    (e) $F = ma$ for m

14. Graph.
    (a) $x > 4$
    (b) $x \le 3$
    (c) $x < -2$
    (d) $x \ge -9$
    (e) $x = 5$

15. Graph.
    (a) $3(2x - 4) \le 6$
    (b) $-(x - 9) > 3 + x$
    (c) $8(2x + 4) \ge 3(5x - 7)$
    (d) $2(3 - x) < 2(2x - 3)$
    (e) $7x \ge 2(3x + 9)$

Answers

1. (a) $-uv$
   (b) $-6y^3$
   (c) $16x - 2$
   (d) $-x^2 - 6x + 7$
   (e) $9p^2 + p$

2. (a) $21p + 14$
   (b) $-24x + 32$
   (c) $12t + 32s$
   (d) $8a$
   (e) $19 - 30a - 21b$

3. (a) 9
   (b) -10
   (c) 60
   (d) 49
   (e) 110

4. (a) $3z + 4$
   (b) $-13 + 2b$
   (c) $8z - 8x + 16$
   (d) $4m - 7$
   (e) $-x - 5$

5. (a) -1
   (b) 10
   (c) 3
   (d) 4
   (e) $-\dfrac{2}{3}$

6. (a) 3
   (b) -2
   (c) 4
   (d) $\dfrac{1}{2}$
   (e) 1

7. (a) 32
   (b) -7
   (c) 147
   (d) -36
   (e) 6

8. (a) $-\dfrac{15}{28}$
   (b) $\dfrac{17}{9}$
   (c) 0
   (d) 0
   (e) 1

9. (a) $\dfrac{1}{x}$
   (b) $x + 7$
   (c) $3x$
   (d) $2x + 4$
   (e) $(x - 2) - 3$

10. (a) 11
    (b) 3
    (c) 3
    (d) 25
    (e) 4

11. (a) 3, 5, 7
    (b) 22, 24, 26
    (c) 34
    (d) 24, 28

12. (a) 10 feet
    (b) 2 inches
    (c) 13 meters
    (d) 5 cm

13. (a) $\dfrac{2\mathbf{A}}{h}$
    (b) $\sqrt{\dfrac{\mathbf{A}}{\pi}}$
    (c) $\dfrac{y - b}{x}$
    (d) $\dfrac{\mathbf{A}}{L}$
    (e) $\dfrac{\mathbf{F}}{a}$

14. See graphs:

(a)

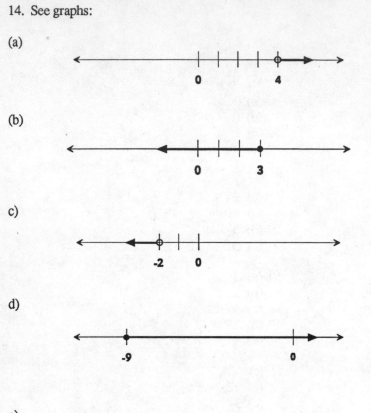

(b)

c)

d)

e)

15. See graphs:

(a)

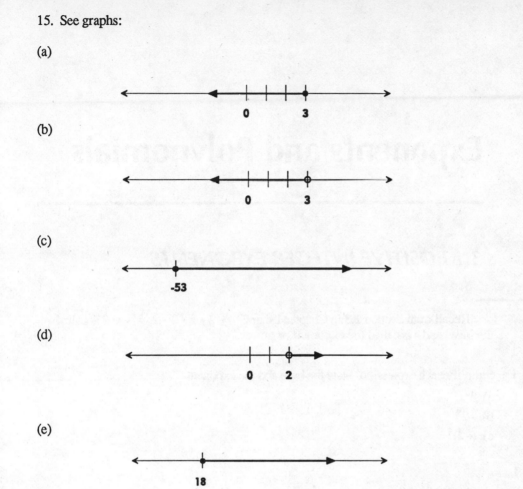

(b)

(c)

(d)

(e)

3

Exponents and Polynomials

3.1 POSITIVE INTEGER EXPONENTS

Review of exponents

Recall from Section 1.3 in Chapter 1 that $2^4 = 2 \cdot 2 \cdot 2 \cdot 2$, where 2 is called the **base**, and 4 is called the **exponent** or **power**.

Example 1   Simplify each expression. State the base and the exponent.

a) 3^2

b) -2^4

c) $(-2)^4$

Solution 1

a) $3^2 = 3 \cdot 3 = 9$ Base 3, exponent 2.

b) $-2^4 = -1 \cdot 2 \cdot 2 \cdot 2 \cdot 2 = -16$ Base 2, exponent 4.

c) $(-2)^4 = (-2)(-2)(-2)(-2) = 16$ Base –2, exponent 4.

Be careful with Examples like b and c. In b, the base is 2, *not* –2!

Exponent laws for positive integer exponents

The following is a list of exponent laws you should memorize:

$a^m a^n = a^{m+n}$	When multiplying, if bases are the same, add the exponents.
$(a^m)n = a^{mn}$	When raising a power to a power, multiply the power.
$(ab)^m = a^m b^m$	When raising a product to a power, raise each factor to the power.
$\left(\dfrac{a}{b}\right)^m = \dfrac{a^m}{b^m}$, $b \neq 0$	When raising a fraction to a power, raise numerato and denominator to the power.

Note in the first law that the bases must be the same in order to add the exponents. $a^m b^n$ is **not** $(ab)^{m+n}$.

Example 2   Simplify each of the following expressions: Leave all answers in exponential form.

a) $4^2 \cdot 4^3$

b) $(-3)^3 (-3)^4$

c) $x^4 \cdot x^2$

d) $y^3 \cdot y$

e) $a^5 \cdot a^3 \cdot a$

f) $3^{2a} \cdot 3^{3a}$

Solution 2

a) $4^2 \cdot 4^3 = 4^{2+3} = 4^5$ When multiplying and bases are equal, add the exponents.

b) $(-3)^3(-3)^4 = (-3)^{3+4} = (-3)^7$ Bases are equal, so add the exponents.

c) $x^4 \cdot x^2 = x^{4+2} = x^6$ Bases are equal, so add the exponents.

d) $y^3 \cdot y = y^3 \cdot y^1 = y^{3+1} = y^4$ Note that no written exponent means an exponent of 1: $y = y^1$.

e) $a^5 \cdot a^3 \cdot a = a^5 \cdot a^3 \cdot a^1$ $a = a^1$.

   $= a^{5+3+1}$ Bases are equal, so add the exponents.

   $= a^9$

f) $3^{2a} \cdot 3^{3a} = 3^{2a+3a}$ Bases are equal, so add the exponents.

$= 3^{5a}$ Combine similar terms: $2a + 3a = 5a$.

Example 3   Simplify each of the following expressions. Leave all answers in exponential form.
a) $(5^4)^2$
b) $(x^2)^3$
c) $(4^a)^3$
d) $(7^x)^y$

Solution 3

a) $(5^4)^2 = 5^4 \cdot 2 = 5^8$ To raise a power to a power, multiply the powers.

b) $x^{2(3)} = x^6$ To raise a power to a power, multiply the powers.

c) $(4^a)^3 = 4^a \cdot 3$ To raise a power to a power, multiply the powers.

$= 4^{3\,a}$ Use the Commutative Property: $a3 = 3a$.

d) $(7^x)^y = 7^{xy}$ To raise a power to a power, multiply the powers.

Example 4   Simplify each of the following expressions.
a) $(3y)^2$
b) $(-5^2)^4$
c) $(-2x^2y^3)^3$
d) $[(3a)^2]^3$

Solution 4

a) $(3y)^2 = 3^2 \cdot y^2 = 9y^2$ To raise a product to a power, raise each factor to the power.

b) $(-5^2)^4 = (-1 \cdot 5^2)^4$ First rewrite s–5 as –1 5.

$= (-1)^4 (5^2)^4$ To raise a product to a power, raise each factor to the power.

$= 1 \cdot 5^8 \, (-1)^4$ $(-1)^4 = (-1)(-1)(-1)(-1) = 1$.
$(5^2)^4 = 5^{2 \cdot 4} = 5^8$

$= 5^8$

c) $(-2x^2y^3)^3 = (-2)^3(x^2)^3(y^3)^3$

$= -8x^6y^9$

d) $[(3a)^2]^3 = (3^1a^1)^2]^3$

$= [(3^2a^2]^3$

$= 3^2 \cdot {}^3a^2 \cdot {}^3$

$= 3^6a^6$

To raise a product to a power, raise each factor to the power.

$(-2)^3 = -2 \cdot -2 \cdot -2 = -8$.

Remember that $3 = 3^11$ and ^{1}.

Work inside parentheses first. To raise a product to a power, raise each factor to the power.

To raise a product to a power, raise each factor to the power. To raise a power to a power, multiply the powers.

Example 5   Simplify each expression.

a) $\left(\dfrac{2}{5}\right)^3$

b) $\left(\dfrac{x}{y}\right)^4$

c) $\left(\dfrac{4c}{3b}\right)^3$

d) $\left(\dfrac{4m2n}{p3}\right)^2$

Solution 5

a) $\left(\dfrac{2}{5}\right)^3 = \dfrac{2^3}{5^3} = \dfrac{8}{125}$

To raise a fraction to a power, raise the numerator and denominator to the power.

b) $\left(\dfrac{x}{y}\right)^4 = \dfrac{x^4}{y^4}$

To raise a fraction to a power, raise the numerator and denominator to the power

c) $\left(\dfrac{4c}{3b}\right)^3 = \dfrac{(4c)^3}{(3b)^3}$

To raise a fraction to a power, raise the numerator and denominator to the power.

$$= \frac{4^3 c^3}{3^3 b^3}$$

To raise a product to a power, raise each factor to the power

$$= \frac{64^3 c^3}{27^3 b^3}$$

$4^3 = 4 \cdot 4 \cdot 4 = 64.$
$3^3 = 3 \cdot 3 \cdot 3 = 27.$

d) $\left(4m^2 \frac{n}{p^3}\right)^2 = \frac{4^2 (m^2)^2 (n^1)^2}{(p^3)^2}$

To raise a fraction to a power, raise the numerator and denominator to the power. To raise a product to a power, raise each factor to the power.

$$= \frac{16m^4 n^2}{p^6}$$

To raise a power to a power, multiply the powers.

3.2 EXPONENT LAWS

Zero and negative integer exponents

We can extend our exponent laws to include all integers with the following definitions for zero and negative integer exponents.

> **Definition:** $a^0 = 1$ for $a \neq 0$.
>
> **Definition:** $a^{-n} = \dfrac{1}{a^n}$ for $a \neq 0$.

Example 6   Simplify the following expressions.

a) 9^0

b) $(-2x^3)^0$

c) $(4x)^0$

d) $4x^0$

Solution 6

a) $9^0 = 1$

Use the definition of 0 as an exponent.

b) $(-2x^3)^0 = 1$

Use the definition of 0 as an exponent.

c) $(4x)^0 = 4^0 x^0$

To raise a product to a power, raise each factor to the power.

$\qquad = 1 \cdot 1$

Use the definition of 0 as an exponent.

$\qquad = 1$

d) $4x^0 = 4 \cdot 1$

Use the definition of 0 as an exponent.

$\qquad = 4$

Note the difference between examples c and d. In c, the product $4x$ is raised to the zero power, while in d only x is raised to the zero power.

Example 7   Evaluate each of the following expressions.

a) 4^{-2}
b) 2^{-3}
c) $(-2)^3$
d) $3x^{-4}$
e) $(2x)^{-3}$

Solution 7

a) $4^{-2} = \dfrac{1}{4^2} = \dfrac{1}{16}$

Use the definition of a negative exponent.

b) $2^{-3} = \dfrac{1}{2^3} = \dfrac{1}{8}$

Use the definition of a negative exponent.

c) $(-2)^3 = (-2)(-2)(-2)$

The exponent is *not* negative. The base, -2, is negative.

$\qquad = -8$

d) $3x^{-4} = 3 \cdot \dfrac{1}{x^4}$

Be careful here—only the x is raised to a negative exponent, not the 3.

$\qquad = \dfrac{3}{x^4}$

e) $(2x)^{-3} = \dfrac{1}{(2x)^3}$

Use the definition of a negative exponent. Since $(2x)$ is raised to the -3 power, $(2x)$ is moved to the denominator.

$$= \frac{1}{2^3 x^3}$$

To raise a product to a power, raise each factor to the power.

$$= \frac{1}{8x^3}$$

Exponents law for division

We need to add one more law to our list of exponent laws.

Exponent Law for Division

$\dfrac{a^m}{a^n} = a^{m-n}$, $a \neq 0$

When dividing, if the bases are the same, subtract the exponent in the denominator from the exponent in the numerator .

Example 8   Simplify each of the following expressions. Write all answers with positive exponents.

a) $\dfrac{4^7}{4^5}$

b) $\dfrac{3}{3^5}$

c) $\dfrac{5^{-3}}{5^4}$

d) $\dfrac{x^7}{x^{-2}}$

Solution 8

a) $\dfrac{4^7}{4^5} = 4^{7-5} = 4^2$

Since the bases are equal, subtract the exponents.

b) $\dfrac{3}{3^5} = \dfrac{3^1}{3^5}$

First rewrite 3 as 3^1.

$= 3^{1-5}$

Since the bases are equal, subtract the exponents.

$$= 3^{-4}$$

You need to write the answer with a positive exponent. Use the definition of negative exponents to rewrite 3^{-4}.

$$= \frac{1}{3^4}$$

c) $\dfrac{5^{-3}}{5^4} = 5^{-3-4}$

Since the bases are equal, subtract the exponents.

$$= 5^{-7}$$

Use the definition of negative exponents to rewrite 5^{-7}.

$$= \frac{1}{5^7}$$

d) $\dfrac{x^7}{x^{-2}} = x^{7-(-2)}$

Since the bases are equal, subtract the exponents. $7 - (-2) = 7 + 2 = 9$.

$$= x^9$$

Example 9 Simplify the following expressions. Write each answer with positive exponents.

a) $\dfrac{(6x^2)^3}{x^4}$

b) $\left(\dfrac{4a^{-3}}{a^2}\right)^2$

c) $\dfrac{(4^{-2}y^{-3}z^5)^{-2}}{(4y^{-2}z^2)^{-1}}$

Solution 9

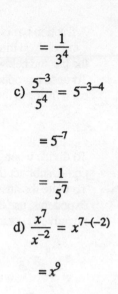

a) $\dfrac{(6x^2)^3}{x^4} = \dfrac{6^3 x^6}{x^4}$

To raise a product to a power, raise each factor to the power.
Since the bases are the same, subtract the exponents.

$$= 216x^{6-4}$$

$$= 216x^2$$

b) $\left(\dfrac{4a^{-3}}{a^2}\right)^2 = (4a^{-3-2})^2$

Simplify inside the parentheses first.

$$= (4a^{-5})^2$$

$$= 4^2 a^{-5 \cdot 2}$$

to raise a product to a power, raise each factor to the power.

$$= 16a^{-10}$$

Use $a^{-10} = \dfrac{1}{a10}$

c) $\dfrac{(4^{-2}y^{-3}z^5)^{-2}}{(4y^{-2}z^2)^{-1}} = \dfrac{4^{-2(-2)}y^{-3(-2)}z^{5(-2)}}{4^{1(-1)}y^{-2(-1)}z^{2(-1)}}$

A fraction bar is a grouping symbol. You must simplify above the bar and below the bar separately. To raise a product to a power, raise each factor to the power.

$$= \dfrac{4^4 y^6 z^{-10}}{4^{-1} y^2 z^{-2}}$$

$$= 4^{4-(-1)} y^{6-2} z^{-10-(-2)}$$

$$= 4^5 y^4 z^{-8}$$

To divide when the bases are equal, subtract the exponents. To write the answer with positive exponents, use the definition of negative exponents.

$$= \dfrac{4^5 y^4}{z^8}$$

Use $z^{-8} = \dfrac{1}{z^8}$

The table below summarizes the exponent laws and definitions we have covered in this chapter.

Exponent Laws

$a^m a^n = a^{m+n}$	When multiplying, if the bases are the same, add the exponents.
$(a^m)^n = a^{mn}$ $(ab)^m = a^m b^m$	When raising a power to a power, multiply the powers. When raising a product to a power, raise each factor to the power.
$\left(\dfrac{a}{b}\right)^m = \dfrac{a^m}{b^m}$, $b \neq 0$	When raising a fraction to a power, raise the numerator and denominator to the power.
$\dfrac{a^m}{a^n} = a^{m-n}$, $a \neq 0$	When dividing, if the bases are the same, subtract the exponent in the denominator from the exponent in the numerator.
$a^0 = 1$ for $a \neq 0$ A	nonzero number raised to the zero power equals 1.
$a^{-n} = \dfrac{1}{a^n}$ for $a \neq 0$	A nonzero number raised to the -n power equals 1 divided by the number raised to the n power.

3.3 SCIENTIFIC NOTATION

Scientific notation is a shorthand method used for writing very large and very small numbers.

Writing numbers in scientific notation

To Write a Number in Scientific Notation:
1. Move the decimal point to the right of the first nonzero digit. Count the number of places you moved the decimal point.
2. Multiply the number from step 1 times 10 raised to + or – the number of places you moved the decimal point.
Use + if you moved the decimal to the left.
Use – if you moved the decimal to the right.

Example 10 Write each number in scientific notation.

a) 247,000

b) 16

c) 3,000,421,000

Solution 10

a) 247,000.

247000

$= 2.47 \times 10^{+5}$

Given number.
Move the decimal to the right of 2.
The decimal point moved 5 places.
Use +5 as the exponent of 10 since the decimal was moved *to the left 5 places*.

b) 16.

1.6

$= 1.6 \times 10^{+1}$

Given number.
Move the decimal to the right of 1.
The decimal point moved 1 place.
Use +1 as the exponent of 10 since the decimal point was moved *to the left 1 place*.

or

$= 1.6 \times 10$

$10^{+1} = 10^1 = 10$ and could be written in any of these forms.

c) 3,000,421,000.
   3.000421000
   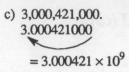
   $= 3.000421 \times 10^9$

Given number.
Move the decimal to the right of 3.
The decimal point moved 9 places.
Use +9 or 9 as the exponent of 10
since the decimal point was moved
to the left 9 places.

Example 11   Write each number in scientific notation.
a) 0.00562
b) 0.0000000048
c) 0.030056

Solution 11

a) 0.00562
   0005.62
   $= 5.62 \times 10^{-3}$

Given number.
Move the decimal to the right of 5.
The decimal point moved 3 places.
Use −3 as the exponent of 10 since
the decimal point was moved *to
the right* 3 places.

b) 0.00000000048
   00000000004.8
   $= 4.8 \times 10^{-10}$

Given number.
Move the decimal to the right of 4.
The decimal point moved 10
places.
Use −10 as the exponent of 10
since the decimal point was moved
to the right 10 places.

c) 0.030056
   003.0056
   $= 3.0056 \times 10^{-2}$

Given number.
Move the decimal to the right of 3.
The decimal point moved 2 places.
Use −2 as the exponent of 10 since
the decimal point was moved *to
the right* 2 places.

Writing numbers in expanded form

To Write a Number in Expanded Form:
1. If the exponent of 10 is positive (+), move the decimal point to the right the same
   number of places as the exponent. Add zeros as necessary.
2. If the exponent of 10 is negative (−), move the decimal point to the left the same
   number of places as the exponent. Add zeros as necessary.

Example 12 Write each number in expanded form.
a) 6.28×10^3
b) 2.15×10^6
c) 4.5896×10^2

Solution 12

a) 6.28×10^3	Given number.
628	Move the decimal point 3 places to the right.
6280	Add necessary 0.
$= 6{,}280$	Answer.
b) 2.15×10^6	Given number.
215 .	Move the decimal point 6 places to the right.
2150000	Add necessary 0s.
$= 2{,}150{,}000$	Answer.
c) $4.5896 + 10^2$	Given number.
458.96	Move the decimal point 2 places to the right.
$= 458.96$	Answer.

Example 13 Write each number in expanded form.
a) 3.79×10^{-5}
b) 2.6×10^{-3}
c) 1.57896×10^{-1}

Solution 13

a) 3.79×10^{-5}	Given number.
. 379	Move the decimal point 5 places to the left.
.0000379	Add necessary 0s.
$= 0.0000379$	Answer. We usually write a 0 to the left of the decimal point.
b) 2.6×10^{-3}	Given number.
. 26	Move the decimal point 3 places to the left.
.0026	Add necessary 0s.
$= 0.0026$	We usually write a 0 to the left of the decimal point.
c) 1.57896×10^{-1}	Given number.
. 157896	Move the decimal point 1 place to the left.
$= 0.157896$	We usually write a 0 to the left of the decimal point.

Using exponent laws with scientific notation

When numbers are written in scientific notation, you can use the exponent laws to simplify products and quotients. Remember that $a^m a^n = a^{m+n}$ and $(\dfrac{a^m}{a^n}) = a^{m-n}$ can be used only when bases are the same!

Example 14 Find the product. Write answers in scientific notation.
a) $(2 \times 10^6) \times (8 \times 10^4)$
b) $(5 \times 10^3) \times (3 \times 10^{-5})$
c) $(4 \times 10^{-2}) \times (9 \times 10^{-4})$
d) $(-3 \times 10^5) \times (-8 \times 10^{-6})$

Solution 14

a) $(2 \times 10^6) \times (8 \times 10^4) =$
$= 2 \times 8 \times 10^6 \times 10^4$ — Use the Commutative and Associative properties.
$= 16 \times 10^{6+4}$ — Equal bases of 10, so add the exponents.
$= 16 \times 10^{10}$ — Not finished yet! Now convert to scientific notation.
$= 16. \times 10^{10}$ — $16 = 16. = 1.6 \times 10^1$.
$= (1.6 \times 10^1) \times 10^{10}$
$= 1.6 \times 10^{11}$ — Equal bases of 10, so add the exponents.

b) $(5 \times 10^3) \times (3 \times 10^{-5})$
$= 5 \times 3 \times 10^3 \times 10^{-5}$
$= 15 \times 10^{3+(-5)}$ — Equal bases of 10, so add the exponents.
$= 15 \times 10{-}2$ — Not finished yet! Now convert to scientific notation.
$= 15. \times 10^{-2}$ — $15 = 15. = 1.5 \times 10^1$.
$= (1.5 \times 10^1) \times 10^{-2}$ — $10^1 \times 10^{-2} = 10^{1+(-2)} = 10^{-1}$.
$= 1.5 \times 10^{-1}$

c) $(4 \times 10^{-2}) \times (9 \times 10^{-4})$
$= 4 \times 9 \times 10^{-2} \times 10^{-4}$
$= 36 \times 10^{-2} + {-4}$ — Equal bases of 10, so add the exponents.
$= 36 \times 10^{-6}$ — Not finished yet! Now convert to scientific notation.
$= (3.6 \times 10^1) \times 10^{-6}$ — $36 = 36. = 3.6 \times 10^1$.
$= 3.6 \times 10^{1 + (-6)}$ — Equal bases of 10, so add the exponents.
$= 3.6 \times 10^{-5}$

d) $(-3 \times 10^5) \times (-8 \times 10^{-6})$

$= (-3) \times (-8) \times 10^5 \times 10^{-6}$

$= 24 \times 10^{5 + (-6)}$

$= 24 \times 10^{-1}$

$= (2.4 \times 10^1) \times 10^{-1}$

$= 2.4 \times 10^{1 + (-1)}$

$= 2.4 \times 10^0$

Equal bases of 10, so add the exponents.
Now convert to scientific notation.
$24 = 24. = 2.4 \times 10^1$.
Equal bases of 10, so add the exponents.

Example 15 Find the quotient. Write answers in scientific notation.

a) $\dfrac{12 \times 10^6}{4 \times -10^{-3}}$

b) $\dfrac{3.6 \times 10^{-2}}{6 \times 10^3}$

c) $\dfrac{-4.8 \times 10^{-7}}{-2.4 \times 10^{-4}}$

Solution 15

a) $\dfrac{12 \times 10^6}{4 \times 10^{-3}}$

$= \dfrac{12}{4} \times 10^{6-(-3)}$

$= 3 \times 10^9$

Equal bases of 10, so subtract the exponents.

$6 - (-3) = 6 + 3 = 9$.

b) $\dfrac{3.6 \times 10^{-2}}{6 \times 10^3}$

$= \dfrac{3.6}{6} \times 10^{-2-(3)}$

$= 0.6 \times 10^{-5}$

$= (6 \times 10^{-1}) \times 10^{-5}$

$= 6 \times 10^{-6}$

Equal bases of 10, so subtract the exponents.
Not finished yet! Now convert to scientific notation.
$0.6 = 6. \times 10^{-1}$.

$10^- \times 10^{-5} = 10^{-1+(-5)} = 10^{-6}$.

c) $\dfrac{-4.8 \times 10^{-7}}{-2.4 \times 10^{-4}}$

$= \dfrac{-4.8}{-2.4} - 4 \times 10^{-7}$

Equal bases of 10, so subtract the exponents.

$= 2 \times 10^{-3}$

$-7 - (-4) = -7 + 4 = -3$.

3.4 ADDING AND SUBTRACTING POLYNOMIALS

Vocabulary for polynomials

The following table presents some language you will need in the remaining sections of this chapter.

VOCABULARY	MEANING	EXAMPLE
Term	A number or a product of a number and one or more variables.	In $6x^2 + 5x + 8$ there are 3 terms: $6x^2$, $5x$, and 8.
Numerical coefficient	Numerical factor in a term.	4 is the numerical coefficient in $4x^3$. -2 is the numerical coefficient in $-2xy^2$.
Polynomial	Expression containing a finite sum of terms.	$4x$ $x^2 + 2x = 1$
Monomial	Polynomial with 1 term	6 $2x$
Binomial	Polynomial with 2 terms.	$x^2 - 9$ $2x + 6$
Trinomial	Polynomial with 3 terms.	$x^2 + 2x + 1$
Degree of a term	Sum of exponents of the variables within the term.	Degree of $6x^2y^3$ is 5. Degree of $2x = 2x^1$ is 1. Degree of $5 = 5x^0$ is 0.
Degree of a polynomial in 1 variable	Highest degree of any term.	Degree of $4x^3-2x$ is 3. Degree of $x^5-2x3=6x$ is 5.
Similar terms or like terms	Terms that have the same variables and exponents.	$4x^3$ and $-6x^3$ $6a$ and $2a$

Example 16 Identify whether each of the following polynomials is a monomial, binomial, or trinomial.
a) $4x + 6$
b) $7x^2 - 5xy + 3y^4$
c) $5xyz$

Solution 16

a) $4x + 6$ is a binomial.
b) $7x^2 - 5xy + 3y^4$ is a trinomial.
c) 5^{xyz} is a monomial.

Example 17 Find the degree of each polynomial.

a) 4^x
b) 6
c) $5xyz$
d) $7x^2 - 5xy + 3y^4$

Solution 17

a) $4x = 4x^1$ has degree 1

b) $6 = 6^{x^0}$ has degree 0

c) $5xyz = 5x^1y^1z^1$ has degree 3

The degree of a term is the sum of the exponents of the variables.

The degree of any constant will be 0 since the constant can be written as the constant times x^0.

The degree of a term is the sum of the exponents of the variables

d) To find the degree of a polynomial, first find the degree of each term:

$7x^2$ has degree 2
$-5xy$ has degree $2 - 5xy = -5x^1y^1.$
$3y^4$ has degree 4

The degree of the polynomial is the highest degree of any term, so the degree of $7x^2 - 5xy + 3y^4$ is 4.

Adding polynomials

Recall from Chapter 2 that only similar terms can be added or subtracted. The following steps will help you add polynomials.

> **To Add Polynomials:**
> 1. Use the definition of subtraction to change subtractions into additions of the additive inverse.
> 2. Group similar terms together, making use of the Commutative and Associative Properties.
> 3. Add the numerical coefficients of similar terms.

Example 18 Add.

a) $(3x^2 + 4x + 7) + (5x^2 + 2x + 12)$
b) $(4x^2 - 6x - 3) + (6x^2 + 8x - 5)$
c) $-2y^3 + 8y - 4 + 7y^3 - y^2 + 5$

Solution 18

a) $(3x^2 + 4x + 7) + (5x^2 + 2x + 12) =$
$(3x^2 + 5x^2) + (4x + 2x) + (7 + 12) =$

Group similar terms together using the Commutative and Associative Properties.

$(3 + 5)x^2 + (4 + 2)x + (19) =$

Add the numerical coefficients of similar terms.

$8x^2 + 6x + 19$

b) $(4x^2 - 6x - 3) + (6x^2 + 8x - 5) =$
$(4x^2 + (-6x) + (-3) + (6x^2 + 8x + (-5) =$

Rewrite each polynomial using the definition of subtraction to change subtractions to addition of the additive inverse.

$(4x^2 + 6x^2) + (-6x + 8x) + (-3 + (-5)) =$
$10x^2 + 2x + (-8) =$

Group similar terms together.
Add numerical coefficients of similar terms.

$10x^2 + 2x - 8$

$+ (-8)$ is usually written -8.

c) $-2y3 + 8y - 4 + 7y^3 - y^2 + 5 =$
$-2y^3 + 8y + (-4) + 7y^3 + (-1y^2) + 5 =$
$(-2y^3 + 7y^3) - y^2 + 8y + (-4 + 5) =$
$5y^3 - y^2 + 8y + 1$

Use the definition of subtraction.
Group similar terms together.
Add numerical coefficients of similar terms.

Subtracting polynomials

To subtract two polynomials, change all the signs on the polynomial behind the subtraction sign and then add the polynomials.

Example 19 Subtract.

a) $(4y^2 - y + 6) - (2y^2 + 5y - 8)$
b) $(5a^4 - 3a^3 - 8) - (-2a^4 + 7a^3 - 2)$

Solution 19

a) $(4y^2 - y + 6) - (2y^2 + 5y - 8) =$
$(4y^2 - y + 6) + (-2y^2 - 5y + 8) =$

Change all signs in the second polynomial.

$(4y^2 - 2y^2) + (-y - 5y) + (6 + 8) =$
$2y^2 - 6y + 14$

Group similar terms.
Combine similar terms.

b) $(5a^4 - 3a^3 - 8) - (-2a^4 + 7a^3 - 2) =$
$(5a^4 - 3a^3 - 8) + (2a^4 - 7a^3 + 2) =$

Change all signs in the second polynomial.

$(5a^4 + 2a^4) + (-3a^3 - 7a^3) + (-8 + 2) =$
$7a^4 - 10a^3 - 6$

Group similar terms.
Combine similar terms.

Example 20 Subtract $6x^2 + 5x - 8$ from $7x^2 - 8$.

Solution 20

$(7x^2 - 8) - (6x^2 + 5x - 8) =$
$(7x^2 - 8) + (-6x^2 - 5x + 8) =$ Change all signs in the second polynomial.

$(7x^2 - 6x^2) - 5x + (-8 + 8) =$ Group similar terms.
$x^2 - 5x$ Combine similar terms.

3.5 MULTIPLYING POLYNOMIALS

Multiplying monomials by monomials

To multiply a monomial times a monomial, multiply the coefficients and add the exponents on equal bases.

Example 21 Multiply.
a) $(4x^2)(-2x^3)$
b) $(3x)(5x)$
c) $y^2(6y^3)$
d) $(-2m^2)(3n^2)$
e) $(4x^2y)(2y^3)(5x^4)$

Solution 21

a) $(4x^2)(-2x^3) = (4)(-2)x^{2+3}$ Multiply coefficients and add exponents on equal bases.

     $= -8x^5$

b) $(3x)(5x) = (3x^1)(5x^1)$ Rewrite each variable with an exponent: $x = x^1$.
Multiply coefficients. Add exponents on equal bases.

     $= (3)(5)x^{1+1}$

     $= 15x^2$

c) $y^2(6y^3) = (1)(6)y^{2+3}$ $y^2 = 1y^2$.
     $= 6y^5$

d) $(-2m^2)(3n^2) = (-2)(3)m^2n^2$ Multiply coefficients. Bases are not equal, so exponents cannot be added.

$$= -6m^2n^2$$

e) $(4x^2y)(2y^3)(5x^4) = (4)(2)(5)x^{2+4}y^3$ Multiply coefficients. Add
exponents on equal bases.

$$= 40x\,6y^3$$

Multiplying
two polynomials

> **To Multiply Two Polynomials:**
> 1. Multiply each term of the second polynomial by each term of the first polynomial.
> 2. Add any similar terms.

Example 22   Multiply.
a) $2y(3y^4 + 4)$
b) $4p(3p^2 - 6p + 2)$
c) $(2a + 4)(3a + 5)$
d) $(3x + 5)(2x - 3)$
e) $(4b - 3)(2b - 7)$

Solution 22

a) $2y(3y^4 + 4) = 2y(3y4) + 2y(4)$ Multiply **each** term of the second
polynomial by $2y$.
$$= 6y^5 + 8y$$
Remember to use $2y = 2y^1$.
Multiply the coefficients, add the exponents on equal bases.

b) $4p(3p^2 - 6p + 2) =$
$4p(3p^2) + 4p(-6p) + 4p(2) =$ Multiply **each** term of the second
polynomial by $4p$.

$$12p^3 - 24p^2 + 8p$$ Multiply the coefficients, add the exponents on equal bases.

STOP HERE!   No similiar terms to add.

c) $(2a + 4)(3a + 5) =$

$2a(3a) + 2a(5) + 4(3a) + 4(5) =$ Multiply each term of the second
polynomial by $2a$ and then by **4**.

$6a2 + 10a + 12a + 20 =$ Multiply coefficients, add the
exponents on equal bases.

$6a^2 + (10a + 12a) + 20 =$ Add similar terms.
$6a2 + 22a + 20$

d) $(3x + 5)(2x - 3) =$
$\qquad 3x(2x) + 3x(-3) + 5(2x) + 5(-3) =$ Multiply each term of the second
      polynomial by $3x$ and then by 5.

$\qquad 6x^2 + (-9x) + 10x + (-15) =$ Multiply coefficients, add the
      exponents on equal bases.

$\qquad 6x^2 + 1x + (-15) =$ $(-9 + 10)x = 1x$
$\qquad 6x^2 + x - 15$ Write $1x$ as x, write $+ (-15)$ as $- 15$.

e) $(4b - 3)(2b - 7) =$
$\qquad (4b + (-3))(2b + (-7)) =$ Use the definition of subtraction.
$\qquad 4b(2b) + 4b(-7) + (-3)(2b) + (-3)(-7) =$ Multiply each term of the second
      polynomial by $4b$ and then
      by -3.

$\qquad 8b^2 + (-28b) + (-6b) + 21 =$ Multiply coefficients, add the
      exponents on equal bases.

$\qquad 8b^2 - 34b + 21$ $(-28b) + (-6b) = (-28 + -6)$
      $b = -34b$.

Example 23 Multiply.

a) $(2x + 3y)^2$
b) $(3x + 2)(4x^2 - 6x + 1)$
c) $(2p^2 + p + 3)(4p^2 + 5p - 3)$
d) $(2m - 1)^3$

Solution 23

a) $(2x + 3y)^2 =$
$\qquad (2x + 3y)(2x + 3y) =$ Write $(2x + 3y)$ two times.
$\qquad 2x(2x) + 2x(3y) + 3y(2x) + 3y(3y) =$ Multiply **each** term of the second
      polynomial by $2x$ and then by $3y$.

$\qquad 4x^2 + 6xy + 6xy + 9y^2 =$ Multiply coefficients, add the
      exponents on equal bases.
      Combine similar terms.

$\qquad 4x^2 + 12xy + 9y^2$

b) $(3x + 2)(4x^2 - 6x + 1)$ This can be done either
      horizontally or vertically. Both
      solutions are presented.

Horizontally:
$3x(4x^2) + 3x(-6x) + 3x(1) + 2$
$(4x^2) + 2(-6x) + 2(1) =$ Multiply each term of second
      polynomial by $3x$ and then by 2.

$12x^3 - 18x^2 + 3x + 8x^2 - 12x + 2 =$ Multiply coefficients, add the
      exponents on equal bases.

$12x^3 + (-18x^2 + 8x^2) + (3x - 12x) + 2 =$ Group similar terms together.
$12x^3 - 10x^2 - 9x + 2$ Add similar terms.

Vertically:

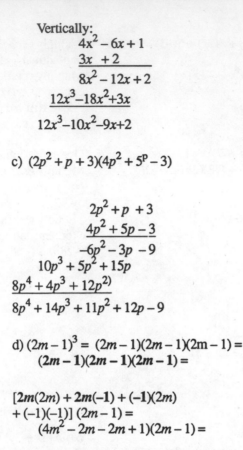

$$4x^2 - 6x + 1$$
$$\underline{3x \ + 2}$$
$$8x^2 - 12x + 2$$ Stack the polynomials.

$$\underline{12x^3 - 18x^2 + 3x}$$ $2(4x2 - 6x + 1)$.

$$12x^3 - 10x^2 - 9x + 2$$ $3x(4x2 - 6x + 1)$.
Add similar terms.

c) $(2p^2 + p + 3)(4p^2 + 5^p - 3)$ You could work horizontally or vertically. The vertical form is shown here.

$$2p^2 + p \ + 3$$
$$\underline{4p^2 + 5p - 3}$$ Stack the polynomials.
$$-6p^2 - 3p \ - 9$$ $-3(2p^2 + p + 3) = -6p^2 - 3p - 9$
$$10p^3 + 5p^2 + 15p$$ $5p(2p^2 + p + 3) = 10p^3 + 5p^2 + 15^p$
$$\underline{8p^4 + 4p^3 + 12p^{2)}}$$ $4p^2(2p^2 + p + 3) = 8p^4 + 4p^3 + 12p^2$
$$8p^4 + 14p^3 + 11p^2 + 12p - 9$$ Combine similar terms.

d) $(2m - 1)^3 = (2m - 1)(2m - 1)(2m - 1) =$ Write $(2m - 1)$ 3 times.
$(2m - 1)(2m - 1)(2m - 1) =$ Multiply two polynomials at a time.

$[2m(2m) + 2m(-1) + (-1)(2m)$ Multiply the first two polynomials.
$+ (-1)(-1)] \ (2m - 1) =$ Multiply coefficients, add the
$(4m^2 - 2m - 2m + 1)(2m - 1) =$ exponents on equal bases.
    You could work horizontally or
$(4m^2 - 4m + 1)(2m - 1) =$ vertically. This is done horizontally.

$4m^2(2m) + 4m^2(-1) + (-4m)(2m) + (-4m)(-1) + 1(2m) + 1(-1) =$
$8m^3 - 4m^2 - 8m^2 + 4m + 2m - 1 =$ Add similar terms.
$8m^3 - 12m^2 + 6m - 1$

3.6 MULTIPLYING USING FOIL AND SPECIAL PRODUCTS

Although all multiplication of polynomials can be done with the techniques discussed in Section 3.5, several shortcuts are available to speed up your work.

Multiplying using FOIL

> **To Multiply Two Binomials Using FOIL:**
> 1. Multiply the **F**irst two terms.
> 2. Multiply the **O**uter two terms.
> 3. Multiply the **I**nner two terms.
> 4. Multiply the **L**ast two terms.
> 5. Add the four terms, combining similar terms whenever possible.

Example 24 Multiply using FOIL.

   a) $(y + 7)(y + 5)$
   b) $(x + 4)(x - 3)$
   c) $(2p - 3)(p + 6)$
   d) $(3m - 1)(4m - 5)$
   e) $(x - 2)(y + 4)$

Solution 24

a) $(y + 7)(y + 5) =$

F: $y(y) = y^2$	Multiply the first two terms.
O: $y(5) = 5y$	Multiply the outer two terms.
I: $7(y) = 7y$	Multiply the inner two terms.
L: $7(5) = 35$	Multiply the last two terms.
$= y^2 + 5y + 7y + 35$	Add the four terms.
$= y^2 + 12y + 35$	Combine similar terms: $5y + 7y = 12y$.

b) $(x + 4)(x - 3) =$

F: $x(x) = x^2$	Multiply the first two terms.
O: $x(-3) = -3x$	Multiply the outer two terms.
I: $4(x) = 4x$	Multiply the inner two terms.
L: $4(-3) = -12$	Multiply the last two terms.
$= x^2 - 3x + 4x - 12$	Add the four terms.
$= x^2 + x - 12$	Combine similar terms: $-3x + 4x = 1x = x$.

c) $(2p - 3)(p + 6) =$

F: $2p(p) = 2p^2$	Multiply the first two terms.
O: $2p(6) = 12p$	Multiply the outer two terms.
I: $-3(p) = -3p$	Multiply the inner two terms.
L: $-3(6) = -18$	Multiply the last two terms.
$= 2p^2 + 12p + (-3p) + (-18)$	Add the four terms.
$= 2p^2 + 9p - 18$	Combine similar terms: $12p + (-3p) = 9p$.

d) $(3m-1)(4m-5) =$

    F: $3m(4m) = 12m^2$ Multiply the first two terms.

    O: $3m(-5) = -15m$ Multiply the outer two terms.

    I: $-1(4m) = -4m$ Multiply the inner two terms.

    L: $-1(-5) = 5$ Multiply the last two terms.

    $= 12m^2 + (-15m) + (-4m) + 5$ Add the four terms.

    $= 12m^2 - 19m + 5$ Combine similar terms:

                                   $(-15m) + (-4m) = -19m.$

e) $(x-2)(y+4) =$

    F: $x(y) = xy$ Multiply the first two terms.

    O: $x(4) = 4x$ Multiply the outer two terms.

    I: $-2(y) = -2y$ Multiply the inner two terms.

    L: $-2(4) = -8$ Multiply the last two terms.

    $= xy + 4x + (-2y + (-8)$ Add the four terms.

    $= xy + 4x - 2y - 8$ There are no similar terms to combine!

Special products: squaring a binomial

To Square a Binomial:
1. Square the first term.
2. Multiply 2 times the first term times the last term.
3. Square the last term.
4. Add these terms together.

This shortcut is based on the fact that when the sum (or) difference of two terms is multiplied using FOIL, the inner and outer terms are similar terms and can be combined. The first example below uses the shortcut and FOIL to demonstrate.

Example 25 Multiply.

    a) $(4+y)^2$

    b) $(a-3)^2$

    c) $(2y+1)^2$

    d) $(2x+3y)^2$

Solution 25

a) $(4+y)^2 =$

    $(4)^2 = 16$

    $2(4)(y) = 8y$

    $(y)^2 = y^2$

    $= 16 + 8y + y^2$

    FOIL:

    $(4+y)^2 = (4+y)$

    F: $4(4) = 16$

    O: $4(y) = 4y$

    I: $y(4) = 4y$

    L: $y(y) = y^2$

    $= 16 + 4y + 4y + y^2$

    $= 16 + 8y + y^2$

Shortcut:
Square the first term.
Multiply 2 times the first term (4) times the last term (y).
Square the last term.
Add the terms together.

Use the definition of exponents to rewrite $(4+y)2 = (4+y)(4+y)$.

Multiply the first two terms.
Multiply the outer two terms.
Multiply the inner two terms.
Multiply the last two terms.
Add the four terms together.
Combine the similar terms: $4y + 4y = 8y$.

Which method do you think is easier?

b) $(a-3)^2 =$

    $(a)^2 = a^2$

    $2(a)(-3) = -6a$

    $(-3)^2 = 9$

    $= a^2 - 6a + 9$

Square the first term.
Multiply 2 times the first term (a) times the last term (−3).
Square the last term.
Add the terms together.

c) $(2y+1)^2 =$

    $(2y)^2 = 4y^2$

    $2(2y)(1) = 4y$

    $(1)^2 = 1$

    $= 4y^2 + 4y + 1$

Square the first term.
Multiply 2 times the first term (2y) times the last term (1).
Square the last term.
Add the terms together.

d) $(2x+3y)^2 =$

    $(2x)^2 = 4x^2$

    $2(2x)(3y) = 12xy$

    $(3y)^2 = 9y^2$

    $= 4x^2 + 12xy + 9y^2$

Square the first term.
Multiply 2 times the first term (2x) times the last term (3y).
Square the last term.
Add the terms together.

Note that example d was worked in Section 3.5 using the Distributive Property. Compare the two techniques. Which do you think is shorter?

Special products: multiplying the sum and difference of two terms

> **To Find the Product of the Sum and Difference of Two Terms:**
> 1. Square the first term.
> 2. Square the last term.
> 3. Subtract these two terms.

This shortcut is based on the fact that when the sum and difference of two terms are multiplied using FOIL, the inner and outer terms sum to 0. The first example below uses the shortcut and FOIL to demonstrate.

Example 26 Multiply.
a) $(x - y)(x + y)$
b) $(2a + 3)(2a - 3)$
c) $(2m - 3n)(2m + 3n)$

Solution 26

Shortcut:

a) $(x - y)(x + y)$ $(x)^2 = x^2$ Square the first term.
$(y)^2 = y^2$ Square the last term.
$= x^2 - y^2$ Subtract.

FOIL:
F: $x(x) = x^2$ Multiply the first two terms.
O: $x(y) = xy$ Multiply the outer two terms.
I: $-y(x) = -xy$ Multiply the inner two terms.
L: $-y(y) = -y^2$ Multiply the last two terms.
$= x^2 + xy - xy - y^2$ Add the terms.
$= x^2 - y^2$ Combine similar terms: $xy - xy = 0$.

b) $(2a + 3)(2a - 3)$ $(2a)^2 = 4a^2$ Square the first term.
$(3)^2 = 9$ Square the last term.
$= 4a^2 - 9$ Subtract.

c) $(2m - 3n)(2m + 3n)$ $(2m)^2 = 4m^2$ Square the first term.
$(3n)^2 = 9n^2$ Square the last term.
$= 4m^2 - 9n^2$ Subtract.

3.7 DIVIDING POLYNOMIALS

Descending order

In dividing polynomials we will need to write terms in descending order.

> **To Write a Polynomial in Descending Order:**
> 1. Write the term with the highest exponent first.
> 2. Write the term with the next highest exponent.
> 3. Continue until all terms are written.

Example 27 Write in descending order.
a) $-15x - 5x^2 + 9 + 2x^3$
b) $100 - 25p^5 + 20p^2 - 75p^3$

Solution 27

a) $-15x - 5x^2 + 9 + 2x^3 = 2x^3 - 5x^2 - 15x + 9$

Note that $9 = 9 \times 0$ and has the lowest exponent. The constant term will always come last when writing a polynomial in descending order.

b) $100 - 25p^5 + 20p^2 - 75p^3 = -25p^5 - 75p^3 + 20p^2 + 100$

Dividing a polynomial by a monomial

> **To Divide a Polynomial by a Monomial:**
> 1. Write the polynomial in descending order, if necessary.
> 2. Divide each term by the monomial.
>   a. Divide the coefficients. Leave as fractions if the numbers do not divide evenly.
>   b. Subtract exponents on equal bases. Leave the answer with positive exponents.

Example 28 Divide.

a) $\dfrac{16x^4 - 8x^3 + 2x}{2x}$

b) $(100 - 25p^5 + 20p^2 - 75p^3)$ by $5p^2$

c) $\dfrac{12a^6 - 8a^4 + 7a}{2a^2}$

Solution 28

a) $\dfrac{16x^4 - 8x^3 + 2x}{2x} =$

Polynomial is already in descending order.

$\dfrac{16x^4}{2x} - \dfrac{8x^3}{2x} + \dfrac{2x}{2x} =$

Divide each term by $2x$.

$8x^3 - 4x^2 + 1$

Divide coefficients, subtract exponents.

b) $(100 - 25p^5 + 20p^2 - 75p^3)$ by $5p^2 =$

$\dfrac{-25p^5 - 75p^3 + 20p^2 + 100}{5p^2} =$

Write polynomial in descending order.

$\dfrac{-25p^5}{5p^2} - \dfrac{75p^3}{5p^2} + \dfrac{20p^2}{5p^2} + \dfrac{100}{5p^2} =$

Divide each term by $5p^2$.

$-5p^3 - 25p + 4 + \dfrac{20}{p^2}$

$\dfrac{20}{p^2} = 20p^{-2}$, but we leave the answer with a positive exponent.

c) $\dfrac{12a^6 - 8a^4 + 7a}{2a^2} =$

$\dfrac{12a^6}{2a^2} - \dfrac{8a^4}{2a^2} + \dfrac{7a}{2a^2} =$

Divide each term by $2a^2$.

$6a^4 - 4a^2 + \dfrac{7}{2a}$

Leave $\dfrac{7}{2}$ since 2 doesn't go evenly into 7.

Dividing polynomials using long division

To divide 265 by 8, we use the following setup:

$$\text{divisor} \rightarrow 8\overline{)265} \leftarrow \text{quotient}$$

with 33 above, $\underline{24} \leftarrow$ dividend, 25, 24, $1 \leftarrow$ remainder

where 8 is called the divisor, 265 is the dividend, 33 is the quotient, and 1 is the remainder. Using this language, here are the rules for dividing a polynomial by a polynomial.

> **Dividing a Polynomial by a Polynomial:**
> 1. Arrange the dividend and the divisor in descending order. Insert 0s for missing powers.
> 2. Divide the first term of the dividend by the first term of the divisor. Write this quotient on the line above the dividend.
> 3. Multiply the quotient times the divisor. Write this product below the dividend. Subtract and bring down the next term.
> 4. This becomes the new dividend. Go back to Step 2 using the new dividend.
> 5. Continue the process until the degree of the remainder is less than the degree of the divisor.
> 6. Check by multiplying the divisor times the quotient, and adding the remainder. This product should equal the dividend.

Example 29 Perform the following divisions.

a) $(2x^2 - 7x + 6) \ (x - 2)$
b) $(9 - 15x + 2x^3 - 5x^2) \ (2x + 1)$
c) $(x^3 - 5x + 2) \div (x + 3)$

Solution 29

a) $x - 2 \overline{)\ 2x^2 - 7x + 6\ } \ =$

Step 1. Dividend and divisor are already in descending order. There are no missing powers.

$$\begin{array}{r} 2x \\ x-2 \overline{)\ 2x^2 - 7x + 6\ } \\ \underline{2x^2 - 4x} \\ -3x + 6 \end{array}$$

Step 2. $\dfrac{2x^2}{x} = 2x$

Step 3. Multiply $2x(x-2) = 2x^2 - 4x$ and write below the dividend. Subtract by changing the signs in $2x^2 - 4x$ to $2x^2 + 4x$. Bring down +6.

Step 4. This is the new dividend.

$$\begin{array}{r} 2x-3 \\ x-2 \overline{)\ 2x^2 - 7x + 6\ } \\ \underline{2x^2 - 4x} \\ -3x + 6 \\ \underline{-3x + 6} \\ 0 \end{array}$$

Step 2. $\dfrac{-3x}{x} = -3$

Step 3. Multiply $-3(x-2) = -3x + 6$ and write below the dividend. Subtract.

Step 5. 0 remainder.

Check: $(x-2)(2x-3) = 2x^2 - 3x - 4x + 6 = 2x^2 - 7x + 6$, which is the dividend, so our work checks.

b) $2x + 1 \overline{)\ 2x^3 - 5x^2 + 15x + 9}$

Step 1: Write dividend and divisor in descending order. Ther are no missing powers.

$$\begin{array}{r} x^2 \\ 2x + 1 \overline{)\ 2x^3 - 5x^2 + 15x + 9} \\ \underline{2x^3 + x^2 } \\ -6x^2 - 15x \end{array}$$

Step 2: $\dfrac{2x^3}{2x} = x^2$

Step 3: Multiply $x^2(2x + 1) = 2x^3 + x^2$ and write below the dividend. Subtract by changing the signs of $2x^3 + x^2$ to $-2x^3 - x^2$. Bring down $-15x^2$.

$$\begin{array}{r} x^2 - 3x \\ 2x + 1 \overline{)\ 2x^3 - 5x^2 + 15x + 9} \\ \underline{2x^3 + x^2 } \\ 6x^2 - 15x \\ \underline{5x^2 - 3x } \\ -12x + 9 \end{array}$$

Step 2: $\dfrac{-6x^2}{2x} = -3x$

Step 3: Multiply $-3x(2x + 1) = -6x^2 - 3x$ and write below $(-6x^2 - 3x)$ the dividend. Subtract and bring down $+ 9$.

$$\begin{array}{r} x^2 - 3x - 6 \\ 2x + 1 \overline{)\ 2x^3 - 5x^2 + 15x + 9} \\ \underline{2x^3 + x^2 } \\ 6x^2 - 15x \\ \underline{5x^2 - 3x } \\ -12x + 9 \\ \underline{-12x - 6} \\ 15 \end{array}$$

Step 2: $\dfrac{-12x}{2x} = -6$

Step 3: Multiply $-6(2x + 1) = -12x - 6$ and write below the dividend. Subtract.

Step 4: Remainder = 15. Degree of $15 = 15x^0$ is 0, and the degree of the divisor is 1 ($2x = 2x^1$). Division stops when the degree of the remainder is lessthan the degree of the divisor.

Check: $(2x + 1)(x^2 - 3x - 6) = 2x^3 - 6x^2 - 12x + x^2 - 3x - 6$

Multiply the divisor times the quotient.

$= 2x^3 - 5x^2 - 15x - 6$

$(2x^3 - 5x^2 - 15x - 6) + 15 = 2x^3 - 5x^2 - 15x + 9$

Add the remainder to the product of the divisor and the quotient. Note that this sum equals the original dividend, so our work checks.

c) $x + 3 \overline{)\, x^3 - 0x^2 - 5x + 2 \,}$

Step 1: Note that there is no x^2 power in the dividend. Insert $0x^2$ for this missing power.

$$\begin{array}{r} x^2 \\ x+3 \overline{)\, x^3 - 0x^2 - 5x + 2 \,} \\ \underline{x^3 + 3x^2 } \\ -3x^2 - 5x \end{array}$$

Step 3: Multiply $x^2(x + 3) = x^3 + 3x^2$ and write below the $-3x^2 - 5x$ dividend. Subtract by changing the signs of $x^3 = 3x^3$ to $x^3 - 3x^2$. Bring down $-5x$.

$$\begin{array}{r} -3x \\ x+3 \overline{)\, x^3 + 0x^2 - 5x + 2 \,} \\ \underline{x^3 + 3x^2 } \\ -3x^2 - 5x \\ \underline{3x^2 + 9x } \\ 4x + 2 \end{array}$$

Step 2: $\dfrac{-3x^2}{x} = -3x$

Step 3: $-3x(x + 3) = -3x^2 - 9x$. Write this below the dividend. Subtract by changing the signs of $-3x^2 - 9x$ to $3x^2 - 9x$. Bring down 2.

$$\begin{array}{r} x^2 - 3x + 4 \\ x+3 \overline{)\, x^3 + 0x^2 - 5x + 2 \,} \\ \underline{x^3 + 3x^2 } \\ -3x^2 - 5x \\ \underline{3x^2 + 9x } \\ 4x + 2 \\ \underline{4x + 12} \\ -10 \end{array}$$

Step 2: $\dfrac{4x}{x} = 4.$

Step 3: $4(x + 3) = 4x + 12$. Write this below the dividend. Subtract.

Step 5: Degree of $-10 = -10x^0$ is 0. Degree of divisor is 1. Thus, -10 is the remainder.

Check: $(x + 3)(x^2 - 3x + 4) + (-10) =$

Multiply the divisor times the quotient and add the remainder.

$(x^3 - 3x^2 + 4x + 3x^2 - 9x + 12) + (-10) =$

$(x^3 - 5x + 12) + (-10) =$

$x^3 - 5x + 2$

This is the original dividend, so the work checks.

Practice Exercises

1. Simplify each of the following expressions.
   (a) 4^2
   (b) -5^3
   (c) $(-2)^3(-2)^7$
   (d) $a^6 \cdot a^4 \cdot a^2$
   (e) $3^{6x} \cdot 3^{4x}$

2. Simplify each of the following expressions.
   Leave all answers in exponential form.
   (a) $(2^4)^3$
   (b) $(x^3)^4$
   (c) $(4y)^3$
   (d) $(-5s^2t^4)^3$
   (e) $[(7a)^2]^2$

3. Simplify each of the following expressions.
   (a) $\left(\dfrac{2}{3}\right)^5$

   (b) $\left(\dfrac{x}{y}\right)^3$

   (c) $\left(\dfrac{7s}{5t}\right)^2$

   (d) $\left(\dfrac{6m \cdot 3n}{p^4}\right)^2$

   (e) $\left(\dfrac{8a}{3b^2}\right)^3$

4. Simplify each of the following expressions.
   (a) 7^0
   (b) $(-4x2)^0$
   (c) $3y^0$
   (d) 2^{-5}
   (e) $(6a)^{-2}$

5. Simplify each of the following expressions.
   (a) $\dfrac{2^6}{2^3}$

   (b) $\dfrac{3^7}{3^2}$

   (c) $\left(\dfrac{5x^{-4}}{x^2}\right)^3$

   (d) $\left(\dfrac{3^{-2}a^{-1}b^5}{3a^0b^2}\right)^{-2}$

6. Write each number in scientific notation.
   (a) 628,000
   (b) 12
   (c) 0.0047230
   (d) 0.3000089

7. Write each number in expanded form.
   (a) 5.89×10^3
   (b) 11.92×10^6
   (c) 9.797×10^{-4}
   (d) 1.3×10^{-8}

8. Find the indicated product or quotients. Write answers in scientific notation.
   (a) $(9 \times 10^3) \times (3 \times 10^2)$
   (b) $(-3 \times 10^7) \times (8 \times 10^{-5})$
   (c) $\left(\dfrac{3.6 \times 10^{-2}}{12 \times 10^4}\right)$
   (d) $\left(\dfrac{-4.8 \times 10^{-7}}{4 \times 10^{-3}}\right)$
   (e) $\left(\dfrac{72 \times 10^8}{6 \times 10^{-9}}\right)$

9. Find the degree of each polynomial.
    (a) 3
    (b) $2abc$
    (c) $9x^2 + 3xy + 4y^3$

10. Perform the indicated operations.
    (a) $(3x^2 + 6x + 4) + (5x^2 + 8x + 5)$
    (b) $(-2x^3 + 7x - 1) + (x^3 - 4x^2 - 4x)$
    (c) $(2a^2 - a + 6) - (4a^2 + 5a + 8)$
    (d) $(-2a^4 - 7a^2 + 2) - (5a^4 - 3a^3 + 8)$

11. Multiply.
    (a) $(2a^2b)(4a^3)(5b^4)$
    (b) $9x^2(10x^{-8})$

(c) $(7a + 9)(6a - 3)$
(d) $4x(5x + 21)$
(e) $(8x + 9y)2$
(f) $(3a^2 + 2a + 1)(5a^2 + 3a + 1)$

12. Perform the following divisions.
    (a) $\dfrac{15x^2 - 15x + 9}{3}$

    (b) $\dfrac{100x^4 - 75x^3 + 50x^2 - 25x}{25x}$

    (c) $(6x^2 + 17x - 45) \div (2x + 9)$
    (d) $(6x^3 + 16x^2 + 9x + 24) \div (8 + 3x)$

Answers

1. (a) 16
   (b) −125
   (c) $(-2)^{10}$
   (d) a^{12}
   (e) 3^{10x}

2. (a) 2^{12}
   (b) x^{12}
   (c) 4^{3y}
   (d) $-125s^6t^{12}$
   (e) $(7a)^4$

3. (a) $\dfrac{32}{243}$
   (b) $\dfrac{x^3}{y^3}$
   (c) $\dfrac{49s^2}{25t^2}$
   (d) $\dfrac{324m^2n^2}{p^8}$
   (e) $\dfrac{512a^3}{27b^6}$

4. (a) 1
   (b) 1
   (c) 3
   (d) $\dfrac{1}{32}$
   (e) $\dfrac{1}{36a^2}$

5. (a) 2^3
   (b) 3^{-9}
   (c) $125x^{-18}$
   (d) $36a^2b^{-6}$

6. (a) 6.28×10^5
   (b) 1.2×10^1
   (c) 4.7230×10^{-3}
   (d) $.000089 \times 10^{-1}$

7. (a) 5,890
   (b) 11,920,000
   (c) 0.0009797
   (d) 0.000000013

8. (a) 27×10^5
   (b) -24×10^2
   (c) 3×10^{-7}
   (d) -1.2×10^{-4}
   (e) 12×1017

9. (a) 0
   (b) 3
   (c) 3

10. (a) $8x^2 + 14x + 9$
    (b) $-x^3 - 4x^2 + 3x - 1$
    (c) $-2a^2 - 6a - 2$
    (d) $-7a^4 + 3a^3 - 7a^2 - 6$

11. (a) $40a^5b^5$
    (b) $90x^{-6}$
    (c) $42a^2 + 33a - 27$
    (d) $20x^2 + 84x$
    (e) $64x^2 + 144xy + 81y^2$
    (f) $15a^4 + 19a^3 + 14a^2 + 5 + 1$

12. (a) $5x^2 - 5x + 3$
    (b) $4x^3 - 3x^2 + 2x - 1$
    (c) $3x - 5$
    (d) $2x^2 + 3$

4

Factoring

4.1 GREATEST COMMON FACTOR AND FACTORING BY GROUPING

Finding the greatest common factor by trial and error

The greatest common factor (GCF) of a list of terms is the largest factor (numerical coefficient and variables) that evenly divides into each term in the list. Often you will be able to find the GCF by trial and error.

> **Finding the GCF by Trial and Error:**
> 1. Write the largest number that evenly divides into each coefficient in the list.
> 2. Write each common variable (variables that appear in every term) to the lowest exponent that appears.
> 3. Multiply your answers from Step 1 and Step 2 together.

Example 1 Find the GCF of $4x^2y$, $32x^3y^2z$, and $8x^4$.

Solution 1 Looking at 4, 32, and 8, you can see that 4 evenly divides into each of these.
x is the only variable that appears in all three terms in the list. The *lowest* exponent that appears on x is 2.
So the GCF = $4x^2$.

Example 2 Find the GCF of $15y^3z^2$, $25yz^3$ and $30y^4z^4$.

Solution 2 Looking at 15, 25, and 30, you can see that 5 evenly divides into each of these.

y and z appear in all three terms in the list. The *lowest* exponent that appears on y is 1. The *lowest* exponent that appears on z is 2. So the GCF = $5y^1z^2 = 5yz^2$.

Finding the greatest common factor by factoring

Following are some useful rules when trial and error either doesn't appeal to you or isn't convenient to use.

Finding the GCF by Factoring:
1. Prime factor each numerical coefficient and rewrite the terms using exponents.
2. Underline common bases (numbers and letters that appear in *every* term).
3. The GCF is the product of the underlined bases raised to the lowest exponent that appears in any of the terms.

Example 3   Find the GCF of $4x^6y^4$ and $8x^3y^5z$.

Solution 3

$$4x^6y^4 = 2^2x^6y^4$$
$$8x^3y^5z = 2^3x^3y^5z$$

$4 = 2 \cdot 2 = 2^2.$
$8 = 2 \cdot 2 \cdot 2 = 2^3.$

$$\begin{cases} \underline{2}^2\underline{x}^6\underline{y}^4 \\ \underline{2}^3\underline{x}^3\underline{y}^5z \end{cases}$$

Underline common bases, 2, x, and y.

$$\text{GCF} = 2^2x^3y^4$$

Lowest exponent on 2 is 2, lowest exponent on x is 3, and lowest exponent on y is 4.

Example 4   Find the GCF of 72, 48, and 36.

Solution 4   This example has no variables, so you only have to work with numbers.

$$72 = 8 \cdot 9 = 2^3 \cdot 3^2$$
$$48 = 16 \cdot 3 = 2^4 \cdot 3^1$$
$$36 = 4 \cdot 9 = 2^2 \cdot 3^2$$

Write each term using exponents.

$$\begin{cases} \underline{2}^3 \cdot \underline{3}^2 \\ \underline{2}^4 \cdot \underline{3}^1 \\ \underline{2}^2 \cdot \underline{3}^2 \end{cases}$$

Underline common bases 2 and 3.

$$\text{GCF} = 2^2 \cdot 3^1 = 12$$

Write common bases to lowest exponent that appears.

Example 5   Find the GCF of $5x^2$, $7yz$, and $12p$.

Solution 5

$5x^2 = 5x^2$
$7yz = 7yz$ Write each term using exponents.
$12p = 2^2 \cdot 3p$

$\begin{cases} 5x^2 \\ 7yz \\ 2^2 \cdot 3p \end{cases}$ There are *no* common bases!

GCF = 1 since 1 is the only number that evenly divides 5, 7, and 12.

Factoring out the GCF

In Chapter 3 we multiplied polynomials using the Distributive Property, FOIL, and several shortcuts. In this chapter we need to reverse the multiplication process, which is called factoring. The first step in any factoring problem is to factor out the greatest common factor.

> **To Factor out the GCF:**
> 1. Write the GCF of all the terms followed by a set of parentheses. Leave room inside the parentheses.
> 2. Divide the GCF into *each* term and write that quotient inside the parentheses.

Example 6   Factor out the GCF.
a) $20x^5 + 10x^3 + 30x^2$
b) $36r^6s^2 - 16r^3s^5$
c) $x(x+3) + 2(x+3)$
d) $2x(x-1) - 3(x-1)$

Solution 6

a) $20x^5 + 10x^3 + 30x^2 =$
$2^2 \cdot 5x^5 + 2 \cdot 5x^3 + 2 \cdot 3 \cdot 5x^2$ Write each term using exponents.
$= 2 \cdot 5x^2(\qquad)$ Write GCF followed by parentheses.

$= 25x^2(2x^3 + x + 3)$ $\dfrac{20x^5}{10x^2} = 2x^3$ and

$\dfrac{10x^3}{10x^2} = x$ and $\dfrac{30x^2}{10x^2} = 3.$

$= 10x^2(2x^3 + x + 3)$

If you can see that 10 evenly divides 20, 10, and 30, you can skip the step in which you write each term using exponents. Just remember to also factor out *common* variables to the *lowest* exponent that appears in any one term.

b) $36r^6s^2 - 16r^3s^5 = 2^2 \cdot 3\,^2r^6s^2 - 2^4r^3s^5$ Write each term using exponents.

$= 2^2r^3s^2($ $)$ Write GCF followed by parentheses.

$= 2^2r^3s^2(9r^3 - 4s^3)$ $\dfrac{36r^6s^2}{4r^3s^2} = 9r^3$ and $\dfrac{16r^3s^5}{4r^3s^2} = 4s^3.$

$= 4r^3s^2(9r^3 - 4s^3)$

c) $x(x + 3) + 2(x + 3) = (x + 3)(x + 2)$ Here, the only common factor is $(x + 3)$, and the lowest exponent that appears is an understood 1.

d) $2x(x - 1) - 3(x - 1) = (x - 1)(2x - 3)$ Note: common factor is $(x - 1)$.

> BEGIN EVERY FACTORING EXAMPLE BY LOOKING FOR THE GCF!

Factoring by grouping

We will do several types of problems involving factoring by grouping. In this section, we will concentrate on problems with four terms that can be grouped as two terms plus two terms. Here are some general rules.

> **To Factor by Grouping:**
> 1. Group together the first two terms and factor out the GCF. Group together the last two terms and factor out the GCF.
> 2. If the expressions in the parentheses are equal, factor out that expression as the GCF.
> 3. If the expressions in the parentheses are not equal, change the order of the terms and go back to step 1.

Example 7   Factor by grouping.
a) $xa + xy + 2a + 2y$
b) $x^2 + 2x + 2x + 4$
c) $mn + 4m - 2n - 8$
d) $pq + 3q + p + 3$
e) $rs + 3t + rt + 3s$

Solution 7

a) $xa + xy + 2a + 2y = (xa + xy) + (2a + 2y)$ Group together the first two terms and the last two terms.

$= x(a + y) + 2(a + y)$ Factor out the GCF, x, from the first two terms.
Factor out the GCF, 2, from the last two terms.

$= (a + y)(x + 2)$ $a + y$ is now the GCF and can be factored out.

b) $x^2 + 2x + 2x + 4 = (x^2 + 2x) + (2x + 4)$ Group together the first two terms and the last two terms.

$= x(x + 2) + 2(x + 2)$ Factor out the GCF, x, from the first two terms.
Factor out the GCF, 2, from the last two terms.

$= (x + 2)(x + 2)$ $x + 2$ is now the GCF and can be factored out.

c) $mn + 4m - 2n - 8 = (mn + 4m) + (-2n - 8)$ Group together the first two terms and the last two terms.

$= m(n + 4) - 2(n + 4)$ Factor out the GCF, m, from the first two terms. The GCF for the last two terms is 2 or –2. Using –2 as the GCF will make the terms in the parentheses equal to the terms in the first set of parentheses.

$= (n + 4)(m - 2)$ $n + 4$ is now the GCF.

d) $pq + 3q + p + 3 = q(p + 3) + 1(p + 3)$ Group the first two terms together and the last two terms together, and factor out the greatest common factors.

$= (p + 3)(q + 1)$ Common factor is now $p + 3$.

e) $rs + 3t + rt + 3s = (rs + 3t) + (rt + 3s)$ Group together the first two terms and the last two terms.

There are no common factors in either set of parentheses.
Change the order of the terms and try again.

$$= rs + rt + 3s + 3t$$

Change order so you can common factor.

$$= (rs + rt) + (3s + 3t)$$

Group together the first terms and the last two terms.

$$= r(s + t) + 3(s + t)$$

Factor out the GCF, r, from the first two terms. Factor out the GCF, 3, from the last two terms.

$$= (s + t)(r + 3)$$

Common factor is now $s + t$.

Note in example e) that you could also reorder the terms as $rs + 3s + rt + 3t$, and will get the same answer, $(s + t)(r + 3)$.

4.2 FACTORING TRINOMIALS OF THE FORM $ax^2 + bx + c$, WHERE $a = 1$

Identifying a, b, and c in a trinomial

In the trinomial $ax^2 + bx + c$, the coefficient of x^2 is a, the coefficient of x is b, and c is the constant term.

Example 8   Identify a, b, and c in each trinomial.
   a) $2x^2 + 4x + 3$
   b) $x^2 - 2x + 5$
   c) $3x^2 - x - 4$
   d) $-4x^2 + 2x - 7$
   e) $7 - 3x + 7x^2$

Solution 8

   a) $2x^2 + 4x + 3$:

   $a = 2$
   $b = 4$
   $c = 3$

b) $x^2 - 2x + 5$:

First rewrite as $1x^2 + (-2x) + 5$.
$a = 1$
$b = -2$
$c = 5$

c) $3x^2 - x - 4$:

First rewrite as $3x^2 + (-1x) + (-4)$.
$a = 3$
$b = -1$
$c = -4$

d) $-4x^2 + 2x - 7$:

First rewrite as $-4x^2 + 2x + (-7)$.
$a = -4$
$b = 2$
$c = -7$

e) $5 - 3x + 7x^2$:

First rewrite in descending order as
$7x^2 - 3x + 5 = 7x^2 + (-3x) + 5$.
$a = 7$
$b = -3$
$c = 5$

Factoring trinomials

When $a = 1$ in $ax^2 + bx + c$, we can factor using the following rules:

1. Identify a, b, and c.
2. List all pairs of factors of c.
3. Find a pair of factors whose sum equals b. If there is no such pair, the trinomial does not factor.
4. Write two sets of parentheses $(x \underline{\quad})(x \underline{\quad})$.
5. Fill in the blanks with the pair from step 2.
6. Check your answer using FOIL.

Example 9   Factor each trinomial.
a) $x^2 + 7x + 10$
b) $x^2 + x - 12$
c) $x^2 - 7x + 6$
d) $x^2 - 2x - 63$
e) $x^2 + 3x + 14$

Solution 9

a) In $x^2 + 7x + 10$, $a = 1$, $b = 7$, $c = 10$.

$$\begin{array}{ll} \underline{c = +10} \\ +1 \quad +10 \\ +2 \quad +5 \\ -1 \quad -10 \\ -2 \quad -5 \end{array}$$

$(x \underline{\quad})(x \underline{\quad})$

$(x + 2)(x + 5)$

Check: $(x + 2)(x + 5) = x^2 + 5x + 2x + 10$

$= x^2 + 7x + 10$

Identify a, b, and c.
List all pairs of factors of +10.
Find a pair whose sum equals 7.

Set up a pair of parentheses.

Fill in the blanks.

Check your answer using FOIL.

This equals the original polynomial, so the answer is correct.

b) In $x^2 + x - 12$, $a = 1$, $b = 1$, $c = -12$.

$$\begin{array}{ll} \underline{c = -12} \\ +1 \quad -12 \\ +2 \quad -6 \\ +3 \quad -4 \\ -1 \quad +12 \\ -2 \quad +6 \\ -3 \quad +4 \end{array}$$

$(x \underline{\quad})(x \underline{\quad})$

$(x - 3)(x + 4)$

Check: $(x - 3)(x + 4) = x^2 + 4x - 3x - 12$

$= x^2 + x - 12$

Identify a, b, and c.

List all pairs of factors of -12.
Find a pair whose sum equals 1.

Set up a pair of parentheses.

Fill in the blanks.

Check your answer using FOIL.

c) In $x^2 - 7x + 6$, $a = 1$, $b = -7$, $c = 6$.

$$\begin{array}{ll} \underline{c = 6} \\ +1 \quad +6 \\ +2 \quad +3 \\ -1 \quad -6 \\ -2 \quad -3 \end{array}$$

$(x \underline{\quad})(x \underline{\quad})$

$(x - 1)(x - 6)$

Check: $(x - 1)(x - 6) = x^2 - x - 6x + 6$

$= x^2 - 7x + 6$

Identify a, b, and c.

List all pairs of factors of +6.
Find a pair that whose sum equals -7.

Set up a pair of parentheses.

Fill in the blanks.

Check your answer using FOIL.

d) In $x^2 - 2x - 63$, $a = 1$, $b = -2$, $c = -63$. Identify a, b, and c.

$$\frac{c = -63}{\begin{array}{rr} +1 & -63 \\ +3 & -21 \\ +7 & -9 \\ -1 & +63 \\ -3 & +21 \\ -7 & +9 \end{array}}$$

List all pairs of factors of -63.
Find a pair whose sum equals -2.

$(x\underline{\quad})(x\underline{\quad})$ Set up a pair of parentheses.

$(x + 7)(x - 9)$ Fill in the blanks.

Check: $(x + 7)(x - 9) = x^2 + 7x - 9x - 63$

$\qquad = x^2 - 2x - 63$ Check your answer using FOIL.

e) In $x^2 + 3x + 14$, $a = 1$, $b = 3$, $c = 14$. Identify a, b, and c.

$$\frac{c = 14}{\begin{array}{rr} +1 & +14 \\ +2 & +7 \\ -1 & -14 \\ -2 & -7 \end{array}}$$

List all pairs of factors of 14.
Find a pair whose sum equals 3.

There is no pair of factors whose sum equals 3. This trinomial does not factor.

Factoring out the GCF

You may need to factor out the GCF before using the rules given for trinomials.

Example 10 Factor.
a) $2x^2 + 4x - 30$
b) $-3x^2 + 30x - 63$
c) $6x^3 - 18x^2 - 24x$
d) $2x^2 + 2x + 12$

Solution 10

a) $2x^2 + 4x - 30 = 2(x^2 + 2x - 15)$ Factor out the GCF 2.

In $x^2 + 2x - 15$, $a = 1$, $b = 2$, $c = -15$.   Identify a, b, and c.

$$\frac{c = -15}{\begin{array}{rr} +1 & -15 \\ +3 & -5 \\ -1 & +15 \\ -3 & +5 \end{array}}$$

List all pairs of factors of -15.
Find a pair whose sum equals 2.

$= 2(x - 3)(x + 5)$

Check: $2(x-3)(x+5) = 2(x^2 + 5x - 3x - 15)$ Use FOIL to multiply the binomials.

$= 2(x^2 + 2x - 15)$ Combine similar terms.

$= 2x^2 + 4x - 30$ Use the Distributive Property.

b) $-3x^2 + 30x - 63 = -3(x^2 - 10x + 21)$ Factor out the GCF -3.

In $x^2 - 10x + 21$, $a = 1$, $b = -10$, $c = 21$.   Identify a, b, and c.

$$\underline{c \;=\; 21}$$
$+1 \;\; +21$
$+3 \;\; +7$
$-1 \;\; -21$
$-3 \;\; -7$
$= -3(x-3)(x-7)$

List all pairs of factors of 21.
Find a pair whose sum equals −10.

Check: $-3(x-3)(x-7) = -3(x^2 - 7x - 3x + 21)$ Use FOIL to multiply the binomials.

$= -3(x^2 - 10x + 21)$ Combine similar terms.

$= -3x^2 + 30x - 63$ Use the Distributive Property.

c) $6x^3 - 18x^2 - 24x = 6x(x^2 - 3x - 4)$ Factor out the GCF $6x$.

In $x^2 - 3x - 4$, $a = 1$, $b = -3$, $c = -4$.   Identify a, b, and c.

$$\underline{c \;=\; -4}$$
$+1 \quad -4$
$+2 \quad -2$
$-1 \quad +4$
$-2 \quad +2$
$= 6x(x+1)(x-4)$

List all pairs of factors of −4.
Find a pair whose sum equals −3.

Check: $6x(x+1)(x-4) = 6x(x^2 - 4x + x - 4)$ Use FOIL to multiply the binomials.

$= 6x(x^2 - 3x - 4)$ Combine similar terms.

$= 6x^3 - 18x^2 - 24x$ Use the Distributive Property.

d) $2x^2 + 2x + 12 = 2(x^2 + x + 6)$ Factor out the GCF 2.

In $x^2 + x + 6$, $a = 1$, $b = 1$, $c = 6$.   Identify a, b, and c.

$$\underline{c \;=\; +6}$$
$+1 \quad +6$
$+2 \quad +3$
$-1 \quad -6$
$-2 \quad -3$

List all pairs of factors of 6.
Find a pair whose sum equals 1.

There is no pair of factors whose sum equals 1. Therefore, the only factoring that can be done is factoring out the GCF. The answer is:

$$2(x^2 + x + 6)$$

4.3 FACTORING TRINOMIALS OF THE FORM $ax^2 + bx + c$, WHERE $a \neq 1$

Factoring by trial and error

The following rules can be used to factor trinomials of the form $ax^2 + bx + c$ particularly when $a \neq 1$. Although the rules given in the previous section apply only when $a = 1$, the following rules can be used for any value of a. We will make use of the fact that the factors of $ax^2 + bx + c$ will be a pair of binomials in which the product of the first two terms must equal ax^2, and the product of the last two terms must equal c.

To Factor $ax^2 + bx + c$ by Trial and Error:
1. List positive pairs of factors of ax^2.
2. List pairs of factors of c.
3. List pairs of binomial factors whose first terms are factors of ax^2 and whose last terms are factors of c.
4. Eliminate combinations that have a GCF. If the original trinomial has no GCF, there cannot be a GCF in any of the factors.
5. Use FOIL to multiply the binomials. Stop when you find a pair of factors whose product equals the original trinomial.

Note: You could use positive and negative factors of ax^2, but students generally find it easier to use positive and negative factors of c. If $a \neq 0$, start by factoring out -1.

Example 11 Factor.
   a) $2x^2 + 7x + 3$
   b) $4x^2 + 7x - 2$
   c) $6x^2 - 7x + 2$
   d) $10x^2 - x - 3$

Solution 11 a)

$$2x^2 + 7x + 3 \quad \begin{array}{c} \underline{ax^2 = 2x^2} \\ 2x \quad x \\ x \quad 2x \end{array} \quad \begin{array}{cc} \underline{c = +3} \\ +1 \quad +3 \\ -1 \quad -3 \end{array} \quad \text{List pairs of factors of } ax^2 \text{ and } c.$$

$(2x + 1)(x + 3)$

$(2x - 1)(x - 3)$

$(x + 1)(2x + 3)$

$(x - 1)(2x - 3)$

List pairs of binomial factors whose first terms are factors of $2x^2$ and whose last terms are factors of +3.

Use FOIL to multiply the binomials:

$(2x + 1)(x + 3) = 2x^2 + 6x + x + 3 = 2x^2 + 7x + 3$

$(2x - 1)(x - 3) = 2x^2 - 6x - x + 3 = 2x^2 - 7x + 3$

$(x + 1)(2x + 3) = 2x^2 + 3x + 2x + 3 = 2x^2 + 5x + 3$

$(x - 1)(2x - 3) = 2x^2 - 3x - 2x + 3 = 2x^2 - 5x + 3$

So $2x^2 + 7x + 3 = (2x + 1)(x + 3)$. We could have stopped after multiplying out the first pair, since its product was equal to the original trinomial.

b) $4x^2 + 7x - 2$

$ax^2 = 4x^2$		$c = -2$
$4x$	x	$+1 \ -2$
$2x$	$2x$	$-1 \ +2$
x	$4x$	

List pairs of factors of ax^2 and c.

$(4x + 1)(x - 2)$

$(4x - 1)(x + 2)$

$(2x + 1)(2x - 2)$

$(2x - 1)(2x + 2)$

$(x + 1)(4x - 2)$

$(x - 1)(4x + 2)$

List pairs of binomial factors whose first terms are factors of $4x^2$ and whose last terms are factors of -2.

Use FOIL to multiply the binomials:

$(4x + 1)(x - 2) = 4x^2 - 8x + x - 2 = 4x^2 - 7x - 2$

$(4x - 1)(x + 2) = 4x^2 + 8x - x - 2 = 4x^2 + 7x - 2$ This is correct!

$(2x + 1)(2x - 2)$ This can be eliminated since $2x - 2$ has a GCF of 2.

$(2x - 1)(2x + 2)$ This can be eliminated since $2x + 2$ has a GCF of 2.

$(x + 1)(4x - 2)$ This can be eliminated since $4x - 2$ has a GCF of 2.

$(x - 1)(4x + 2)$ This can be eliminated since $4x + 2$ has a GCF of 2.

Notice that we listed $4x$ and x, as well as x and $4x$ in our list of factors for $4x^2$. By using the Commutative Property to form our list of factors of $4x^2$, we do not need to list -2 and $+1$, and $+2$ and -1 in our list of factors of c. If you do list factors of c in both orders, you will find duplicates in the list of pairs of binomial factors (such as $(4x - 2)(x + 1)$).

c) $6x^2 - 7x + 2$

$ax^2 = 6x^2$		$c = +2$
$6x$	x^2	$+1$ $+2$
$3x$	$2x$	-1 -2
x	$6x$	
$2x$	$3x$	

List pairs of factors of ax^2 and c.

$(6x + 1)(x + 2)$
$(6x - 1)(x - 2)$
$(3x + 1)(2x + 2)$
$(3x - 1)(2x - 2)$
$(x + 1)(6x + 2)$
$(x - 1)(6x - 2)$
$(2x + 1)(3x + 2)$
$(2x - 1)(3x - 2)$

List pairs of binomial factors whose first terms are factors of $6x^2$ and whose last terms are factors of $+2$.

Use FOIL to multiply the binomials:

$(6x + 1)(x + 2) = 6x^2 + 12x + x + 2 = 6x^2 + 13x + 2$
$(6x - 1)(x - 2) = 6x^2 - 12x - x + 2 = 6x^2 - 13x + 2$

$(3x + 1)(2x + 2)$ This can be eliminated since $2x + 2$ has a GCF of 2.

$(3x - 1)(2x - 2)$ This can be eliminated since $2x - 2$ has a GCF of 2.

$(x + 1)(6x + 2)$ This can be eliminated since $6x + 2$ has a GCF of 2.

$(x - 1)(6x - 2)$ This can be eliminated since $6x - 2$ has a GCF of 2.

$(2x + 1)(3x + 2) = 6x^2 + 4x + 3x + 2 = 6x^2 + 7x + 2$
$(2x - 1)(3x - 2) = 6x^2 - 4x - 3x + 2 = 6x^2 - 7x + 2$ This is it!

So $6x^2 - 7x + 2 = (3x - 2)(2x - 1)$.

d) $10x^2 - x - 3$

$ax^2 = 10x^2$		$c = -3$
x	$10x$	$+1$ -3
$2x$	$5x$	-1 $+3$
$10x$	x	
$5x$	$2x$	

List pairs of factors of ax^2 and c.

$(x + 1)(10x - 3)$
$(x - 1)(10x + 3)$
$(2x + 1)(5x - 3)$
$(2x - 1)(5x + 3)$
$(10x + 1)(x - 3)$
$(10x - 1)(x + 3)$
$(5x + 1)(2x - 3)$
$(5x - 1)(2x + 3)$

List pairs of binomial factors whose first terms are factors of $10x^2$ and whose last erms are factors of -3.

Use FOIL to multiply the binomials:

$(x + 1)(10x - 3) = 10x^2 - 3x + 10x - 3 = 10x^2 + 7x - 3$
$(x - 1)(10x + 3) = 10x^2 + 3x - 10x - 3 = 10x^2 - 7x - 3$
$(2x + 1)(5x - 3) = 10x^2 - 6x + 5x - 3 = 10x^2 - x - 3$ This is it!

So $10x^2 - x - 3 = (5x - 3)(2x + 1)$.

Factoring $ax^2 + bx + c$ by grouping

If there are many choices for factors of a and factors of c, you may prefer the following method. These steps assume that you have already factored out any common factor.

Factoring $ax^2 + bx + c$ by Grouping:
1. Multiply $a \cdot c$.
2. List pairs of factors of $a \cdot c$.
3. Find a pair of factors whose sum equals b.
4. Rewrite $ax^2 + bx + c$ by replacing bx with the pair of factors found in Step 3.
5. Factor this new four-term polynomial by grouping.

To help you find factors more quickly, consider the signs of b and c, assuming that a is a positive number. If b and c are both positive, the factors of c must be positive. If b is negative and c is positive, the factors of c must both be negative. If b is positive and c is negative, the larger factor of c must be positive, and the smaller factor must be negative. If b is negative and c is negative, the larger factor must be negative, and the smaller factor must be positive. Go back and check the answers from Example 11 to verify these cases.

Sign of b	Sign of c	Sign of Factors of c	Example 11
+	+	Both must be a +.	See 11 a)
−	+	Both must be −.	See 11 c)
+	−	Larger factor must be +, smaller factor must be −.	See 11 b)
−	−	Larger factor must be −, smaller factor must be +.	See 11 d)

Example 12 Factor.

    a) $8x^2 + 18x + 9$

    b) $8x^2 + 14x - 15$

    c) $x^2 - 10x + 24$

    d) $3x^2 - 2x - 8$

Solution 12

a) $8x^2 + 18x + 9$

$$\underline{8x^2 \cdot 9 = 72x^2}$$

$1x$	$72x$
$2x$	$36x$
$3x$	$24x$
$4x$	$18x$
$6x$	**$12x$**
$8x$	$9x$

Multiply $a \cdot c$.
List pairs of factors of $a \cdot c$.
Sign of b is +, sign of c is +,
so both factors must
be positive.
Find a pair whose sum equals $18x$.

$8x^2 + 6x + 12x + 9$

$2x(4x + 3) + 3(4x + 3)$

$= (4x + 3)(2x + 3)$

Replace $18x$ with $6x + 12x$.
Factor by grouping.

b) $8x^2 + 14x - 15$

$$\underline{8x^2 \cdot -15 = -120x^2}$$

$-1x$	$120x$
$-2x$	$60x$
$-3x$	$40x$
$-4x$	$30x$
$-5x$	$24x$
$-6x$	**$20x$**
$-8x$	$15x$
$-10x$	$12x$

Multiply $a \cdot c$.
List pairs of factors of $a \cdot c$.
Sign of b is +, sign of c is −,
so the larger factor must
be positive and the smaller
factor must be negative.
Find a pair whose sum equals $+14x$.

$8x^2 - 6x + 20x - 15$

$2x(4x - 3) + 5(4x - 3)$

$= (4x - 3)(2x + 5)$

Replace $14x$ with $-6x + 20x$.

Factor by grouping.

c) $x^2 - 10x + 24$

$$\underline{1x^2 \cdot 24 = 24x^2}$$

$-1x$	$-24x$
$-2x$	$-12x$
$-3x$	$-8x$
$-4x$	**$-6x$**

Multiply $a \cdot c$.
List pairs of factors of $a \cdot c$.
Sign of b is −, sign of c is +,
so both factors must be negative.
Find a pair whose sum equals $-10x$.

$x^2 - 4x - 6x + 24$

$x(x - 4) - 6(x - 4)$

$= (x - 4)(x - 6)$

Replace $-10x$ with $-4x - 6x$.
Factor by grouping.

d) $3x^2 - 2x - 8$

$3x^2 \cdot -8 = -24x^2$	
$1x$	$-24x$
$2x$	$-12x$
$3x$	$-8x$
$4x$	$-6x$

Multiply $a \cdot c$.
List pairs of factors of $a \cdot c$.
Sign of b is –, sign of c is –,
so the larger factor must be
negative and the smaller factor
must be positive.
Find a pair whose sum equals $-2x$.

$3x^2 + 4x - 6x - 8$

Replace $-2x$ with $4x - 6x$.

$x(3x + 4) - 2(3x + 4)$
$= (3x + 4)(x - 2)$

Factor by grouping.

Choosing methods for factoring

You may find that trial and error works best for problems in which a and/or c are prime, and that grouping works well otherwise. Remember to start every factoring example looking for the greatest common factor.

Example 13 Factor as completely as possible. Remember to look for the GCF first! Use either method.

a) $20a^3b + 15a^2b - 50ab$
b) $4x^3 + 10x^2y - 24xy^2$
c) $2s^2 - 2s - 12$

Solution 13

a) $20a^3b + 15a^2b - 50ab = 5ab(4a^2 + 3a - 10)$ The GCF is $5ab$.

$4a^2 + 3a - 10$

$4a^2 \cdot -10 = -40a^2$	
$-1a$	$40a$
$-2a$	$20a$
$-4a$	$10a$
$-5a$	$8a$

Neither a nor c is prime, so try
factoring by grouping.
List pairs of factors of $a \cdot c$.
Sign of b is +, sign of c is –,
so the larger factor must be
positive and the smaller factor
must be negative.
Find a pair whose sum equals $+3a$.

$4a^2 - 5a + 8a - 10$
$a(4a - 5) + 2(4a - 5)$
$(4a - 5)(a + 2)$
$= 5ab (4a - 5)(a + 2)$

Replace $+3a$ with $-5a + 8a$.
Factor by grouping.

Remember to write the GCF in
your answer.

b) $4x^3 + 10x^2y - 24xy^2 = 2x(2x^2 + 5xy - 12y^2)$ The GCF is $2x$.

$2x^2 + 5xy - 12y^2$ $\quad 2x^2 \cdot -12y^2 = -24x^2y^2$ Since a is prime, this could be
$\qquad\qquad$ $-1xy \quad 24xy$ done by either method.
$\qquad\qquad$ $-2xy \quad 12xy$ Sign of b is +, sign of c is −,
$\qquad\qquad$ $\mathbf{-3xy \quad 8xy}$ so the larger factor must be
$\qquad\qquad$ $-4xy \quad 6xy$ positive and the smaller factor
$\qquad\qquad\qquad\qquad\qquad\qquad$ must be negative.
$\qquad\qquad\qquad\qquad\qquad\qquad$ Find a pair whose sum equals $+5xy$.

$2x^2 - 3xy + 8xy - 12y^2$ Replace $+5xy$ with $-3xy + 8xy$.
$x(2x - 3y) + 4y(2x - 3y)$ Factor by grouping.
$(2x - 3y)(x + 4y)$
$= 2x(2x - 3y)(x + 4y)$ Remember to write the GCF in
$\qquad\qquad\qquad\qquad\qquad\qquad$ your answer.

c) $2s^2 - 2s - 12 = 2(s^2 - s - 6)$ The GCF is 2.

$s^2 - s + 6$ $\quad \dfrac{ax^2 = s^2}{s \quad s}$ $\quad \underline{c = -6}$
$\qquad\qquad\qquad\qquad\qquad$ $+1 \quad -6$ Since a is prime, use trial
$\qquad\qquad\qquad\qquad\qquad$ $+2 \quad -3$ and error.
$\qquad\qquad\qquad\qquad\qquad\qquad$ Sign of b is −, sign of c is −, so the
$\qquad\qquad\qquad\qquad\qquad\qquad$ larger factor must be negative.
$(s + 1)(s - 6)$ List pairs of binomial factors.
$(s + 2)(s - 3)$

Use FOIL to multiply the binomials:
$(s + 1)(s - 6) = s^2 - 6s + s - 6 = s^2 - 5s - 6$
$(s + 2)(s - 3) = s^2 - 3s + 2s - 6 = s^2 - s - 6$ This is it!
$= 2(s + 2)(s - 3)$ Remember to write the GCF in
$\qquad\qquad\qquad\qquad\qquad\qquad$ your answer.

4.4 FACTORING SPECIAL POLYNOMIALS

In this section we will factor several special polynomials. The following table summarizes the formulas we will be using:

Difference of Two Squares	$x^2 - y^2 = (x - y)(x + y)$
Sum of Two Squares	$x^2 + y^2$ does not factor.
Perfect Square Trinominal	$x^2 + 2xy + y^2 = (x + y)^2 = (x + y)(x + y)$ $x^2 - 2xy + y^2 = (x - y)^2 = (x - y)(x - y)$
Sum of Two Cubes	$x^3 + y^3 = (x + y)(x^2 - xy + y^2)$
Difference of Two Cubes	$x^3 - y^3 = (x - y)(x^2 + xy + y^2)$

Difference and sum of two squares

To recognize either a difference or sum of two squares, try writing each term as a perfect square. A difference of two squares has a subtraction sign between the two terms; a sum of two squares has an addition sign between the two terms.

$$4x^2 - 9 = (2x)^2 - (3)^2$$ Difference of two squares.

$$25y^2 - 1 = (5y)^2 - (1)^2$$ Difference of two squares.

$$81p^2 - 49q^2 = (9p)^2 - (7q)^2$$ Difference of two squares.

$$x^2 + 16 = (x)^2 + (4)^2$$ Sum of two squares.

$$16a^2 - 7 = (4a)^2 - (7)$$ *Not* a difference of two squares.

To Factor a Difference of Two Squares:
1. Write each term as a perfect square $(x)^2 - (y)^2$.
2. Write two sets of parentheses $(\_ + \_)(\_ - \_)$.
3. Use each term in parentheses from step 1 to fill in the blanks $(x + y)(x - y)$.
4. Check using FOIL.

Example 14   Factor each difference of two squares.
a) $4x^2 - 9$
b) $25y^2 - 1$
c) $81p^2 - 49q^2$

Solution 14

a) $4x^2 - 9 = (2x)^2 - (3)^2$ $(2x)^2 = 4x^2$.
    $(3)^2 = 9$.

$\quad = (\_ + \_)(\_ - \_)$ Write two sets of parentheses.

$\quad = (2x + 3)(2x - 3)$ Use terms in parentheses from Step 1 to fill in the blanks.

Check: $(2x + 3)(2x - 3) = 4x^2 - 6x + 6x - 9 = 4x^2 - 9$

b) $25y^2 - 1 = (5y)^2 - (1)^2$ $(5y)^2 = 25y^2$.
    $(1)^2 = 1$.

$\quad = (\_ + \_)(\_ - \_)$ Write two sets of parentheses.

$\quad = (5y + 1)(5y - 1)$ Use terms in parentheses from Step 1 to fill in the blanks.

Check: $(5y + 1)(5y - 1) = 25y^2 - 5y + 5y - 1 = 25y^2 - 1$

c) $81p^2 - 49q^2 = (9p)^2 - (7q)^2$ $(9p)^2 = 81p^2$.
    $(7q)^2 = 49q^2$.

$$= (\_ + \_)(\_ - \_)$$ Write two sets of parentheses.

$$= (9p + 7q)(9p - 7q)$$ Use terms in parentheses from Step 1 to fill in the blanks.

$$Check: (9p + 7q)(9p - 7q) = 81p^2 - 63pq + 63pq - 49q^2$$
$$= 81p^2 - 49q^2$$

A sum of two squares, such as $x^2 + y^2$, cannot be factored. The only possible factoring would involve factoring out the GCF. (If you take more mathematics courses you may find that a sum of two squares factors over the complex numbers, but that is beyond our needs at this point.)

To Factor a Sum of Two Squares:
1. Factor out the GCF.
2. That's it!

Example 15   Factor, if possible.
a) $x^2 + 16$
b) $4a^2 + 16$
c) $162p^2 + 98q^2$
d) $162p^2 - 98q^2$

Solution 15

a) $x^2 + 16 = x^2 + 16$ No GCF.

b) $4a^2 + 16 = 4(a^2 + 4)$ GCF, sum of two squares.

c) $162p^2 + 98q^2 = 2(81p^2 + 49q^2)$ GCF, sum of two squares.

d) $162p^2 - 98q^2 = 2(81p^2 - 49q^2)$ GCF, difference of two squares.

$$81p^2 - 49q^2 = (9p)^2 - (7q)^2$$ Write each term as a perfect square.

$$= (9p + 7q)(9p - 7q)$$ Write two sets of parentheses and fill in the perfect squares from the step above.

$$= 2(9p + 7q)(9p - 7q)$$ Remember to write the GCF in your final answer.

Notice the difference between c and d. A sum of two squares does not factor, while a difference of two squares does factor!

Example 16   Factor completely.
a) $x^4 - y^4$
b) $(x - 2)^2 - 16$
c) $3x^6 - 48$

Solution 16

a) $x^4 - y^4 = (x^2)^2 - (y^2)^2$ Write each term as a perfect square.

     $= (x^2 + y^2)(x^2 - y^2)$ Keep going! $x^2 - y^2$ is a difference of two squares.

     $= (x^2 + y^2)[(x)^2 - (y)^2]$ Write each term as a perfect square.

     $= (x^2 + y^2)(x + y)(x - y)$ Note that $x^2 + y^2$ is a sum of two squares and cannot be factored further.

b) $(x - 2)^2 - 16 = (x - 2)^2 - (4)^2$ Write each term as a perfect square. $(x - 2)^2$ is already written as a perfect square. $16 = (4)^2$.

     $= (\underline{} + \underline{})(\underline{} - \underline{})$ Write two sets of parentheses.

     $= (x - 2 + 4)(x - 2 - 4)$ Fill in the blanks with the perfect squares.

     $= (x + 2)(x - 6)$ Simplify: $-2 + 4 = 2.$
                                                   $-2 - 4 = -6.$

c) $3x^6 - 48 = 3(x^6 - 16)$ Factor out the GCF, 3.

     $x^6 - 16 = (x^3)^2 - (4)^2$ Write each term as a perfect square. To raise a power to a power, multiply the exponents, so $(x^3)2 = x^{3 \cdot 2} = x^6$.

     $= (x^3 + 4)(x^3 - 4)$ Write two sets of parentheses and fill in the perfect squares.

     $= 3(x^3 + 4)(x^3 - 4)$ Remember to write the GCF in your final answer.

Identifying perfect square trinomials

A perfect square trinomial can be written as $(x)^2 \pm 2\,(x)(y) + (y)^2$

                                              ↑   ↑

                                     perfect   perfect
                                     square   square

The first and third terms are perfect squares. The middle term is twice the product of the terms in the parentheses. The sign stands for plus or minus and means that the middle sign could be plus or could be minus.

Example 17   Which of the following are perfect square trinomials?

     a) $4a^2 + 20a + 25$

     b) $25x^2 - 30xy + 9y^2$

   c) $x^2 - 2xy + 4y^2$

   d) $16p^2 + 8pq + 15$

Solution 17

   a) $4a^2 + 20a + 25$

Are the first and third terms perfect squares?

$4a^2 = (2a)^2 \quad 25 = (5)^2$ Yes.

Is the middle term $2(2a)(5)$?

$2(2a)(5) = 20a$ Yes.

Thus, this is a perfect square trinomial.

   b) $25x^2 - 30xy + 9y^2$

Are the first and third terms perfect squares?

$25x^2 = (5x)^2 \quad 9y^2 = (3y)^2$ Yes.

Is the middle term $2(5x)(3y)$?

$2(5x)(3y) = 30xy$ Yes.

Thus, this is a perfect square trinomial.

   c) $x^2 - 2xy + 4y^2$

Are the first and third terms perfect squares?

$x^2 = (x)^2 \quad 4y^2 = (2y)^2$ Yes.

Is the middle term $2(x)(2y)$?

$2(x)(2y) = 4xy$ No!

Thus, this is not a perfect square trinomial.

   d) $16p^2 + 8pq + 15$

Are the first and third terms perfect squares?

$16p^2 = (4p)^2 \quad 15 \neq (\quad)^2$ No!

Thus, this is not a perfect square trinomial.

Factoring perfect square trinomials

> **To Factor a Perfect Square Trinomial:**
> 1. Write the trinomial as a perfect square trinomial: $(x)^2 \pm 2(x)(y) + (y)^2$.
> 2. Write a set of parentheses with a square outside. Use the sign of the middle term inside the parentheses: $(\_ \pm \_)^2$
> 3. Fill in the blanks with the perfect squares of the first and third terms.
> $(x)^2 \pm 2(x)(y) + (y)^2 = (x \pm y)^2$

Example 18 Factor.

a) $4a^2 + 20a + 25$

b) $25x^2 - 30xy + 9y^2$

c) $121 - 22m + m^2$

d) $r^2 + 10rs + 9s^2$

Solution 18

a) $4a^2 + 20a + 25 = (2a)^2 + 2(2a)(5) + (5)^2$ Write the trinomial as a perfect square trinomial.

$= (\_ + \_)^2$ Write a set of parentheses with a square outside. Use a plus sign inside because the middle term is $+ 20a$.

$= (2a + 5)^2$ Fill in the blanks from the perfect squares of the first and third terms.

b) $25x^2 - 30xy + 9y^2 = (5x)^2 - 2(5x)(3y) + (3y)^2$ Write the trinomial as a perfect square trinomial.

$= (\_ - \_)^2$ Write a set of parentheses with a square outside. Use a minus sign inside because the middle term is $- 30xy$.

$= (5x - 3y)^2$ Fill in the blanks from the perfect squares of the first and third terms.

c) $121 - 22m + m^2 = (11)^2 - 2(11)(m) + (m)^2$ Write the trinomial as a perfect square trinomial.

$= (\underline{\hspace{0.4cm}} - \underline{\hspace{0.4cm}})^2$ Write a set of parentheses with a square outside. Use a minus sign inside because the middle term is $-22m$.

$= (11 - m)^2$ Fill in the blanks from the perfect squares of the first and third terms.

d) $r^2 + 10rs + 9s^2$ This is not a perfect square trinomial!

Are the first and third terms perfect squares?

$r^2 = (r)^2 \quad 9s^2 = (3s)^2$ Yes.

Is the middle term $2(r)(3s)$?

$2(r)(3s) = 6rs$ No!

Try factoring by trial and error or by grouping:

$r^2 + 10rs + 9s^2 = (r + 9s)(r + s)$ Trial and error works well because $a = 1$.

Factoring a perfect square trinomial and a difference of two squares

Sometimes a problem involves both a perfect square trinomial *and* a difference of two squares.

Example 19 Factor completely.

a) $x^2 - 2x + 1 - b^2$

b) $(4p - q)^2 - 16$

Solution 19

a) $x^2 - 2x + 1 - b^2 = (x^2 - 2x + 1) - b^2$ $x^2 - 2x + 1$ is a perfect square trinomial.

$x^2 - 2x + 1 = (x)^2 - 2(x)(1) + (1)^2$ Write the trinomial as a perfect square trinomial.

$= (x - 1)^2$ Write a set of parentheses with a square outside. Use the sign of the middle term $(-2x)$ inside the parentheses.

$= (x-1)^2 - b^2$ This is a difference of two squares.

$= (\underline{\quad} + \underline{\quad})(\underline{\quad} - \underline{\quad})$ Write two sets of parentheses.

$= (x-1+b)(x-1-b)$ Fill in the blanks from the perfect squares $(x-1)$ and b.

b) $(4p-q)^2 - 16 = (4p-q)^2 - (4)^2$ Write as a difference of two squares.

$= (\underline{\quad} + \underline{\quad})(\underline{\quad} - \underline{\quad})$ Write two sets of parentheses.

$= (4p-q+4)(4p-q-4)$ Fill in the blanks from the perfect squares $(4p-q)$ and 4.

Factoring the sum or difference of two cubes

Here is a list of perfect cubes:

$(1)^3 = 1$	$(5)^3 = 125$	$(9)^3 = 729$
$(2)^3 = 8$	$(6)^3 = 216$	$(10)^3 = 1000$
$(3)^3 = 27$	$(7)^3 = 343$	
$(4)^3 = 64$	$(8)^3 = 512$	

To Factor a Sum or Difference of Two Cubes:
1. Write each term as a perfect cube.
2. Use these formulas to factor:
$$(x)^3 + (y)^3 = (x + y)(x^2 - xy + y^2)$$
$$(x)^3 - (y)^3 = (x - y)(x^2 + xy + y^2)$$

You will have to memorize these formulas! There are some similarities about the two formulas that will help you:

1. Each factorization consists of a binomial times a trinomial (two terms times three terms).

2. The terms in the binomial are the cube roots (the numbers in the parentheses) when you write the original terms as perfect cubes.

3. The sign in the binomial is the same sign as in the original problem.

4. The first and third terms of the trinomial are the squares of the terms of the binomial.

5. The middle term of the trinomial is the product of the terms in the binomial, with the opposite sign of the binomial.

Example 20 Factor.

a) $8a^3 - 27$
b) $125r^3 + 216s^3$
c) $1000p^6 + 1$

Solution 20

a) $8a^3 - 27 = (2a)^3 - (3)^3$ Rewrite each term as a perfect cube.

$= (2a - 3)[(2a)^2 + (2a)(3) + (3)^2]$ The terms in the binomial are the numbers in parentheses, $2a$ and 3. The first and third terms in the trinomial are the squares of $2a$ and 3. The middle term is the product of $2a$ and 3, with the opposite sign of the binomial, so use a + sign.

$= (2a - 3)(4a^2 + 6a + 9)$ $(2a)^2 = 4a^2, (2a)(3) = 6a,$ and $(3)^2 = 9.$

b) $125r^3 + 216s^3 = (5r)^3 + (6s)^3$ Rewrite each term as a perfect cube.

$= (5r + 6s)[(5r)^2 - (5r)(6s) + (6s)^2]$ The terms in the binomial are the numbers in parentheses, $5r$ and $6s$. The first and third terms in the trinomial are the squares of $5r$ and $6s$. The middle term is the product of $5r$ and $6s$, with the opposite sign of the binomial, so use a − sign. Simplify inside the parentheses.

$= (5r + 6s)(25r^2 - 30rs + 36s^2)$

c) $1000p^6 + 1 = (10p^2)^3 + (1)^3$ Rewrite each term as a perfect cube.

$= (10p^2 + 1)[(10p^2)^2 - (10p^2)(1) + (1)^2]$ The terms in the binomial are the numbers in parentheses, $10p^2$ and 1. The first and third terms in the trinomial are the squares of $10p^2$ and 1. The middle term is the product of $10p^2$ and 1, with the opposite sign of the binomial, so use a − sign.

$= (10p^2 + 1)(100p^4 - 10p^2 + 1)$ Simplify inside the parentheses.

4.5 SOLVING EQUATIONS BY FACTORING

A quadratic equation in standard form can be written as

$$ax^2 + bx + c = 0,$$

where a, b, and c are real numbers and $a \neq 0$. Many quadratic equations can be solved by factoring and using the zero-factor property: If a and b are real numbers and $a \cdot b = 0$, then $a = 0$ or $b = 0$.

Solving factorable quadratic equations

> **To Solve a Factorable Quadratic Equation:**
> 1. Write the quadratic equation in standard form by getting 0 alone on one side of the equal sign.
> 2. Factor completely.
> 3. Set each factor containing a variable equal to 0.
> 4. Solve each equation.
> 5. Check your answers in the original equation.

Example 21   Solve each equation.

a) $(x + 3)(x + 2) = 0$

b) $m^2 + m - 12 = 0$

c) $2p^2 = p + 3$

d) $32r^2 = 18$

e) $2y^2 = 10y$

f) $x(2x + 1) = 15$

Solution 21

a) $(x + 3)(x + 2) = 0$ This is already completely factored.

    $x + 3 = 0$ or $x + 2 = 0$ Set each factor equal to 0.

    $x = -3$ or $x = -2$ Solve each equation.

Check:

$(-3+3)(-3+2) \overset{?}{=} 0$ Substitute −3 into original equation.

$0(-1) = 0$ −3 checks.

$(-2+3)(-2+2) \overset{?}{=} 0$ Substitute −2 into original equation.

$(1)0 = 0$ −2 checks.

b) $m^2 + m - 12 = 0$ Equation already equals 0.

$(m+4)(m-3) = 0$ Factor completely.

$m+4 = 0 \text{ or } m-3 = 0$ Set each factor equal to 0.

$m = -4 \text{ or } m = 3$ Solve each equation.

Check:

$(-4)^2 + (-4) - 12 \overset{?}{=} 0$ Substitute −4 into original equation.

$16 - 4 - 12 = 0$ −4 checks.

$(3)^2 + (3) - 12 \overset{?}{=} 0$ Substitute 3 into original equation.

$9 + 3 - 12 = 0$ 3 checks.

c) $2p^2 = p + 3$ Write equation in standard form.

$2p^2 - p - 3 = 0$ Get 0 on one side of the equation.

$(2p-3)(p+1) = 0$ Factor completely.

$2p-3 = 0 \text{ or } p+1 = 0$ Set each factor equal to 0.

$2p = 3 \text{ or } p = -1$ Solve each equation.

$p = \frac{3}{2} \text{ or } p = -1$ Proposed solutions.

Check:

$2\left(\frac{3}{2}\right)^2 \overset{?}{=} \left(\frac{3}{2}\right) + 3$ Substitute $\frac{3}{2}$ into original equation.

$2\left(\frac{9}{4}\right) \overset{?}{=} \frac{3}{2} + \frac{6}{2}$

$\frac{9}{2} = \frac{9}{2}$ $\frac{3}{2}$ checks.

$2(-1)^2 \overset{?}{=} (-1) + 3$ Substitute −1 into original equation.

$2(1) = 2$ −1 checks.

d) $32r^2 = 18$ Write equation in standard form.

$32r^2 - 18 = 0$ Get 0 alone on one side.

$2(16r^2 - 9) = 0$ Common factor.
$2(4r - 3)(4r + 3) = 0$ Factor the difference of two
                                              squares.

$4r - 3 = 0$ or $4r + 3 = 0$ Set each factor with a variable
                                              equal to 0.

$4r = 3$ or $4r = -3$ Solve each equation.

$r = \dfrac{3}{4}$ or $r = -\dfrac{3}{4}$ Proposed solutions. Try the check
                                              on your own.

e) $2y^2 = 10y$ Write equation in standard form.

$2y^2 - 10y = 0$ Get 0 alone on one side.

$2y(y - 5) = 0$ Factor completely.

$2y = 0$ or $y - 5 = 0$ Set each factor equal to 0.

$y = 0$ or $y = 5$ Proposed solutions. Try the check
                                              on your own.

f) $x(2x + 1) = 15$ Be careful! This looks factored,
                                              but 0 is not on one side!

$2x^2 + x = 15$

$2x^2 + x - 15 = 0$ Get 0 alone on one side.

$(2x - 5)(x + 3) = 0$ Factor completely.

$2x - 5 = 0$ or $x + 3 = 0$ Set each factor equal to 0.

$2x = 5$ or $x = -3$ Solve each equation.

$x = \dfrac{5}{2}$ or $x = -3$ Proposed solutions. Try the check
                                              on your own.

Solving equations with more than two factors

The zero-factor property can be used to solve equations with more than two factors. You must get zero alone on one side of the equal sign. Then set each factor containing a variable equal to 0 after the polynomial is factored.

Example 22 Solve each equation.

a) $x(x - 2)(2x + 5) = 0$

b) $(3x + 1)(x^2 - x - 6) = 0$

Solution 22

a) $x(x - 2)(2x + 5) = 0$ Equation is already factored, with 0 on one side.

$x = 0$ or $x - 2 = 0$ or $2x + 5 = 0$ Set each factor equal to 0.

$x = 0$ or $x = 2$ or $x = -\dfrac{5}{2}$ Solve each equation.

Check:

$(0)((0) - 2)(2(0) + 5) \stackrel{?}{=} 0$ Substitute 0 into the original equation.

$0(-2)(5) \stackrel{?}{=} 0$ Simplify inside parentheses first.

$0 = 0$ 0 checks.

$(2)((2) - 2)(2(2) + 5) \stackrel{?}{=} 0$ Substitute 2 into the original equation.

$2(0)(9) \stackrel{?}{=} 0$ Simplify inside parentheses first.

$0 = 0$ 2 checks.

$\left(-\dfrac{5}{2}\right)\left(\left(-\dfrac{5}{2}\right) - 2\right)\left(2\left(-\dfrac{5}{2}\right) + 5\right) \stackrel{?}{=} 0$ Substitute $-\dfrac{5}{2}$ into the original equation.

$\left(-\dfrac{5}{2}\right)\left(-\dfrac{9}{2}\right)(0) \stackrel{?}{=} 0$ $-\dfrac{5}{2} - 2 = -\dfrac{5}{2} - \dfrac{4}{2} - \dfrac{9}{2}.$

$2\left\{-\dfrac{5}{2}\right\} + 5 = -5 + 5 = 0.$

$0 = 0$ $-\dfrac{5}{2}$ checks.

b) $(3x + 1)(x^2 - x - 6) = 0$ Equation is not completely factored!

$(3x + 1)(x - 3)(x + 2) = 0$ Factor equation completely.

$3x + 1 = 0$ or $x - 3 = 0$ or $x + 2 = 0$ Set each factor equal to 0.

$x = -\dfrac{1}{3}$ or $x = 3$ or $x = -2$ Solve each equation.

Try the check on your own.

4.6 APPLICATIONS INVOLVING FACTORING

Some geometry formulas you will need in this section are listed below:

Area of a rectangle	$A = L \cdot W$, where L is the length and W is the width of the rectangle.
Area of a triangle	$A = \frac{1}{2} b h$, where b is the base and h is the height of the triangle.
Pythagorean Theorem	$c^2 = a^2 + b^2$, where c is the length of the hypotenuse and a and b are the lengths of the legs.

Example 23 The length of a rectangle is 4 feet more than the width. The area of the rectangle is 21 square feet. Find the dimensions.

Solution 23 Let x = the width, so $x = W$.
Then $x + 4$ = the length, so $x + 4 = L$.

$x(x + 4) = 21$	$L \cdot W$ = Area.
$x^2 + 4x - 21 = 0$	Get 0 alone on one side.
$(x + 7)(x - 3) = 0$	Factor.
$x = -7$ or $x = 3$	Set each factor equal to 0 and solve.

Check:

$(-7)((-7) + 4) \overset{?}{=} 21$	Substitute -7 into the original equation.
$(-7)(-3) = 21$	-7 checks in the original equation.
$(3)((3) + 4) \overset{?}{=} 21$	Substitute 3 into the original equation.
$(3)(7) = 21$	3 checks in the original equation.

Even though both answers check in the original equation, only a length of 3 feet makes sense. No length can be negative, so we cannot give -7 as an answer.

Thus, the dimensions of the rectangle are 3 feet by 7 feet.

Example 24 The base of a triangle is twice the height. The area of the triangle is 16 square inches. Find the base of the triangle.

Solution 24

Let x = the height of the triangle, so $x = h$.
$2x$ = the base of the triangle, so $2x = b$.

$$A = \frac{1}{2}bh$$

Formula for the area of a triangle.

$$16 = \frac{1}{2}(2x)(x)$$

Substitute $b = 2x$ and $h = x$ into the formula.

$$16 = x^2$$

Simplify the right side of the equation.

$$x^2 - 16 = 0$$

Get 0 alone on one side.

$$(x-4)(x+4) = 0$$

Factor.

$$x - 4 = 0 \text{ or } x + 4 = 0$$

Set each factor equal to 0 and solve.

$$x = 4 \text{ or } x = -4$$

But a base cannot have a negative length, so we eliminate $x = -4$.

Check: $16 \overset{?}{=} \frac{1}{2}(2(4))(4)$

Substitute 4 into the original equation.

$$16 \overset{?}{=} \frac{1}{2}(32)$$

$$16 = 16$$

4 checks.

If $x = 4$, then $2x = 2(4) = 8$, so the base is 8 inches.

Example 25 The hypotenuse of a right triangle is 10 cm. One leg is 2 cm shorter than the other leg. Find the lengths of the legs.

Solution 25 Let x = the length of one leg, so $x = a$
$x - 2$ = the length of the shorter leg, so $(x - 2) = b$

$$c^2 = a^2 + b^2$$

Pythagorean Theorem, where c is the length of the hypotenuse and a and b are the lengths of the legs.

$$(10)^2 = (x)^2 + (x-2)^2$$

Substitute $a = x$ and $b = (x-2)$ into the formula.

$$100 = x^2 + x^2 - 4x + 4$$

$$100 = 2x^2 - 4x + 4 \qquad \text{Add similar terms.}$$

$$0 = 2x^2 - 4x - 96 \qquad \text{Get 0 alone on one side.}$$

$$2x^2 - 4x - 96 = 0$$

$$2(x^2 - 2x - 48) = 0 \qquad \text{Factor out the GCF, 2.}$$

$$2(x - 8)(x + 6) = 0 \qquad \text{Factor } x^2 - 2x - 48 = (x - 8)(x + 6).$$

$$x - 8 = 0 \text{ or } x + 6 = 0 \qquad \text{Set each factor equal to 0 and solve}$$

$$x = 8 \text{ or } x = -6$$

But a length cannot be negative, so we eliminate –6.

Check: $10^2 \overset{?}{=} (8)^2 + ((8) - 2)^2 \qquad$ Substitute 8 into the original equation.

$$100 \overset{?}{=} 64 + (6)^2 \qquad \text{Simplify inside parentheses.}$$

$$100 \overset{?}{=} 64 + 36$$

$$100 = 100$$

8 checks.

If $x = 8$, $x - 2 = 8 - 2 = 6$, so the legs are 8 cm and 6 cm.

Integer applications

Recall from Section 2.5 that consecutive even or odd integers can be represented by $x, x + 2, x + 4$, etc.

Example 26   The product of two consecutive even integers is 14 more than 7 times their sum. Find the integers.

Solution 26   Let $x =$ the first even integer.
$x + 2 =$ the next consecutive even integer.

product is 14 more than 7 times their sum

$$x(x + 2) = 14 + 7(x + (x + 2)) \qquad \text{Write an equation.}$$

$$x^2 + 2x = 14 + 7(2x + 2) \qquad \text{Simplify both sides of the equation.}$$

$$x^2 + 2x = 14 + 14x + 14$$

$$x^2 + 2x = 28 + 14x$$

$$x^2 - 12x - 28 = 0$$ Get 0 alone on one side.

$$(x - 14)(x + 2) = 0$$ Factor.

$$x - 14 = 0 \text{ or } x + 2 = 0$$ Set each factor equal to 0.

$$x = 14 \text{ or } x = -2$$ Solve each equation.

Check:

$$(14)((14) + 2) \overset{?}{=} 14 + 7((14) + (14 + 2))$$ Substitute 14 into the original equation.

$$(14)(16) \overset{?}{=} 14 + 7(14 + 16)$$ Simplify inside parentheses.

$$224 \overset{?}{=} 14 + 7(30)$$

$$224 \overset{?}{=} 14 + 210$$ Multiply before adding.

$$224 = 224$$ 14 checks.

$$(-2)((-2) + 2) \overset{?}{=} 14 + 7((-2) + ((-2) + 2))$$ Substitute –2 into the original equation.

$$(-2)(0) \overset{?}{=} 14 + 7(-2 + 0)$$ Simplify inside parentheses.

$$0 \overset{?}{=} 14 + 7(-2)$$

$$0 = 14 - 14$$ –2 checks.

There are two sets of answers! If $x = 14$, $x + 2 = 16$. If $x = -2$, $x + 2 = 0$. So the integers are either 14 and 16 *or* -2 and 0.

Practice Exercises

1. Find the GCF.
   (a) $32x^2y, 4x^4, 8x^2y$
   (b) $15x^3y^2z, 35x^4yz^2, 40xy^3z$
   (c) $13, 52, 104$
   (d) $9x^2y^8, 27x^3y^7z^2$
   (e) $3x^2y, 5ab, 7s^3t^4$

2. Factor.
   (a) $30x^5 + 10x^3 + 20x$
   (b) $9a(5a + 7) - 2(5a + 7)$
   (c) $st + 4t + 2rs + 8r$
   (d) $pq + 2r + pr + 2q$

3. Factor.
   (a) $x^2 + 3x + 2$
   (b) $2x^2 + 9x + 4$
   (c) $x^2 + 7x + 12$
   (d) $12x^2 + 25x + 12$
   (e) $10x^2 - x - 3$

4. Factor.
   (a) $6x^2 - 7x - 20$
   (b) $6p^2 - 13p + 5$
   (c) $8y^2 + 30y - 27$
   (d) $24m^2 - 114m + 135$

5. Factor.
   (a) $15x^2 + 8y + 10x + 12xy$
   (b) $6x^3 + 2x^2 - 27xy - 9y$
   (c) $4x + 5y + 35xy + 28x^2$
   (d) $48p^3r + 120p^3 + 18p^2qr + 45p^2q$
   (e) $12ab + 3ac - 20b - 5c$

6. Factor.
   (a) $9x^2 - 49$
   (b) $49t^2 - 64$
   (c) $a^2 - 28a + 196$
   (d) $9y^2 + 24y + 16$
   (e) $18a^2 - 12ab + 2b^2$

. Factor.
   (a) $x^2 + 9$
   (b) $16a^2 + 25$
   (c) $98s^2 + 162t^2$
   (d) $169a^2 - 36b^2$

8. Factor.
   (a) $144 - 24x + x^2$
   (b) $361 + 38a + a^2$
   (c) $9s^2 + 24st + 16t^2$
   (d) $9u^2 - 12uv + 4v^2$
   (e) $(2a + 1)^2 - 4$

9. Factor.
   (a) $125x^3 - y^3$
   (b) $8m^3n^3 + 343$
   (c) $128r^3 - 250s^3$
   (d) $24 + 81p^3$

10. Factor.
   (a) $6a^3 - 39a^2 + 60a$
   (b) $12a^3 - 34a^2 + 10a$
   (c) $12a^3 - 40a^2 + 28a$
   (d) $10a^3 - 55a^2 + 75a$
   (e) $14a^3 - 34a^2 + 12a$

11. Solve each equation.
   (a) $(x - 3)(2x + 1) = 0$
   (b) $2x(x + 5) = 0$
   (c) $a^2 - 10a + 24 = 0$
   (d) $y^2 = 4y$
   (e) $6b^2 + 7b = -2$

10. Solve each equation.
   (a) The hypotenuse of a right triangle is 25 cm. One leg is 5 cm longer than the other. Find the lengths of both legs.
   (b) The product of two integers is 54 and the sum of the numbers is 15. Find both integers.

Answers

1. (a) $4x^2$
   (b) $5xyz$
   (c) 13
   (d) $9x^2y^7$
   (e) 1

2. (a) $10x(3x^4 + x^2 + 2)$
   (b) $(5a + 7)(9a - 2)$
   (c) $(s + 4)(t + 2r)$
   (d) $(p + 2)(q + r)$

3. (a) $(x + 2)(x + 1)$
   (b) $(2x + 1)(x + 4)$
   (c) $(x + 4)(x + 3)$
   (d) $(3x + 4)(4x + 3)$
   (e) $(5x - 3)(2x + 1)$

4. (a) $(2x - 5)(3x + 4)$
   (b) $(3p - 5)(2p - 1)$
   (c) $(4y - 3)(2y + 9)$
   (d) $3(2m - 5)(4m - 9)$

5. (a) $(5x + 4y)(3x + 2)$
   (b) $(2x^2 - 9y)(3x + 1)$
   (c) $(4x + 5y)(7x + 1)$
   (d) $3p^2(8p + 3q)(2r + 5)$
   (e) $(3a - 5)(4b + c)$

6. (a) $(3x + 7)(3x - 7)$
   (b) $(7t - 8)(7t + 8)$
   (c) $(a - 14)^2$
   (d) $(3y + 4)^2$
   (e) $2(3a - b)^2$

7. (a) cannot factor
   (b) cannot factor
   (c) $2(48s^2 + 81t^2)$
   (d) $(13a + 6b)(13a - 6b)$

8. (a) $(12 - x)^2$
   (b) $(19 + a)^2$
   (c) $(3s + 4t)^2$
   (d) $(3u - 2v)^2$
   (e) $(2a + 3)(2a - 1)$

9. (a) $(5x - y)(25x^2 + 5xy + y^2)$
   (b) $(2mn + 7)(4m^2n^2 - 14mn + 49)$
   (c) $2(4r - 5s)(16r^2 + 20rs + 25s^2)$
   (d) $3(2 + 3p)(4 - 6p + 9p^2)$

10. (a) $3a(2a - 5)(a - 4)$
    (b) $2a(3a - 1)(2a - 5)$
    (c) $4a(3a - 7)(a - 1)$
    (d) $5a(2a - 5)(a - 3)$
    (e) $2a(7a - 3)(a - 2)$

11. (a) $3, -\dfrac{1}{2}$
    (b) $0, -5$
    (c) $4, 6$
    (d) $0, 4$
    (e) $-\dfrac{1}{2}, -\dfrac{2}{3}$

12. (a) 15 cm, 20 cm
    (b) 6, 9

5

Rational Expressions

5.1 REDUCING RATIONAL EXPRESSIONS

In this section, we will reduce *rational expressions*, that is, expressions in which the numerator and denominator are polynomials. Because the denominator may now contain variables, we may need to state restrictions to keep the denominator from equaling 0.

Restricting variables in denominators

> **To Find Restrictions on Variables:**
> 1. There are no restrictions if the denominator does not contain a variable.
> 2. Set the denominator equal to 0.
> 3. Solve the resulting equation, remembering to factor if necessary.
> 4. Use the solutions from Step 3 as restrictions.

Example 1   State the restrictions on the variable in the following rational expressions:

a) $\dfrac{4x - 5}{2}$

b) $\dfrac{x + 1}{x - 4}$

c) $\dfrac{2x + 1}{x^2 - x - 6}$

Solution 1

a) $\dfrac{4x - 5}{2}$ No variable in the denominator, so there are no restrictions on x.

b) $\dfrac{x + 1}{x - 4}$ $x - 4 = 0$ Set denominator = 0.

$x = 4$ Solve.

$x \neq 4$ State restriction.

c) $\dfrac{2x + 1}{x^2 - x - 6}$ $x^2 - x - 6 = 0$

$(x - 3)(x + 2) = 0$ Set denominator = 0

$x - 3 = 0$ or $x + 2 = 0$ Factor.

$x = 3$ or $x = -2$ Set each factor = 0.

$x \neq 3$ and $x \neq -2$ Solve.

State restrictions.

Reducing rational expressions

In the past you have reduced fractions like

$$\frac{6}{9} = \frac{2 \cdot 3}{3 \cdot 3} = \frac{2 \cdot \mathbf{3}}{3 \cdot \mathbf{3}} = \frac{2}{3},$$

where the common factor of 3 was divided out of the numerator and denominator.

Although you may do the factoring step in your head for an example like $\frac{6}{9}$, you will need to *write* your factors for the polynomials in the numerator and denominator of rational expressions.

> **To Reduce Rational Expressions:**
> 1. Factor the numerator.
> 2. Factor the denominator.
> 3. Divide out the common factor(s).

Example 2   Reduce to lowest terms.

a) $\dfrac{4x - 8}{5x - 10}$

b) $\dfrac{x^2 + 2x - 3}{x^2 + 7x + 12}$

c) $\dfrac{3x^2 - 75}{6x^2 + 42x + 60}$

d) $\dfrac{x^2 + 2x - xy - 2y}{px + 2p + qx + 2q}$

Solution 2

a) $\dfrac{4x - 8}{5x - 10} =$

$\dfrac{4(x - 2)}{5(x - 2)} =$ Factor the numerator.

Factor the denominator.

$$\frac{4(x - 2)}{5(x - 2)} =$$

Divide out the common factor $x - 2$.

$$\frac{4}{5}$$

b) $$\frac{x^2 + 2x - 3}{x^2 + 7x + 12} =$$

$$\frac{(x - 1)(x + 3)}{(x + 4)(x + 3)} =$$

Factor the numerator.
Factor the denominator.

$$\frac{(x - 1)(x + 3)}{(x + 4)(x + 3)} =$$

Divide out the common factor $x + 3$.

$$\frac{x - 1}{x + 4}$$

c) $$\frac{3(x^2 - 25)}{6x^2 + 42x + 60} =$$

$$\frac{3x^2 - 75}{6(x^2 + 7x + 10)} =$$

$$\frac{3(x - 5)(x + 5)}{6(x + 2)(x + 5)} =$$

Factor out the GCF.

Numerator is difference of two squares. Denominator factored by trial-and-error.

$$\frac{3(x - 5)(x + 5)}{3 \cdot 2(x + 2)(x + 5)} =$$

Divide out the common factors 3 and $x + 5$.

$$\frac{x - 5}{2(x + 2)}$$

d) $$\frac{x^2 + 2x - xy - 2y}{px + 2p + qx + 2q} =$$

$$\frac{x(x + 2) - y(x + 2)}{p(x + 2) + q(x + 2)} =$$

Four terms, so factor by grouping.

$$\frac{(x + 2)(x - y)}{(x + 2)(p + q)} =$$

Finish factoring by grouping before dividing out common factors.

$$\frac{(x + 2)(x - y)}{(x + 2)(p + q)} =$$

Divide out the common factor $x + 2$.

$$\frac{(x - y)}{(p + q)}$$

Recognizing rational expressions that reduce to -1

At first glance an expression like $\dfrac{b - a}{a - b}$ may not look like it can be reduced. But

$$\frac{b - a}{a - b} = \frac{-a + b}{a - b}$$

Commutative Property: $b - a = -a + b$.

$$\frac{-1(a - b)}{a - b}$$

Factor out -1.

$$\frac{-1(a - b)}{a - b}$$

Divide out the common factor $a - b$.

$$= -1$$

You do not need to do all the steps if you understand and recognize these forms of -1.

How to Recognize Rational Expressions That Reduce to -1:
1. The factor in the numerator and denominator must have subtraction signs between the terms.
2. The Commutative Property can be used to change the order of the terms.
Then:
3. Write -1 as a factor in the numerator and divide out the common factors.

Example 3 Write in lowest terms:

a) $\dfrac{p - 2}{2 - p}$

b) $\dfrac{3x - 3}{2 - 2x}$

c) $\dfrac{x^2 - 9}{3 - x}$

d) $\dfrac{m - 2n}{2n + m}$

E) $\dfrac{2x + y}{y + 2x}$

Solution 3

a) $\dfrac{p - 2}{2 - p} = \dfrac{-2 + p}{2 - p}$

Commutative Property:
$p - 2 = -2 + p$.

$$= \frac{-1(2 - p)}{2 - p}$$

$$= -1$$

Factor out -1.
Divide out the common factor $2 - p$.

b) $\dfrac{3x - 3}{2 - 2x} = \dfrac{3(x - 1)}{2(1 - x)}$

Factor the numerator and the denominator.
$\dfrac{x - 1}{1 - x} = -1$.

$$= \frac{3 \cdot -1}{2}$$

$$= \frac{-3}{2} = -\frac{3}{2}$$

c) $\dfrac{x^2 - 9}{3 - x} = \dfrac{(x - 3)(x + 3)}{3 - x}$

Factor the numerator.

$$= -1(x + 3)$$

$\dfrac{x - 3}{3 - x} = -1.$

d) $\dfrac{m - 2n}{2n + m}$

This is already in lowest terms. No subtraction sign in denominator!

e) $\dfrac{2x + y}{y + 2x} = \dfrac{2x + y}{2x + y}$

No subtraction signs, but this can be reduced.

$$= 1$$

Warning: It is very tempting to divide out *terms* instead of *factors!*

$\dfrac{2x + 6}{2} \neq \dfrac{2x + 6}{2} \neq 2x + 3$ Here 6 is a term, not a factor.

$\dfrac{2x + 6}{2} = \dfrac{2(x + 3)}{2} = x + 3$ Here 2 is a factor and *can* be divided out.

5.2 MULTIPLYING AND DIVIDING RATIONAL EXPRESSIONS

The same rules used for multiplying and dividing rational numbers are used for multiplying and dividing rational expressions:

$$\frac{A}{B} \cdot \frac{C}{D} = \frac{AC}{BD} \qquad\qquad B, D \neq 0$$

$$\frac{A}{B} + \frac{C}{D} = \frac{A}{B} \cdot \frac{D}{C} = \frac{AD}{BC} \qquad\qquad B, D, C \neq 0$$

We will use factoring to simplify this process.

Practice multiplying and dividing rational expressions

Example 4   Multiply or divide the expressions on the following page as indicated. Reduce all answers to lowest terms.

a) $\dfrac{3x^2}{9x} \cdot \dfrac{18x}{15x}$

b) $\dfrac{25y^8}{15y^6} \div \dfrac{9y}{10y^4}$

c) $\dfrac{a^2 - 5a + 6}{2a + 4} \cdot \dfrac{a + 2}{2a - 6}$

d) $\dfrac{6x^2 - 54}{2x^2 + 3x + 1} \div \dfrac{4x - 12}{2x^2 - 9x - 5}$

e) $\dfrac{x^2 - 6x + 9}{x^2 - 1} \div \dfrac{3 - x}{1 + x}$

Solution 4

a) $\dfrac{3x^2}{9x} \cdot \dfrac{18x}{15x} =$

$\dfrac{3x^2 \cdot 18x}{9x \cdot 15x} =$ Multiply numerators. Multiply denominators.

$\dfrac{3 \cdot x \cdot x \cdot 9 \cdot 2 \cdot x}{9 \cdot x \cdot 5 \cdot 3 \cdot x} =$ Factor.

$\dfrac{2x}{5}$ Divide out the common factors 3, 9, x, and x.

If you had completed the multiplication in the numerator and denominator before factoring your work would look like:

$\dfrac{3x^2 \cdot 18x}{9x \cdot 15x} = \dfrac{54x^3}{135x^2}$

You would now have to factor:

$\dfrac{2 \cdot 3 \cdot 3 \cdot 3 \cdot x \cdot x \cdot x}{3 \cdot 3 \cdot 3 \cdot 5 \cdot x \cdot x},$

which would still reduce to $\dfrac{2x}{5}$. It is usually easier to factor first, rather than multiplying out the numerator and denominator, but either method will work.

b) $\dfrac{25y^8}{15y^6} \div \dfrac{9y}{10y^4} =$

$\dfrac{25y^8}{15y^6} \cdot \dfrac{10y^4}{9y} =$ Invert divisor and multiply.

$\dfrac{25y^8 \cdot 10y^4}{15y^6 \cdot 9y} =$ Multiply numerators. Multiply denominators.

$\dfrac{5 \cdot 5 \cdot y^6 \cdot y \cdot y \cdot 10y^4}{5 \cdot 3 \cdot y^6 \cdot 9 \cdot y} =$ Factor.

$$\frac{50y^5}{27}$$

Divide out the common factors 5, y6, and *y*

c) $\dfrac{a^2 - 5a + 6}{2a + 4} \cdot \dfrac{a + 2}{2a - 6}$

$\dfrac{(a - 3)(a - 2)}{2(a + 2)} \cdot \dfrac{a + 2}{2(a - 3)}$

Factor.

$\dfrac{(a - 3)(a - 2)(a + 2)}{2(a + 2)\, 2(a - 3)}$

Multiply numerators.
Multiply denominators.

$\dfrac{a - 2}{4}$

Divide out the common factors (*a* - 3) and (*a* + 2).

d) $\dfrac{6x^2 - 54}{2x^2 + 3x + 1} \div \dfrac{4x - 12}{2x^2 - 9x - 5} =$

$\dfrac{6x^2 - 54}{2x^2 + 3x + 1} \cdot \dfrac{2x^2 - 9x - 5}{4x - 12} =$

Invert divisor and multiply.

$\dfrac{6(x^2 - 9)}{(2x + 1)(x + 1)} \cdot \dfrac{(2x + 1)(x - 5)}{4(x - 3)} =$

Factor.

$\dfrac{2 \cdot 3(x - 3)(x + 3)(2x + 1)(x - 5)}{(2x + 1)(x + 1)2 \cdot 2(x - 3)} =$

Factor and multiply.

$\dfrac{3(x + 3)(x - 5)}{2(x + 1)}$

Divide out common factors 2, (x – 3), and (2x + 1).

Answers are usually left in factored form.

e) $\dfrac{x^2 - 6x + 9}{x^2 - 1} \div \dfrac{3 - x}{1 + x} =$

$\dfrac{x^2 - 6x + 9}{x^2 - 1} \cdot \dfrac{1 + x}{3 - x} =$

Invert divisor and multiply.

$\dfrac{(x - 3)(x - 3)(1 + x)}{(x - 1)(x + 1)(3 - x)} =$

Factor and multiply.

$\dfrac{-1(x - 3)}{x - 1}$

Divide out common factors
$\dfrac{x - 3}{3 - x} = -1$ and $\dfrac{1 + x}{x + 1} = 1.$

You may find an answer like $\dfrac{-1(x - 3)}{x - 1}$ rewritten as

$\dfrac{-1(x - 3)}{x - 1} = \dfrac{-x + 3}{x - 1}$

Use the Distributive Property.

$= \dfrac{3 - x}{x - 1}$

Use the Commutative Property:
$-x + 3 = 3 - x.$

5.3 WRITING RATIONAL EXPRESSIONS USING THE LEAST COMMON MULTIPLE

To add or subtract rational expressions, you *must* have a common denominator. The least common denominator is the least common multiple of the given denominators. You may want to review Method 2 for finding the least common denominator in Chapter 1. First we'll find the least common multiple (LCM).

To Find the Least Common Multiple:
1. Factor each expression, using exponents where possible.
2. The LCM is the product of each different factor raised to the highest exponent that appears in any of the given expressions.

Example 5 Find the LCM.

a) $12x^2y$ and $8xy^3$

b) $x^2 + 6x + 9$ and $4x + 12$

c) $x^2 + x - 2$ and $x^2 - 6x + 5$

Solution 5

a) $12x^2y = 2^2 \cdot 3^1 \cdot x^2 \cdot y^1$
    $8xy^3 = 2^3 \cdot x^1 \cdot y^3$
    $\text{LCM} = 2^3 \cdot 3^1 \cdot x^2 \cdot y^3$

Factor $12 = 4 \cdot 3 = 2^2 \cdot 3^1$.
Factor $8 = 2^3$.
The highest power of 2 is 3, so use 2^3.
The highest power of 3 is 1, so use 3^1.
The highest power of x is 2, so use x^2.
The highest power of y is 3, so use y^3.

   $= 24x^2y^3$

Multiply out the numerical coefficient and write the variables with exponents.

b) $x^2 + 6x + 9 = (x + 3)^2$
    $4x + 12 = 2^2(x + 3)^1$

    $\text{LCM} = 2^2(x + 3)^2$

Factor $x^2 + 6x + 9 = (x + 3)^2$.
Factor
$4x + 12 = 4(x + 3)^1 = 2^2(x + 3)^1$
The highest power of 2 is 2, so use 2^2. The highest power of $(x + 3)$ is 2, so use $(x + 3)^2$.

   $= 4(x + 3)^2$

Multiply out the numerical coefficient.

c) $x^2 + x - 2 = (x + 2)(x - 1)$

Factor.

$$x^2 - 6x + 5 = (x - 5)(x - 1)$$
$$LCM = (x+2)(x-1)(x-5)$$

Factor.
The highest power of each factor is 1. Be careful here—do not try to use $(x - 1)^2$, there is no power of 2 on either factor of $(x - 1)$.

Leave the LCM in factored form.

Finding the least common denominator

The least common denominator is the least common multiple of all the denominators. Follow the rules given for finding the least common multiple using the denominators of the rational expressions.

Example 6   Find the LCD.

$$\frac{4}{x^2 - x - 6}, \frac{6}{x^2 + x - 2}$$

Solution 6

$$x^2 - x - 6 = (x - 3)(x + 2)$$
$$x^2 + x - 2 = (x + 2)(x - 1)$$
$$LCD = (x - 3)(x + 2)(x - 1)$$

Factor each denominator.

Use each factor raised to the highest exponent.

Example 7   Find the LCD.

$$\frac{3}{x^2 - 2x + 1}, \frac{5}{x^2 - 2x - 3}, \frac{6}{x^2 - 4x + 3}$$

Solution 7

$$x^2 - 2x - 1 = (x - 1)^2$$
$$x^2 - 2x - 3 = (x - 3)(x + 1)$$
$$x^2 - 4x + 3 = (x - 1)(x - 3)$$
$$LCD = (x - 1)^2(x + 1)(x - 3)$$

Factor each denominator.

The highest power of $(x - 1)$ is 2, so use $(x - 1)^2$.
The highest power of $(x + 1)$ is 1, so use $(x + 1)$.
The highest power of $(x - 3)$ is 1, so use $(x - 3)$.

Writing rational expressions with the LCD

Recall from our work with fractions that a fraction can be "built up" by multiplying the numerator and denominator by a common factor. We will use that same idea to write rational expressions with the least common denominator.

Example 8   Rewrite $\dfrac{4}{x^2 - x - 6}$ and $\dfrac{6}{x^2 + x - 2}$ with the LCD.

Solution 8   The LCD of $\dfrac{4}{x^2-x-6}$ and $\dfrac{6}{x^2+x-2}$ is $(x-3)(x+2)(x-1)$ (see Example 6).

After writing the denominators in factored form, compare the given denominator to the LCD. Multiply by the factor (or factors) that are needed to make the given denominator equal the LCD. Remember that you must then multiply the numerator *and* denominator by this factor (or factors) to obtain equivalent rational expressions.

$$\frac{4}{x^2-x-6} = \frac{4}{(x-3)(x+2)} \cdot \left(\frac{x-1}{x-1}\right)$$

Multiply the numerator and denominator by $(x-1)$ to make the denominator equal the LCD.

$$= \frac{4x-4}{(x-3)(x+2)(x-1)}$$

Multiply numerators; keep the denominator in factored form.

$$\frac{6}{x^2+x-2} = \frac{6}{(x+2)(x-1)} \cdot \left(\frac{x-3}{x-3}\right)$$

Multiply the numerator and denominator by $(x-3)$ to make the denominator equal the LCD.

$$= \frac{6x-18}{(x+2)(x-1)(x-3)}$$

Multiply numerators; keep the denominator in factored form.

Example 9   Rewrite $\dfrac{3}{x^2-1}$, $\dfrac{5}{x^2-2x-3}$ and $\dfrac{6}{x^2-4x+3}$ with the LCD.

Solution 9   First find the LCD:

$$x^2-1 = (x-1)(x+1)$$
$$x^2-2x-3 = (x-3)(x+1)$$
$$x^2-4x+3 = (x-3)(x-1)$$
$$LCD = (x-1)(x+1)(x-3)$$

Factor each denominator.

The highest exponent of $(x-1)$ is 1, so use $(x-1)$.
The highest exponent of $(x+1)$ is 1, so use $(x+1)$.
The highest exponent of $(x-3)$ is 1, so use $(x-3)$.

$$\frac{3}{(x-1)(x+1)} = \frac{3}{(x-1)(x+1)} \cdot \left(\frac{x-3}{x-3}\right)$$

Multiply the numerator and denominator by $(x-3)$ to make the denominator equal the LCD.

$$= \frac{3x-9}{(x-1)(x+1)(x-3)}$$

Multiply the numerators; keep the denominator in factored form.

$$\frac{5}{(x-3)(x+1)} = \frac{5}{(x-3)(x+1)} \cdot \left(\frac{x-1}{x-1}\right)$$

Multiply the numerator and denominator by $(x-1)$ to make the denominator equal the LCD.

$$= \frac{5x-5}{(x-3)(x+1)(x-1)}$$

Multiply the numerators; keep the denominator in factored form.

$$\frac{6}{(x-3)(x-1)}$$

$$= \frac{6}{(x-3)(x-1)} \cdot \left(\frac{x+1}{x+1}\right)$$

Multiply the numerator and denominator by $(x+1)$ to make the denominator equal the LCD.

$$= \frac{6x+6}{(x-3)(x-1)(x+1)}$$

Multiply the numerators; keep the denominator in factored form.

5.4 ADDING AND SUBTRACTING RATIONAL EXPRESSIONS

You *must* have a common denominator to add or subtract rational expressions. If the given denominators are equal, start with Step 4 of these rules.

To Add or Subtract Rational Expressions:
1. Factor each denominator.
2. Find the LCD.
3. Rewrite each rational expression with the LCD.
4. Add or subtract numerators. Distribute the subtraction sign across the *whole* numerator. The LCD is the denominator.
5. Reduce the answer, if possible, by factoring and dividing out common factors.

Adding and subtracting rational expressions with common denominators

Example 10   Find the sums or differences.

a) $\dfrac{7}{x} - \dfrac{9}{x}$

b) $\dfrac{4}{y + 2} + \dfrac{2y}{y + 2}$

c) $\dfrac{x^2}{x^2 + 3x - 18} + \dfrac{x - 12}{x^2 + 3x - 18}$

Solution 10

a) $\dfrac{7}{x} - \dfrac{9}{x} = \dfrac{7 - 9}{x}$

Given denominators are equal. Subtract the numerators; use LCD of x as the denominator.

$= \dfrac{-2}{x}$ or $-\dfrac{2}{x}$

The negative can be written in the numerator, or in front of the entire fraction.

b) $\dfrac{4}{y + 2} + \dfrac{2y}{y + 2} =$

$\dfrac{4 + 2y}{y + 2} =$

Given denominators are equal. Add the numerators; use LCD of $y + 2$ as the denominator.

$\dfrac{2(2 + y)}{y + 2} =$

Factor the numerator.

2

Divide out the common factor $2 + y = y + 2$.

c) $\dfrac{x^2}{x^2 + 3x - 18} + \dfrac{x - 12}{x^2 + 3x - 18} =$

$\dfrac{x^2 + x - 12}{x^2 + 3x - 18} =$

Given denominators are equal. Add the numerators, use LCD of $x^2 + 3x - 18$ as the denominator.

$\dfrac{(x - 3)(x + 4)}{(x - 3)(x + 6)} =$

Factor the numerator and the denominator.

$\dfrac{x + 4}{x + 6}$

Divide out the common factor $x - 3$

Adding and subtracting rational expressions without common denominators

Example 11 Find the sums or differences.

a) $\dfrac{5x}{6} - \dfrac{2x}{3}$

b) $\dfrac{6}{x^2 + x - 2} - \dfrac{4}{x^2 - x - 6}$

c) $\dfrac{10}{x^2 - 25} - \dfrac{9}{x^2 - x - 20}$

d) $\dfrac{2}{p - 4} + \dfrac{5}{4 - p}$

Solution 11

a) $\dfrac{5x}{6} - \dfrac{2x}{3} =$

$\dfrac{5x}{2 \cdot 3} - \dfrac{2x}{3} =$ Factor the denominators.

$\dfrac{5x}{2 \cdot 3} - \dfrac{2x}{3} \cdot \left(\dfrac{2}{2}\right) =$ LCD $= 2 \cdot 3$.

$\dfrac{5x}{2 \cdot 3} - \dfrac{(2x)(2)}{2 \cdot 3} =$

Rewrite $\dfrac{2x}{3}$ with LCD of 6.

$\dfrac{5x - 4x}{6} =$

Subtract the numerators. Use LCD of 6 as the denominator.

$\dfrac{x}{6}$ Simplify the numerator.

b) $\dfrac{6}{x^2 + x - 2} - \dfrac{4}{x^2 - x - 6} =$

$\dfrac{6}{(x + 2)(x - 1)} - \dfrac{4}{(x - 3)(x + 2)} =$ Factor the denominators.

$\dfrac{6}{(x + 2)(x - 1)} \cdot \left(\dfrac{x - 3}{x - 3}\right) - \dfrac{4}{(x - 3)(x + 2)} \cdot \left(\dfrac{x - 1}{x - 1}\right) =$

See LCD work from Example 8.

$\dfrac{6x - 18}{(x + 2)(x - 1)(x - 3)} - \dfrac{4x - 4}{(x - 3)(x + 2)(x - 1)}$

Multiply the numerators. Keep the denominators in factored form.

$\dfrac{6x - 18 - (4x - 4)}{(x + 2)(x - 1)(x - 3)} =$

Subtract the numerators. Be careful to distribute the subtraction sign across the whole numerator!

$\dfrac{6x - 18 - 4x + 4}{(x + 2)(x - 1)(x - 3)} =$

Combine similar terms in the numerator.

$$\frac{2x - 14}{(x + 2)(x - 1)(x - 3)}$$

Even though the numerator factors to $2(x-7)$, there are no common factors to divide out, so the answer is usually left in the form shown.

c) $\dfrac{10}{x^2 - 25} - \dfrac{9}{x^2 - x - 20} =$

$\dfrac{10}{(x - 5)(x + 5)} - \dfrac{9}{(x - 5)(x + 4)} =$ Factor the denominators. LCD = $(x - 5)(x + 5)(x + 4)$

$\dfrac{10}{(x - 5)(x + 5)} \cdot \left(\dfrac{x + 4}{x + 4}\right) - \dfrac{9}{(x - 5)(x + 4)} \cdot \left(\dfrac{x + 5}{x + 5}\right) =$

Rewrite each expression with the LCD.

$\dfrac{10x + 40}{(x - 5)(x + 5)(x + 4)} - \dfrac{9x + 45}{(x - 5)(x + 4)(x + 5)}$

Multiply the numerators. Leave the denominators in factored form.

$\dfrac{10x + 40 - (9x + 45)}{(x - 5)(x + 5)(x + 4)} =$

Subtract the numerators. Use the LCD as the denominator.

$\dfrac{10x + 40 - 9x - 45}{(x - 5)(x + 5)(x + 4)} =$

Be careful to distribute the subtraction sign!

$\dfrac{x - 5}{(x - 5)(x + 5)(x + 4)} =$

$\dfrac{1}{(x + 5)(x + 4)}$

Divide out common factor $x - 5$.

Reduced answer.

d) $\dfrac{2}{p - 4} + \dfrac{5}{4 - p} =$

These denominators are negatives of each other. Use the Commutative Property and sign rules for fractions to rewrite $\dfrac{5}{4 - p}$.

$\dfrac{2}{p - 4} + \dfrac{5}{-1(p - 4)} =$

$4 - p = -p + 4 = -1(p - 4)$.

$\dfrac{2}{p - 4} - \dfrac{5}{p - 4} =$

$+\dfrac{5}{-1(p - 4)} = -\dfrac{5}{+(p - 4)}$

$= -\dfrac{5}{p - 4}$.

$\dfrac{2 - 5}{p - 4} =$

Denominators are now equal. Subtract the numerators. Use the LCD of $p - 4$ as the denominator.

$$\frac{-3}{p-4}$$

Since $4-p=-p+4=-1(p-4)$, you can use either $p-4$ or $4-p$ as the LCD!

5.5 COMPLEX FRACTIONS

A complex fraction is a rational expression that contains fractions in the numerator and/or denominator. There are two methods used to simplify complex fractions. If your instructor uses only Method 1, study Example 12. If your instructor uses only Method 2, study Example 13. If you want to compare these two methods, study Example 14.

Method 1
1. Write the numerator of the complex fraction as a single fraction.
2. Write the denominator of the complex fraction as a single fraction.
3. Perform indicated division by inverting divisor and multiplying.
4. Reduce, if possible.

Method 2 (Sometimes Called the LCD Method)
1. Find the LCD of *all* the denominators within the complex fraction.
2. Multiply the numerator and denominator of the complex fraction by the LCD.
3. Reduce, if possible.

Simplifying complex fractions using method 1

Example 12 Simplify each complex fraction.

a) $\dfrac{\frac{2}{5}}{4}$

b) $\dfrac{\frac{3x^2}{y}}{\frac{9x^6}{10y^3}}$

---

c) $\dfrac{\dfrac{m+1}{m^2-9}}{\dfrac{4m+4}{m^2+5m+6}}$

Solution 12

a) $\dfrac{\dfrac{2}{5}}{\dfrac{4}{}}=$

$\dfrac{\dfrac{2}{5}}{\dfrac{4}{1}}=$

Numerator and denominator are single fractions.

$\dfrac{\dfrac{2}{5}\cdot\dfrac{1}{4}}{}=$

Invert and multiply.

$\dfrac{2\cdot 1}{5\cdot 2\cdot 2}=$

Reduce by dividing out common factors.

$\dfrac{1}{10}$

b) $\dfrac{\dfrac{3x^2}{y}}{\dfrac{9x^6}{10y^3}}$

Numerator and denominator are single fractions.

$\dfrac{3x^2}{y}\cdot\dfrac{10y^3}{9x^6}=$

Invert and multiply.

$\dfrac{3x^3\cdot 10y^3}{y\cdot 3\cdot 3x^6}=$

Reduce by dividing out common factors 3, x^2 and y.

$\dfrac{10y^2}{3x^4}$

c) $\dfrac{\dfrac{m+1}{m^2-9}}{\dfrac{4m+4}{m^2+5m+6}}=$

Numerator and denominator are single fractions.

$$\frac{m + 1}{m^2 - 9} \cdot \frac{m^2 + 5m + 6}{4m + 4} =$$

Invert and multiply.

$$\frac{m + 1}{(m + 3)(m - 3)} \cdot \frac{(m + 2)(m + 3)}{4(m + 1)} =$$

Divide out common factors of $m + 1$ and $m + 3$.

$$\frac{m + 2}{4(m - 3)}$$

Simplifying complex fractions using method 2

Example 13 Simplify each complex fraction.

a) $\dfrac{\dfrac{2}{a} - 3}{\dfrac{2}{a} + 3}$

b) $\dfrac{\dfrac{4}{p^2 q} - \dfrac{3}{pq^2}}{\dfrac{5}{p^2 q^2} + \dfrac{1}{pq}}$

Solution 13

a) $\dfrac{\dfrac{2}{a} - 3}{\dfrac{2}{a} + 3} = \dfrac{a\left(\dfrac{2}{a} - \dfrac{3}{1}\right)}{a\left(\dfrac{2}{a} + \dfrac{3}{1}\right)}$

Multiply the numerator and denominator by the LCD.

$$= \dfrac{a\left(\dfrac{2}{a}\right) - a\left(\dfrac{3}{1}\right)}{a\left(\dfrac{2}{a}\right) + a\left(\dfrac{3}{1}\right)}$$

Use the Distributive Property to multiply the LCD times each term.

$$= \dfrac{2 - 3a}{2 + 3a}$$

$a\left(\dfrac{2}{a}\right) = \dfrac{2a}{a} = 2.$

$a\left(\dfrac{3}{1}\right) = \dfrac{3a}{1} = 3a.$

b) $\dfrac{\dfrac{4}{p^2 q} - \dfrac{3}{pq^2}}{\dfrac{5}{p^2 q^2} + \dfrac{1}{pq}} = \dfrac{p^2 q^2 \left(\dfrac{4}{p^2 q} - \dfrac{3}{pq^2}\right)}{p^2 q^2 \left(\dfrac{5}{p^2 q^2} + \dfrac{1}{pq}\right)}$

Multiply the numerator and denominator by the LCD.

$$= \frac{p^2q^2\left(\frac{4}{p^2q}\right) - p^2q^2\left(\frac{3}{pq^2}\right)}{p^2q^2\left(\frac{5}{p^2q^2}\right) + p^2q^2\left(\frac{1}{pq}\right)}$$

Use the Distributive Property to multiply the LCD times each term.

$$= \frac{4q - 3p}{5 + pq}$$

Simplifying complex fractions—a comparison of methods 1 and 2

Generally, either method can be used to simplify a complex fraction. The following example demonstrates both methods. Which method do you prefer?

Example 14 Simplify.

$$\frac{2 + \frac{3}{4}}{3 - \frac{1}{8}}$$

Solution 14 *Method 1:*

$$\frac{2 + \frac{3}{4}}{3 - \frac{1}{8}} = \frac{\frac{2}{1}\left(\frac{4}{4}\right) + \frac{3}{4}}{\frac{3}{1}\left(\frac{8}{8}\right) - \frac{1}{8}}$$

Write the numerator as a single fraction. Write the denominator as a single fraction.

$$= \frac{\frac{8}{4} + \frac{3}{4}}{\frac{24}{8} - \frac{1}{8}}$$

Find the LCD for the numerator (4) and rewrite each fraction with the LCD. Find the LCD for the denominator (8) and rewrite each fraction with the LCD

$$= \frac{\frac{11}{4}}{\frac{23}{8}}$$

Add the fractions in the numerator. Subtract the fractions in the denominator.

$$\frac{11}{4} \cdot \frac{8}{23}$$

Invert and multiply.

$$= \frac{22}{23}$$

Method 2:

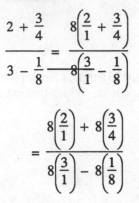

$$\frac{2 + \frac{3}{4}}{3 - \frac{1}{8}} = \frac{8\left(\frac{2}{1} + \frac{3}{4}\right)}{8\left(\frac{3}{1} - \frac{1}{8}\right)}$$

Find the LCD of all the denominators: LCD of 1, 4, and 8 is 8.

$$= \frac{8\left(\frac{2}{1}\right) + 8\left(\frac{3}{4}\right)}{8\left(\frac{3}{1}\right) - 8\left(\frac{1}{8}\right)}$$

Use the Distributive Property to multiply the LCD times each term.

$$8\left(\frac{2}{1}\right) = \frac{16}{1} = 16$$

$$8\left(\frac{3}{4}\right) = \frac{24}{4} = 6$$

$$8\left(\frac{3}{1}\right) = \frac{24}{1} = 24$$

$$8\left(\frac{1}{8}\right) = \frac{8}{8} = 1$$

$$= \frac{16 + 6}{24 - 1} = \frac{22}{23}$$

5.6 RATIOS AND PROPORTIONS

Ratios

A **ratio** provides a way of comparing two quantities with the same units. The ratio of two numbers a and b is written as $\frac{a}{b}$ or $a : b$ or a to b.

Reducing a ratio is equivalent to reducing a fraction.

Example 15 Write each word phrase as a ratio. Write each ratio in lowest terms.

   a)   8 hours to 4 hours

b)   20 miles : $\frac{3}{4}$ mile

c)   6 days : 12 hours

Solution 15

a)   8 hours to 4 hours $= \dfrac{8 \text{ hours}}{4 \text{ hours}}$

Write the ratio as a fraction.

$= \dfrac{2 \text{ hours}}{1 \text{ hour}}$

Reduce the fraction.

We would ordinarily write $\dfrac{2}{1}$ as 2, but with ratios we generally write denominators of 1.

b)   20 miles : $\dfrac{3}{4}$ miles $= \dfrac{20 \text{ miles}}{\frac{3}{4} \text{ miles}}$

Write the ratio as a fraction.

$= \dfrac{\dfrac{20}{1}}{\dfrac{3}{4}}$

Simplify the complex fraction. It is easier to work without the units (miles); just remember to put them in the answer.

$= \dfrac{20}{1} \cdot \dfrac{4}{3}$

Invert and multiply.

$= \dfrac{80}{3}$

Multiply the numerators; multiply the denominators.

$= \dfrac{80 \text{ miles}}{3 \text{ miles}}$

Put the units back in the numerator and denominator.

c)   6 days : 12 hours $= 6 \text{ days} : \dfrac{1}{2} \text{ day}$

The units must be the same.

Rewrite 12 hours as $\dfrac{1}{2}$ day

$= \dfrac{\dfrac{6}{1}}{\dfrac{1}{2}}$

Write the ratio as a complex fraction.

$= \dfrac{\dfrac{6}{1}}{\dfrac{1}{2}}$

Simplify the complex fraction.

$$= \frac{6}{1} \cdot \frac{2}{1}$$

Invert and multiply.

$$= \frac{12}{1}$$

Multiply the numerators, multiply the denominators.

$$= \frac{12 \text{ days}}{1 \text{ day}}$$

Put the units back in the numerator and denominator.

Proportions

An equation that consists of two equal ratios is called a **proportion**. If $\frac{a}{b}$ and $\frac{c}{d}$ are two equal ratios, then $\frac{a}{b} = \frac{c}{d}$ is called a proportion. In the proportion $\frac{a}{b} = \frac{c}{d}$, a, b, c, and d are called terms of the proportion. Also, b and c are called the **means** of the proportion, and a and d are called the **extremes** of the proportion. We will use the following formula when working with proportions:

> If $\frac{a}{b} = \frac{c}{d}$, then $ad = bc$.
>
> In words, the product of the extremes equals the product of the means.

Example 16 Solve and check each proportion.

a) $\frac{x}{6} = \frac{8}{4}$

b) $\frac{x}{2} = \frac{3}{4}$

c) $\frac{8}{r + 24} = \frac{2}{r}$

Solution 16

a) $\frac{x}{6} = \frac{8}{4}$

The extremes are x and 4. The means are 6 and 8.

$4x = 6 \cdot 8$

The product of the extremes equals the product of the means.

$4x = 48$

Solve the equation.

$\frac{4x}{4} = \frac{48}{4}$

Divide both sides by 4.

$x = 12$

Check:

$\frac{x}{6} = \frac{8}{4}$

Original proportion.

$\frac{12}{6} \overset{?}{=} \frac{8}{4}$

Substitute 12 into the original proportion.

$$2 = 2$$

12 checks.

b) $\dfrac{x}{2} = \dfrac{3}{4}$

The extremes are x and 4. The means are 2 and 3.

$$4x = 2 \cdot 3$$

The product of the extremes equals the product of the means.

$$4x = 6$$

Solve the equation.

$$\dfrac{4x}{4} = \dfrac{6}{4}$$

Divide both sides by 4.

$$x = \dfrac{3}{2}$$

Reduce the fraction.

Check:

$$\dfrac{x}{2} = \dfrac{3}{4}$$

Original proportion.

$$\dfrac{\frac{3}{2}}{2} \stackrel{?}{=} \dfrac{3}{4}$$

Substitute $\dfrac{3}{2}$ into the original proportion.

$$\dfrac{\frac{3}{2}}{\frac{2}{1}} = \dfrac{3}{4}$$

Simplify the complex fraction: $\dfrac{3}{2} \cdot \dfrac{1}{2} = \dfrac{3}{4}$.

$$\dfrac{3}{4} = \dfrac{3}{4}$$

$\dfrac{3}{2}$ checks.

c) $\dfrac{8}{r + 24} = \dfrac{2}{r}$

The extremes are 8 and r. The means are $(r + 24)$ and 2.

$$8r = 2(r + 24)$$

The product of the extremes equals the product of the means.

$$8r = 2r + 48$$

Solve the equation.

$$6r = 48$$

Subtract $2r$ from both sides of the equation.

$$\dfrac{6r}{6} = \dfrac{48}{6}$$

Divide both sides of the equation by 6.

$$r = 8$$

Check:

$$\dfrac{8}{r + 24} = \dfrac{2}{r}$$

Original proportion.

$$\frac{8}{(8) + 24} \stackrel{?}{=} \frac{2}{8}$$

Substitute 8 into the original proportion.

$$\frac{8}{32} = \frac{2}{8}$$

Simplify the fraction.

$$\frac{1}{4} = \frac{1}{4}$$

8 checks.

5.7 SOLVING EQUATIONS CONTAINING RATIONAL EXPRESSIONS

This section presents techniques for *solving equations* with rational expressions, not simplifying rational expressions. To use these techniques, make sure the directions say "Solve," not "Simplify."

Practice solving equations

To Solve Equations with Rational Expressions:
1. Factor each denominator as necessary to find the LCD.
2. Multiply both sides of the equation by the LCD.
3. Divide out common factors. There should be *no* fractions remaining after this step.
4. Solve the resulting equation.
5. Check each solution in the original equation.

Example 17 Solve each equation and check your answers.

a) $\frac{x}{6} + 1 = \frac{1}{3}$

b) $1 + \frac{3}{x} = \frac{10}{x^2}$

c) $\frac{x}{x - 4} = 2 + \frac{4}{x - 4}$

d) $\frac{2}{x - 2} + \frac{1}{x^2 - 4} = \frac{3}{x + 2}$

e) $\frac{2x}{x - 3} - \frac{x}{x + 2} = \frac{-6}{x^2 - x - 6}$

f) $\frac{x + 3}{x^2 - 3x - 4} - \frac{2}{x^2 + 3x + 2} = \frac{8}{x^2 - 2x - 8}$

g) $\dfrac{r}{r-1} = \dfrac{2}{r^2-1}$

Solution 17

a) $\dfrac{x}{6} + 1 = \dfrac{1}{3}$

$6\left(\dfrac{x}{6} + 1\right) = 6\left(\dfrac{1}{3}\right)$

Multiply both sides of equation by LCD = 6.

$6 \cdot \dfrac{x}{6} + 6 \cdot 1 = 6 \cdot \dfrac{1}{3}$

Distribute.

$x + 6 = 2$

Divide out common factors.

$x = -4$

Check:

$\dfrac{-4}{6} + 1 \overset{?}{=} \dfrac{1}{3}$

Substitute x = –4.

$\dfrac{-4}{6} + \dfrac{6}{6} = \dfrac{1}{3}$

$\dfrac{2}{6} = \dfrac{1}{3}$

True.

b) $1 + \dfrac{3}{x} = \dfrac{10}{x^2}$

$x^2\left(1 + \dfrac{3}{x}\right) = x2\left(\dfrac{10}{x^2}\right)$

Multiply both sides of equation by LCD = x^2.

$x^2 \cdot 1 + x^2 \cdot \dfrac{3}{x} = x^2 \cdot \dfrac{10}{x^2}$

Distribute.

$x^2 + 3x = 10$

Quadratic equation.

$x^2 + 3x - 10 = 0$

Get 0 on one side.

$(x + 5)(x - 2) = 0$

Factor.

$x = -5$ or $x = 2$

Set each factor equal to 0 and solve.

Check:

When $x = -5$,

$1 + \dfrac{3}{(-5)} \overset{?}{=} \dfrac{10}{(-5)^2}$

When $x = 2$,

$1 + \dfrac{3}{(2)} \overset{?}{=} \dfrac{10}{(2)^2}$

$1 - \dfrac{3}{5} \overset{?}{=} \dfrac{10}{25}$

$1 + \dfrac{3}{2} \overset{?}{=} \dfrac{10}{4}$

$\dfrac{2}{5} = \dfrac{2}{5}$

$\dfrac{5}{2} = \dfrac{5}{2}$

Both solutions check.

c) $\dfrac{x}{x-4} = 2 + \dfrac{4}{x-4}$

$(x-4)\dfrac{x}{x-4} = (x-4)\left(2 + \dfrac{4}{x-4}\right)$ Multiply by LCD $= (x-4)$.

$(x-4)\dfrac{x}{x-4} = (x-4)2 + (x-4)\left(\dfrac{4}{x-4}\right)$

  Distribute.

$x = 2x - 8 + 4$ Solve first–degree equation.

$-x = -4$

$x = 4$ Proposed solution.

Check: When $x = 4$, the denominator equals 0! Recall from our earlier work that 4 is a restricted value and that x cannot equal 4. Thus, this equation has *no solution*.

d) $\dfrac{2}{x-2} + \dfrac{1}{x^2-4} = \dfrac{3}{x+2}$ Since $x^2 - 4 = (x-2)(x+2)$,

  LCD $= (x-2)(x+2)$.

$(x-2)(x+2)\left(\dfrac{2}{x-2} + \dfrac{1}{x^2-4}\right) = (x-2)(x+2)\left(\dfrac{3}{x+2}\right)$

$(x-2)(x+2)\left(\dfrac{2}{x-2}\right) + (x-2)(x+2)\left(\dfrac{1}{(x-2)(x+2)}\right) =$

$(x-2)(x+2)\left(\dfrac{3}{x+2}\right)$

$(x+2)(2)+1 = (x-2)(3)$ Solve the first–degree equation.

$2x+4+1 = 3x-6$

$-x = -11$

$x = 11$ Proposed solution.

Check: Try the check on your own.

e) $\dfrac{2x}{x-3} - \dfrac{x}{x+2} = \dfrac{-6}{x^2-x-6}$

$(x-3)(x+2)\left(\dfrac{2x}{x-3} - \dfrac{x}{x+2}\right) = (x-3)(x+2)\left(\dfrac{-6}{(x-3)(x+2)}\right)$

  Since $x^2 - x - 6 = (x-3)(x+2)$,

  the LCD $= (x-3)(x+2)$.

$(x-3)(x+2)\left(\dfrac{2x}{x-3}\right) - (x-3)(x+2)\left(\dfrac{x}{x+2}\right) =$

$(x-3)(x+2)\left(\dfrac{-6}{(x-3)(x+2)}\right)$

$(x+2)(2x)-(x-3)(x) = -6$ Simplify each side of the equation.

$2x^2 + 4x - x^2 + 3x = -6$ This is a quadratic equation.

$x^2 + 7x + 6 = 0$ Get 0 alone on one side of the equation.

$(x+6)(x+1) = 0$ Factor.

$x + 6 = 0$ or $x + 1 = 0$ — Set each factor equal to 0 to solve.

$x = -6$ or $x = -1$ — Proposed solutions.

Check: Both -6 and -1 check in the original equation and are solutions.

f) $\dfrac{x+3}{x^2 - 3x - 4} - \dfrac{2}{x^2 + 3x + 2} = \dfrac{8}{x^2 - 2x - 8}$ ~

Factor the denominators to find the LCD.

$$\dfrac{x+3}{(x-4)(x+1)} - \dfrac{2}{(x+2)(x+1)} = \dfrac{8}{(x-4)(x+2)}$$

LCD $= (x-4)(x+1)(x+2)$.

$$(x-4)(x+1)(x+2)\left[\dfrac{x+3}{(x-4)(x+1)} - \dfrac{2}{(x+2)(x+1)}\right] =$$

$$(x-4)(x+1)(x+2)\left[\dfrac{8}{(x-4)(x+2)}\right]$$

Multiply both sides of the equation by the LCD.

$$(x-4)(x+1)(x+2)\left(\dfrac{x+3}{(x-4)(x+1)}\right)$$

$$- (x-4)(x+1)(x+2)\left(\dfrac{2}{(x+2)(x+1)}\right)$$

$$= (x-4)(x+1)(x+2)\left(\dfrac{8}{(x-4)(x+2)}\right)$$

Use the Distributive Property to multiply the LCD times each term.

$(x+2)(x+3)-(x-4)(2)=(x+1)8$ — Simplify both sides of the equation.

$x^2 + 5x + 6 - 2x + 8 = 8x + 8$ — Solve the quadratic equation.

$x^2 + 3x + 14 = 8x + 8$ — Combine similar terms.

$x^2 - 5x + 6 = 0$ — Get 0 alone on one side.

$(x-2)(x-3) = 0$ — Factor and set each factor equal to 0 to solve.

$x - 2 = 0$ or $x - 3 = 0$

$x = 2$ or $x = 3$ — Proposed solutions.

Check: Both 2 and 3 will check when substituted into the original equation.

g) $\dfrac{r}{r-1} = \dfrac{2}{r^2 - 1}$

$$(r-1)(r+1)\left(\dfrac{r}{r-1}\right) = (r-1)(r+1)\left(\dfrac{2}{(r-1)(r+1)}\right)$$

Multiply both sides of the equation by the LCD $(r-1)(r+1)$.

$(r+1)r = 2$ — Distribute.

$r^2 + r = 2$ — Solve the quadratic equation.

$r^2 + r - 2 = 0$ — Get 0 alone on one side of the equation.

$(r+2)(r-1)=0$ Factor.

$r+2=0$ or $r-1=0$ Set each factor equal to 0 to solve.

$r=-2$ or $r=1$ Proposed solutions.

Check: $r=1$ makes the denominators of the original equation equal 0, so 1 is *not* a solution. Recall from our earlier work that 1 is called a restricted value and that r cannot equal 1.

If $r=-2$, $\dfrac{-2}{(-2)-1} \stackrel{?}{=} \dfrac{2}{(-2)^2-1}$

$\dfrac{-2}{-2} = \dfrac{2}{3}$

So -2 *is* a solution to the original equation.

5.8 APPLICATIONS

In this section we will solve four basic types of applications that lead to equations with rational expressions: number problems, motion problems ($D = R\ T$), work problems, and variation problems. In working the number problems, remember that the numerator is the top of the fraction, the denominator is the bottom of the fraction, and the reciprocal of a number a is $\dfrac{1}{a}$.

Number problems

Example 18   If twice the reciprocal of a number is subtracted from the number, the result is $\dfrac{7}{3}$. Find the number.

Solution 18   Let a = original number

Then $\dfrac{1}{a}$ = reciprocal

Twice the reciprocal $= 2\left(\dfrac{1}{a}\right)$, so to subtract twice the reciprocal from the number (a), we write:

$a - 2\left(\dfrac{1}{a}\right) = \dfrac{7}{3}$ Write an equation.

$a - \left(\dfrac{2}{a}\right) = \dfrac{7}{3}$ LCD = 3a.

$$3a\left(a - \frac{2}{a}\right) = 3a\left(\frac{7}{3}\right)$$

Multiply both sides of the equation by 3a.

$3a2 - 6 = 7a$

Solve the quadratic equation.

$3a2 - 7a - 6 = 0$

Get 0 alone on one side of the equation.

$(3a + 2)(a - 3) = 0$

Factor and set each factor equal to 0.

$3a + 2 = 0$ or $a - 3 = 0$

Solve each first degree equation.

$3a = -2$

$a = -\frac{2}{3}$

or $a = 3$

If $a = -\frac{2}{3}$, $\frac{1}{a} = \frac{3}{2}$

If $a = 3\frac{1}{a}$, $= \frac{1}{3}$

Check:

For $a = -\frac{2}{3}$

For $a = \frac{1}{3}$

$-\frac{2}{3} - 2\left(\frac{3}{2}\right) = \frac{7}{3}$ $3 - 2\left(\frac{1}{2}\right) = \frac{7}{3}$

Substitute each value into the original equation.

$-\frac{2}{3} + 3 = \frac{7}{3}$

$3 - \frac{2}{3} = \frac{7}{3}$

$\frac{7}{3} = \frac{7}{3}$

$\frac{7}{3} = \frac{7}{3}$

Both solutions check.

Motion problems

Motion problems involve a moving object, often a plane, car, boat, or person on a bicycle. These problems may ask you to account for the rate of the object when it is affected by the speed of the wind (for the plane or bicyclist) or the speed of the current (for the boat). Remember that an object moves faster *with* the wind or *with* the current (downstream!). The following table contains some sample language:

Boat	Plane	Symbol
speed in still water	speed in still air	x
current	windspeed	y
speed upstream	speed against wind	x − y
speed downstream	speed with wind	x + y

These problems will make use of the formula
$D = R \cdot T$, where D is distance, R is the rate, and T is time.

Example 19 A boat can travel 20 miles up the river in the same amount of time it takes to travel 40 miles down the river. If the current is 10 miles per hour, what is the speed of the boat in still water?

Solution 19

	R	T	D
Upstream	$x - 10$		20
Downstream	$x + 10$		40

Let x = speed of the boat in still water. Then,
since $R \cdot T = D$

$$\frac{R \cdot T}{R} = \frac{D}{R}$$

$$T = \frac{D}{R}$$

Solve for T.

Divide both sides by R.

Now we can complete the table:

	R	T	D
Upstream	$x - 10$	$\dfrac{20}{x - 10}$	20
Downstream	$x + 10$	$\dfrac{40}{x + 10}$	40

Now, since the time upstream must be equal to the time downstream:

$$\frac{20}{x - 10} = \frac{40}{x + 10}$$

$$(x - 10)(x + 10)\left(\frac{20}{x - 10}\right) = (x - 10)(x + 10)\left(\frac{40}{x + 10}\right)$$

Multiply by LCD.

$(x + 10)(20) = (x - 10)(40)$ Solve the first–degree equation.
$20x + 200 = 40x - 400$ Subtract 200 and 40x from both sides.

$-20x = -600$

$$\frac{-20x}{-20} = \frac{-600}{-20}$$

Divide both sides of the equation by –20.

$x = 30$ miles per hour   Speed of boat in still water.

Check:

$$\frac{20}{x - 10} = \frac{40}{x + 10}$$

Original equation.

$$\frac{20}{(30)-10}=\frac{40}{(30)+10}$$

Substitute 30 into the original equation.

$$\frac{20}{20}=\frac{40}{40}$$

30 checks.

Work problems

Work problems involve the length of time to do a job and usually involve two or more people or machines working at a task such as painting or typing. These techniques are also used for pipes that fill and drain sinks or swimming pools. Study the following table that relates total job time to the fractional part of the job completed in 1 hour.

Time to Complete Job	Part of Job Completed in 1 Hour	Part of Job Completed in 2 Hours
5 hours	$\frac{1}{5}$	$\frac{2}{5}$
8 hours	$\frac{1}{8}$	$\frac{2}{8}$
x hours	$\frac{1}{x}$	$\frac{2}{x}$

Example 20 Joan can type a manuscript in 30 hours. Lisa can do the job in 60 hours. How long would it take them if they worked together?

Solution 20 Let x = time to complete the job working together.

In 1 hour, Joan completes $\frac{1}{30}$ of the job.

Lisa completes $\frac{1}{60}$ of the job.

Together they complete $\frac{1}{x}$ of the job.

So, $\dfrac{1}{30}+\dfrac{1}{60}=\dfrac{1}{x}$

$$60x\left(\frac{1}{30}+\frac{1}{60}\right)=60x\left(\frac{1}{x}\right)$$

Multiply by the LCD.

$$60x\left(\frac{1}{30}\right)+60x\left(\frac{1}{60}\right)=60x\left(\frac{1}{x}\right)$$

Distribute.

$2x+x=60$ Solve.

$3x=60$

$x=20$ hours

Example 21 A cold–water faucet can fill a sink in 15 minutes, and a hot–water faucet can fill it in 10 minutes. The drain can empty the sink in 18 minutes. If both faucets are on and the drain is accidentally left open, how long will it take to fill the sink?

Solution 21 Let x = time to fill the sink.

In 1 minute: The cold–water faucet fills $\dfrac{1}{15}$ of the sink.

The hot–water faucet fills $\dfrac{1}{10}$ of the sink.

The drain empties $\dfrac{1}{18}$ of the sink.

Then $\dfrac{1}{15} + \dfrac{1}{10} - \dfrac{1}{18} = \dfrac{1}{x}$

$90x\left(\dfrac{1}{15} + \dfrac{1}{10} - \dfrac{1}{18}\right) = 90x\left(\dfrac{1}{x}\right)$ Multiply by the LCD.

$90x\left(\dfrac{1}{15}\right) + 90x\left(\dfrac{1}{10}\right) - 90x\left(\dfrac{1}{18}\right) = 90x\left(\dfrac{1}{x}\right)$ Distribute.

$6x + 9x - 5x = 90$ Solve.

$10x = 90$

$x = 9$ minutes

It takes 9 minutes to fill the sink.

Variation

Two quantities vary directly when one quantity is a constant multiple of the other. For example, if you buy 3 cans of cat food for 2 cats, you would buy 6 cans of cat food for 4 cats. (Two times as many cats means two times as many cans of cat food.) The constant is usually represented by k. In an indirect variation, one quantity increases as the other decreases. Some types of variations are:

Type	Language	Symbols
directindirect	y varies directly as x	$y = kx$
indirect	y varies inversely as x or y varies indirectly as x	$y = \dfrac{k}{x}$

Example 22 If t varies directly as s, and $t = 9$ when s = 6, find t when s is $\dfrac{2}{5}$.

Solution 22 Find k first:

$t = ks$ Direct variation.

$9 = k(6)$ Substitute $t = 9, s = 6.$

$\dfrac{9}{6} = k$

Solve for k.

$$\frac{3}{2} = k$$

Find *t*:

$$t = \frac{3}{2}s$$

Direct variation, $k = \frac{3}{2}$.

$$t = \frac{3}{2}\left(\frac{2}{5}\right)$$

Substitute $s = \frac{2}{5}$.

$$t = \frac{3}{5}$$

Solve for *t*.

Example 23 If *p* varies indirectly as *q*2 and p = 12 when q = 2, find p when q = 4.

Solution 23 First find *k*:

$$p = \frac{k}{q^2}$$

Indirect variation.

$$12 = \frac{k}{(2)^2}$$

Substitute $p = 12$, $q = 2$.

$$12 = \frac{k}{4}$$

$$4(12) = 4\left(\frac{k}{4}\right)$$

Multiply by LCD.

$$48 = k$$

Now, use *k* to find *p* when *q* = 4.

$$p = \frac{48}{q^2}$$

Indirect variation, $k = 48$.

$$p = \frac{48}{(4)^2}$$

Substitute $q = 4$.

$$p = \frac{48}{16}$$

$$p = 3$$

Solution.

Practice Exercises

1. State the restrictions on the variable in the following rational expressions.

   (a) $\dfrac{2x - 3}{8}$

   (b) $\dfrac{x + 3}{x - 7}$

   (c) $\dfrac{9x^2}{5x + 6}$

   (d) $\dfrac{11x}{x^2 - 3x + 2}$

2. Reduce to lowest terms.

   (a) $\dfrac{3x + 6}{7x + 14}$

   (b) $\dfrac{x^2 + 3x + 2}{x^2 - x - 2}$

   (c) $\dfrac{4x^2 + 4x + 1}{6x^2 + 7x + 2}$

   (d) $\dfrac{x^2 + xy + xz + yz}{2x^2 + 3xz + 2xy + 3yz}$

3. Write in lowest terms.

   (a) $\dfrac{5a - b}{b - 5a}$

   (b) $\dfrac{a - 2b}{2b + a}$

   (c) $\dfrac{x^2 - 36}{6 - x}$

   (d) $\dfrac{x^2 + x - 2}{-x^2 + 1}$

4. Solve.

   (a) $\dfrac{3x^2}{27x^3} \cdot \dfrac{12x}{16x}$

   (b) $\dfrac{x^2 - 4}{2y} \cdot \dfrac{2 - x}{6xy}$

   (c) $\dfrac{a^2 + 5a + 6}{2a^2 + 9a + 4} \cdot \dfrac{2a^2 + 7a - 4}{2a^2 + 7a + 6}$

   (d) $\dfrac{a^2 + 3a + 2}{a^2 + 5a + 6} \cdot \dfrac{a^2 + 2a + 1}{a^2 + 4a + 3}$

5. Find the LCM.
   (a) $6x3y$ and $8xy2$
   (b) $x2 + 4x + 3$ and $x2 + 5x + 6$

6. Find the LCD.

   (a) $\dfrac{2}{x^2 - x - 6}$ and $\dfrac{4}{x^2 - 5x + 6}$

   (b) $\dfrac{1}{8}$ and $\dfrac{1}{14}$

7. Solve.

   (a) $\dfrac{3}{y^2} + \dfrac{8}{y^2}$

   (b) $\dfrac{4x + 3}{2x + 7} + \dfrac{3x - 8}{2x + 7}$

   (c) $\dfrac{2}{m^2 - 4} - \dfrac{3}{m + 2}$

   (d) $\dfrac{6z}{(z - 1)^2} - \dfrac{2z}{z^2 - 1}$

8. Simplify.

   (a) $\dfrac{\dfrac{36x^4}{5y^4z^5}}{\dfrac{9xy^2}{15z^5}}$

   (b) $\dfrac{\dfrac{9}{x} + \dfrac{3}{x^2}}{\dfrac{4}{5} + \dfrac{1}{x}}$

   (c) $\dfrac{\dfrac{4x + 8}{3x^2}}{\dfrac{4}{6x}}$

9. Solve.

(a) $\dfrac{x}{7} = \dfrac{3}{21}$

(b) $\dfrac{6}{x + 18} = \dfrac{2}{x}$

(c) $\dfrac{5}{x^2 - 25} = \dfrac{1}{x - 5}$

10. Solve.

(a) $\dfrac{x}{x + 4} = \dfrac{2}{x + 4} + 5$

(b) $\dfrac{2}{x - 3} - \dfrac{3}{x + 3} = \dfrac{12}{x^2 - 9}$

(c) $\dfrac{1}{2x^2 - x - 1} + \dfrac{2}{2x^2 + 3x + 1} = \dfrac{3}{x^2 - 1}$

(d) $\dfrac{2}{x} + \dfrac{20}{x^2 + 5x} = \dfrac{x + 1}{x + 5}$

(e) $\dfrac{x + 3}{x^2 - x} = \dfrac{8}{x^2 - 1}$

11. Solve.

(a) The sum of a number and 3 times its reciprocal is $\dfrac{13}{2}$. Find the number

(b) Bill can type 5 forms of a test in 4 hours. Lisa can type the same 5 forms in 6 hours. If they work together, how long would it take to type all 5 forms?

(c) Triangles ABC and XYZ are similar. The lengths of the corresponding sides are a and x, b and y, and c and z. If $a = 10$, $x = 15$, $y = 12$, and $z = 14$, find b.

Answers

1. (a) none
    (b) $x \neq 7$
    (c) $x \neq -\dfrac{6}{5}$
    (d) $x \neq 1, 2$

2. (a) $\dfrac{3}{7}$
    (b) $\dfrac{x + 2}{x - 2}$
    (c) $\dfrac{2x + 1}{3x + 2}$
    (d) $\dfrac{x + z}{2x + 3z}$

3. (a) -1
    (b) $\dfrac{a - 2b}{2b + a}$
    (c) $-x - 6$
    (d) $-\dfrac{(x + 2)}{(x + 1)}$

4. (a) $\dfrac{1}{12x}$
    (b) $-3x - 6$
    (c) $\dfrac{(a + 3)(2a - 1)}{(2a + 1)(2a + 3)}$
    (d) 1

5. (a) $24x3y2$
    (b) $x3 + 6x2 + 11x + 6$

6. (a) $x3 - 3x2 - 4x + 12$
    (b) 56

7. (a) $\dfrac{11}{y^2}$
    (b) $\dfrac{7x - 5}{2x + 7}$
    (c) $\dfrac{8 - 3m}{m^2 - 4}$
    (d) $\dfrac{4z(z + 2)}{(z - 1)^2(z + 1)}$

8. (a) $\dfrac{12x^3}{y^6}$
    (b) $\dfrac{15(3x + 1)}{x(4x + 5)}$
    (c) $\dfrac{2x + 4}{x}$

9. (a) 1
    (b) 9
    (c) 0

10. (a) $-\dfrac{11}{2}$
    (b) 3
    (c) $-\dfrac{4}{3}$
    (d) 6 (-5 is a restricted value)
    (e) 3

11. (a) $6, \dfrac{1}{2}$
    (b) 2.5 hours
    (c) 8

6

Graphing Linear Equations

6.1 SOLUTIONS TO LINEAR EQUATIONS IN TWO VARIABLES

Ordered pairs and solutions to equations

In this chapter, we will solve linear equations in two variables, such as

$$3x - 2y = 6$$

and graph the solutions. A **linear equation in two variables** is an equation that can be written in the form $ax + by = c$, where a, b, and c are real numbers and a and b are not both 0. Recall that a solution to an equation like $4x + 6 = 14$ is a number that replaces the variable and makes the equation a true statement. For example, if $x = 2$,

$$4(2) + 6 = 14$$

is a true statement. Solutions to linear equations in two variables will need replacements for both variables. For example, substituting $x = 4$ and $y = 3$ into $3x - 2y = 6$ we have

$$3x - 2y = 6$$
$$3(4) - 2(3) = 6,$$

which is a true statement. We call $x = 4$ and $y = 3$ a solution to the linear equation in two variables and write it as (4, 3). When a pair of numbers is written in a specific order in parentheses it is called an **ordered pair**.

Just as our equations in Chapters 2, 4, and 5 used variables other than x, linear equations in two variables may involve x's and y's or a's and b's, etc. The numbers written in an ordered pair are called **coordinates**. In our example (4, 3), we call 4 the x-coordinate and 3 the y-coordinate because the equation contained the variables x and y. We generally list the coordinates of an ordered pair in alphabetical order. Consider the following examples.

Linear Equation in Two Variables	Ordered Pairs	Example of Solution
$3a + b = 9$	(a, b)	$(2, 3)$ is a solution since $3(2) + (3) = 9$
$p - 5q = 10$	(p, q)	$(0, -2)$ is a solution since $0 - 5(-2) = 10$
$-2r + 5s = 15$	(r, s)	$(10, 7)$ is a solution since $-2(10) + 5(7) = 15$

Example 1 Determine whether the given ordered pair is a solution of the given equation.

a) $4x + y = 6$; $(2, -2)$
b) $y = 5x - 1$; $(3, 14)$
c) $2a - 7b = 6$; $(1, 3)$
d) $x = 3$; $(3, -1)$

Solution 1

a) $4x + y = 6$; $(2, -2)$ The ordered pair is in alphabetical order, so $x = 2$ and $y = -2$.

$4(2) + (-2) = 6$ Substitute $x = 2, y = -2$.
$8 + (-2) = 6$ A true statement.

Since this is a true statement, the ordered pair $(2, -2)$ is a solution to $4x + y = 6$.

b) $y = 5x - 1$; $(3, 14)$ The ordered pair is in alphabetical order, so $x = 3$ and $y = 14$.

$14 = 5(3) - 1$ Substitute $x = 3, y = 14$.
$14 = 15 - 1$ A true statement.

Since this is a true statement, the ordered pair $(3, 14)$ is a solution to $y = 5x - 1$.

c) $2a - 7b = 6$; $(1, 3)$ The ordered pair is in alphabetical order, so $a = 1$ and $b = 3$.

$2(1) - 7(3) = 6$ Substitute $a = 1, b = 3$.
$2 - 21 =$ Multiply before subtracting.
$-19 = 6$ A false statement.

Since this is a false statement, the ordered pair $(1, 3)$ is *not* a solution to $2a - 7b = 6$.

d) $x = 3$; $(3, -1)$ The ordered pair is in alphabetical order, so $x = 3$ and $y = -1$.

$x + 0y = 3$ There is no y written in the given equation, which means the equation can be written $x + 0y = 3$.

$(3) + 0(-1) = 3$ Substitute $x = 3$ and $y = -1$.
$3 + 0 = 3$ A true statement.

Since this is a true statement, the ordered pair $(3, -1)$ is a solution to $x = 3$.

Solving linear equations in two variables

> **Given one coordinate, you can find the solution by**
> 1. Substituting the given coordinate.
> 2. Solve the resulting equation.

Example 2 Complete the given ordered pairs for the equation $3x - 2y = 6$.
a) (6,)
b) (, 0)
c) (-3,)

Solution 2

a) $3x - 2y = 6$
   $3(6) - 2y = 6$

   $\dfrac{18 - 2y = 6}{-18 \quad -18}$

   $-2y = -12$

   $\dfrac{-2y}{-2} = \dfrac{-12}{-2}$

   $y = 6$
   (6, 6)

   Check:
   $3x - 2y = 6$
   $3(6) - 2(6) \overset{?}{=} 6$

   $18 - 12 \overset{?}{=} 6$
   $6 = 6$

Substitute $x = 6$.
Solve for y.

Subtract 18 from each side of the equation.

Divide each side by -2.

Solution.

Original equation.
Substitute $x = 6$ and $y = 6$ into the original equation.
Multiply before subtracting.

(6, 6) checks.

b) $3x - 2y = 6$
   $3x - 2(0) = 6$
   $3x - 0 = 6$
   $3x = 6$
   $\dfrac{3x}{3} = \dfrac{6}{3}$
   $x = 2$
   (2, 0)

   Check:
   $3x - 2y = 6$
   $3(2) - 2(0) \overset{?}{=} 6$

   $6 - 0 \overset{?}{=} 6$
   $6 = 6$

Substitute y = 0.
Solve for x.
Divide each side by 3.

Solution.

Original equation.
Substitute $x = 2$ and $y = 0$ into the original equation.
Multiply before subtracting.
(2, 0) checks.

c) $3x - 2y = 6$

$\quad\quad 3(-3) - 2y = 6$ Substitute $x = -3$.

$\quad\quad -9 - 2y \;=\; 6$ Solve for y. Add 9 to both sides of the equation

$$\underline{\quad +9 \quad\quad\quad +9\quad}$$
$$-2y \;=\; 15$$

$$\frac{-2y}{-2} = \frac{15}{-2}$$ Divide each side by -2.

$$y = \frac{-15}{2}$$

$$\left(-3, \; -\frac{15}{2}\right)$$ Solution.

Check:

$\quad 3x - 2y = 6$ Original equation.

$\quad 3(-3) - 2\dfrac{15}{2} \overset{?}{=} 6$ Substitute $x = -3$ and $y = -\dfrac{15}{2}$ into the original equation. Multiply before adding.

$\quad -9 + 15 \overset{?}{=} 6$

$\quad 6 = 6$ $\left(-3, -\dfrac{15}{2}\right)$ checks.

Example 3   Complete the given ordered pairs for the equation $y = 4$.

a) (2,)
b) (-3,)
c) (0,)

Solution 3   Since *y* must equal 4, all the missing *y* coordinates are 4. Thus,

a) (2, 4)
b) (-3, 4)
c) (0, 4)

are the required solutions.

Example 4   Complete the given ordered pairs for the equation $x = -6$.

a) (, 3)
b) (, -2)
c) (, 0)

Solution 4   Since *x* must equal -6, all the missing *x* coordinates are -6. Thus,

a) (-6, 3)
b) (-6, -2)
c) (-6, 0)

are the required solutions.

6.2 GRAPHING LINEAR EQUATIONS

The coordinate system

We can solve $2x - 4 = 10$ as follows:

$$2x - 4 = 10$$
$$\underline{+4 = +4}$$
$$2x = 14$$

Add 4 to both sides of the equation.

$$\frac{1}{2}(2x) = \frac{1}{2}(1)4$$

Multiply each side by $\frac{1}{2}$ (or divide by 2).

$$x = 7$$

and graph the solution on a number line:

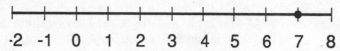

To graph ordered pairs, we use a rectangular coordinate system made up of two number lines: the horizontal number line is called the *x-axis*, and the vertical number line is called the *y-axis*.

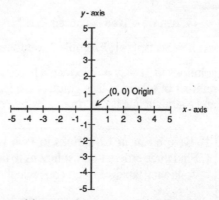

On a number line, positive numbers are to the right of 0, and negative numbers are to the left of 0. Notice that the *x-axis* is arranged in the same way. On the *y-axis*, positive numbers are written up the axis, and negative numbers are written down the axis. Where the two axes (the plural of axis) intersect, the *x-coordinate* equals 0 and the *y* coordinate equals 0. The point (0, 0) is called the **origin**.

To Plot the Ordered Pair (x, y):
1. Place your pencil point at the origin (0, 0).
2. Go right *x* units if $x > 0$ or left *x* units if $x < 0$.
3. Go up *y* units if $y > 0$ or down *y* units if $y < 0$.
4. Put a point where your movement ended and label it with (x, y).

Example 5   Plot the points (0, 0), (2, 4), (–2, 4), (–2, –4), (2, –4), (0, 4) and (2,0).

Solution 5

(0, 0) is at the intersection of the axes.

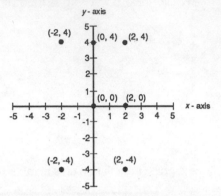

(2, 4) is 2 units to the right and 4 units up from the origin (0, 0).
(–2, 4) is 2 units to the left and 4 units up from the origin (0, 0).
(–2, –4) is 2 units to the left and 4 units down from the origin.
(2, –4) is 2 units to the right and 4 units down from the origin.
(0, 4) is 0 units left or right and 4 units up from the origin.
(2, 0) is 2 units to the right and 0 units up or down from the origin.

Graphing Linear Equations in Two Variables

When we solved equations like $2x - 4 = 10$, we found one solution. From our work in Section 6.1, Example 2, we found that (6, 6), (2, 0), and $(-3, \frac{-15}{2})$ were *all* solutions to $3x - 2y = 6$. In fact, a linear equation in two variables has an *infinite* number of solutions. The graph of a linear equation in two variables is a straight line, and a straight line is determined by two points.

To Graph Linear Equations in Two Variables:
1. Find three ordered-pair solutions to the given equation. Completing either of the following tables is often convenient:

x	y		x	y
0			1	
	0		2	
1			3	

2. Plot the three points.
3. Draw a straight line through these points. If they are not in line, go back and check your arithmetic. Put arrows on both ends of the line to show that the line continues forever in both directions.
Note: Although two points determine a line, we usually plot three as a check on our arithmetic.

Example 6   Graph.

a) $x - 2y = -6$
b) $x + y = 4$
c) $y = 2x$

Solution 6

a) $x - 2y = -6$ Let's complete the table:

x	y
0	
	0
2	

$x - 2y = -6$
If $x = 0$, $0 - 2y = -6$
$\qquad\qquad -2y = -6$
$\qquad\qquad\quad y = 3$

x	y
0	3
	0
2	

If $y = 0$, $x - 2(0) = -6$
$\qquad\qquad\quad x = -6$

x	y
0	3
-6	0
2	

If $x = 2$, $(2) - 2y = -6$
$\qquad\qquad -2y = -8$
$\qquad\qquad\quad y = 4$

x	y
0	3
-6	0
2	

The values in the table give the following ordered pairs as solutions to $x - 2y = -6$:
(0, 3)
(-6, 0)
(2, 4)
Now, plot your points and connect with a straight line.

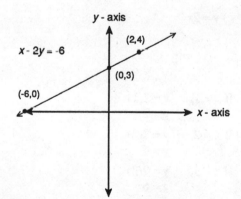

Notice that we used $(2, \ )$ rather than $(1, \ )$ to produce an integer solution. $(1, \frac{7}{2})$ is, of course, also on the line.

b) $x + y = 4$ Let's complete the table:

x	y
1	
2	
3	

$x + y = 4$
If $x = 1$, $(1) + y = 4$
                         $y = 3$
If $x = 2$, $2 + y = 4$
                         $y = 2$
If $x = 3$, $+ y = 4$
                         $y = 1$

x	y
1	3
2	2
3	1

The values in the table give the following ordered pairs as solutions to $x + y = 4$:
(1, 3)
(2, 2)
(3, 1)
Now, plot these points and connect with a straight line.

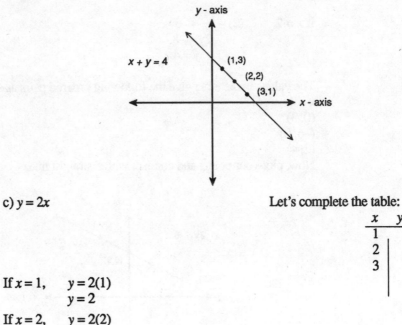

c) $y = 2x$ Let's complete the table:

x	y
1	
2	
3	

If $x = 1$, $y = 2(1)$
                    $y = 2$
If $x = 2$, $y = 2(2)$
                    $y = 4$
If $x = 3$, $y = 2(3)$
                    $y = 6$

The values in the table give the following ordered pairs as solutions to $y = 2x$:
(1, 2)
(2, 4)
(3, 6)
Now, plot these points and connect with a straight line.

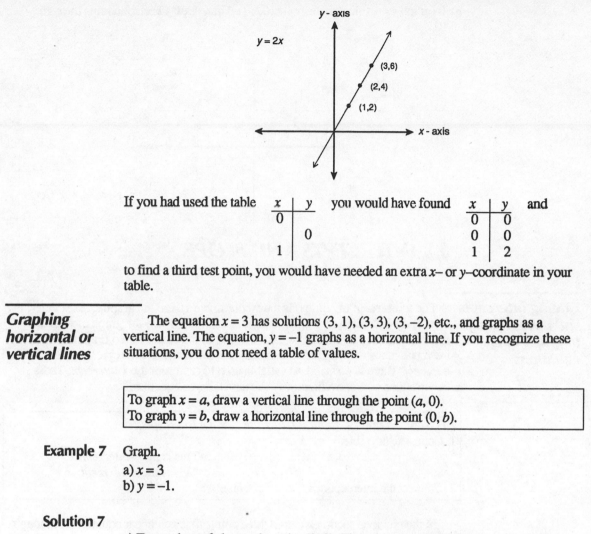

$y = 2x$

If you had used the table

x	y
0	
	0
1	

you would have found

x	y
0	0
0	0
1	2

and

to find a third test point, you would have needed an extra x– or y–coordinate in your table.

Graphing horizontal or vertical lines

The equation $x = 3$ has solutions $(3, 1)$, $(3, 3)$, $(3, -2)$, etc., and graphs as a vertical line. The equation, $y = -1$ graphs as a horizontal line. If you recognize these situations, you do not need a table of values.

To graph $x = a$, draw a vertical line through the point $(a, 0)$.
To graph $y = b$, draw a horizontal line through the point $(0, b)$.

Example 7 Graph.
a) $x = 3$
b) $y = -1$.

Solution 7

a) To graph $x = 3$, locate the point $(3, 0)$. Then draw a vertical line through $(3, 0)$.

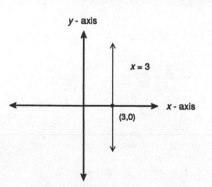

b) To graph $y = -1$, locate the point $(0, -1)$. Then draw a horizontal line through $(0, -1)$.

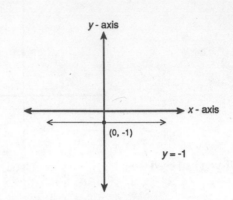

6.3 INTERCEPTS AND SLOPE

Finding intercepts and using them to graph linear equations

The **x-intercept** of a graph is the *x-coordinate* where the graph crosses the *x-axis*. The **y-intercept** of a graph is the *y* coordinate where the graph crosses the *y-axis*. To find the *x-intercept*, replace *y* with 0 in the equation. To find the *y-intercept*, replace *x* with 0. We generally use the variable *b* to represent the *y-intercept*. There is no standard variable used to represent the *x-intercept*. These intercepts give us a convenient way to graph a linear equation.

To Graph a Linear Equation Using the x and y Intercepts:

1. Complete the table:

x	y
0		This is the *y-intercept*.
	0	This is the *x-intercept*.

2. Connect the intercepts with a straight line.

In the previous section we used three points to graph linear equations. Although two points determine a line, we often use a third point as a check. You may want to use a third point to check the following graphs.

Example 8   Find the *x-* and *y-*intercepts for each linear equation and use them to draw the graph.

a) $2x - y = 2$

b) $y = \dfrac{3}{2}x + 3$

c) $y = 2x$

Solution 8

a) $2x - y = 2$

If $x = 0$, $2(0) - y = 2$ Find the *y-intercept*, *b*.
                        $-y = 2$
                        $y = -2$ $(0, -2)$

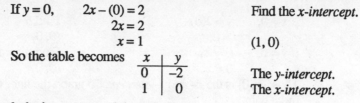

So the table becomes

x	y
0	-2
1	0

The *y-intercept.*
The *x-intercept.*

Graph the intercepts and draw the line:

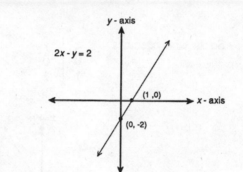

b) $y = \dfrac{3}{2}x + 3$

If $x = 0$, $y = \dfrac{3}{2}(0) + 3$ Find the *y-intercept, b.*

             $y = 3$ (0, 3)

If $y = 0$, $0 = \dfrac{3}{2}x + 3$ Find the *x-intercept.*

            $-3 = \dfrac{3}{2}x$

$\dfrac{2}{3}(-3) = \dfrac{2}{3}\left(\dfrac{3}{2}\right)x$

                               Multiply by $\dfrac{2}{3}$.

$-2 = x$ (-2, 0)

So the table becomes

x	y
0	3
-2	0

The *y-intercept.*
The *x-intercept.*

Graph the intercepts and draw the line:

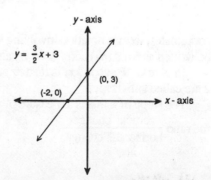

c) $y = 2x$

If $x = 0$, $y = 2(0)$ Find b.
                $y = 0$ $(0, 0)$
If $y = 0$, $0 = 2x$ Find the x-*intercept*.
                $0 = x$ $(0, 0)$

Thus, $(0, 0)$ is the x– and y-*intercept*. To graph the line, we will need at least one more point.

If $x = 1$, $y = 2(1)$ Substitute $x = 1$ into the original equation.

            $y =$ $(1, 2)$ is another point on the line.

So the table becomes

x	y
0	0
1	2

The x– and y-*intercept*

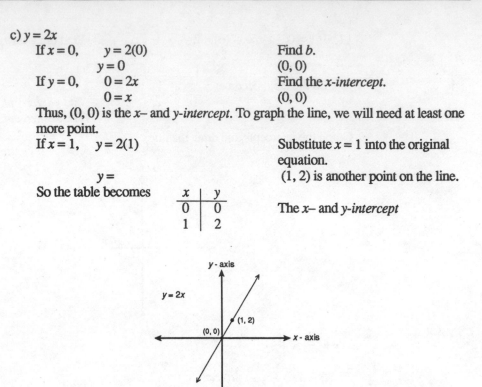

Graph the points and draw the line:

Slope

When we want to work with several points on a line, but not with specific

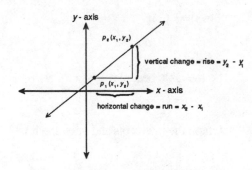

coordinates, we use notation involving subscripts. Thus, two points on a line could be written as $P_1(x_1, y_1)$ and $P_2(x_2, y_2)$ and shown on a graph as follows:

P_1 is read "P sub 1," x_1 is read "x sub 1," and y_2 is read "y sub 2," etc.; the 1 and 2 are called **subscripts**.

The **slope** of a line is a measure of the steepness of the line. It is calculated by the ratio $\dfrac{\text{vertical change}}{\text{horizontal change}}$.

> The slope of a line containing points $P_1(x_1, y_1)$ and $P_2(x_2, y_2)$ is:
>
> $$\text{slope} = m = \frac{\text{rise}}{\text{run}} = \frac{y_2 - y_1}{x_2 - x_1} = \frac{y_1 - y_2}{x_1 - x_2}$$

Note that the letter m is the standard variable used to represent slope.

Example 9   Find the slope of each of the following lines.

a) the line through $(1, 2)$ and $(3, 5)$
b) the line through $(-2, 1)$ and $(1, -4)$
c) the line through $(2, 3)$ and $(-1, 3)$
d) the line through $(-1, -2)$ and $(-1, 4)$

Solution 9

a) (x_1, y_1) (x_2, y_2) Label the points as (x_1, y_1) and (x_2, y_2).

$(1, 2)$ $(3, 5)$

$$m = \frac{y_2 - y_1}{x_2 - x_1}$$

Write the formula for slope.

$$= \frac{5 - 2}{3 - 1}$$

Substitute $y_2 = 5$, $y_1 = 2$ and $x_2 = 3$, $x_1 = 1$.

$$= \frac{3}{2}$$

Simplify the numerator and denominator.

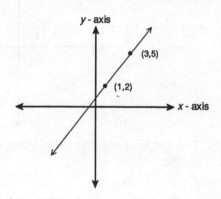

This line has positive slope. When the slope of a line is positive, it *rises* from left to right.

If you had labeled the points as (x_1, y_1) (x_2, y_2)
                                     $(3, 5)$ $(1, 2)$

your work would have looked like:

$$m = \frac{y_2 - y_1}{x_2 - x_1}$$

Write the formula for slope.

$$= \frac{2 - 5}{1 - 3}$$

Substitute $y_2 = 2$, $y_1 = 5$ and $x_2 = 1$, $x_1 = 3$.

$$= \frac{-3}{-2} = \frac{3}{2}$$

Simplify the numerator and denominator.

Notice that the slope equals $\frac{3}{2}$ regardless of which point you choose as P_1 and which you choose as P_2.

b) (x_1, y_1) (x_2, y_2)

Label the points as (x_1, y_1) and (x_2, y_2).

    $(-2, 1)$ $(1, -4)$

$$m = \frac{y_2 - y_1}{x_2 - x_1}$$

Write the formula for slope.

$$= \frac{-4 - 1}{1 - (-2)}$$

Substitute $y_2 = -4$, $y_1 = 1$ and $x_2 = 1$, $x_1 = -2$.

$$= \frac{-5}{3}$$

Simplify the numerator and denominator.

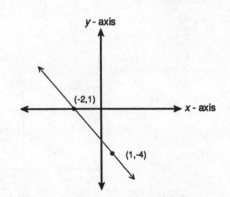

This line has a negative slope. When the slope of a line is negative, it *falls* from left to right.

c) (x_1, y_1) (x_2, y_2)

Label the points as (x_1, y_1) and (x_2, y_2).

    $(2, 3)$ $(-1, 3)$

$$m = \frac{y_2 - y_1}{x_2 - x_1}$$

Write the formula for slope.

$$= \frac{3 - 3}{-1 - 2}$$

Substitute $y_2 = 3$, $y_1 = 3$ and $x_2 = -1$, $x_1 = 2$.

$$= \frac{0}{-3} = 0$$

Simplify the numerator and denominator.

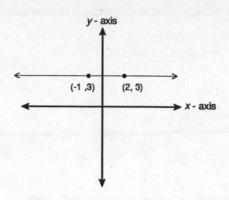

This line has 0 slope. When the slope is 0, the graph is a horizontal line.

d) (x_1, y_1) (x_2, y_2)

$(-1, -2)$ $(-1, 4)$

$$m = \frac{y_2 - y_1}{x_2 - x_1}$$

$$= \frac{4 - (-2)}{-1 - (-1)}$$

$$= \frac{6}{0}$$

which is *undefined*.

Label the points as (x_1, y_1) and (x_2, y_2).

Write the formula for slope.

Substitute $y_2 = 4$, $y_1 = -2$ and $x_2 = -1$, $x_1 = -1$.

Simplify the numerator and denominator.

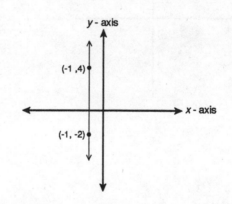

This line has undefined slope. When the slope is undefined, the graph is a vertical line.

Here are some slope concepts to remember:

Positive Slope
Rises from left to right

Negative Slope
 Falls from left to right

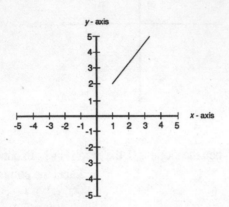

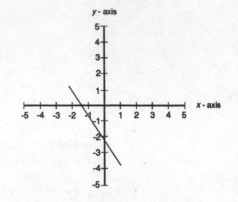

When the slope = 0,
graph is a horizontal line.

When the slope is undefined,
 graph is a vertical line.

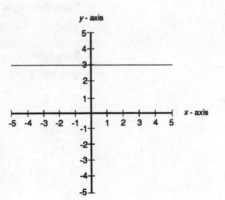

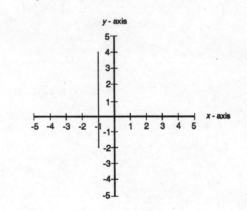

Graphing using the slope and a point on the line

If you know the slope of a line and any point on the line, you can graph the line using the following steps.

To Graph the Line through the Point (x^1, y^1) with Slope $m = \dfrac{a}{b}$:

1. Put a point on (x^1, y^1) and use this as your starting point.
2. Use $m = \dfrac{\text{rise}}{\text{run}} = \dfrac{a}{b}$ and rise (or go up) a units *from* your starting point. Then move to the right b units and put a second point there.
3. Draw a line through the two points.

Note: If the given slope is an integer, write it as a fraction using 1 for the denominator. If the given slope is negative, carry the negative in the numerator and *fall* (go down) a units instead of rising a units.

Example 10 Graph the lines with the given slopes and containing the given points.

a) $m = \dfrac{3}{2}, (-1, -2)$

b) $m = 2, (0, 1)$

c) $m = -\dfrac{1}{3}, (-1, 2)$

Solution 10

a) Start at $(-1, -2)$. $m = \dfrac{3}{2} = \dfrac{\text{rise}}{\text{run}}$, rise (go up) 3 units, run 2 units to the right.

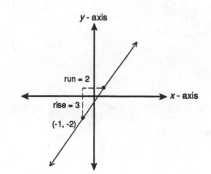

b) Start at $(0, 1)$.

$m = 2$	Given slope.
$= \dfrac{2}{1}$	Rewrite 2 as the fraction $\dfrac{2}{1}$.
$\dfrac{2}{1} = \dfrac{\text{rise}}{\text{run}}$	Rise (go up) 2 units, run 1 unit to the right.

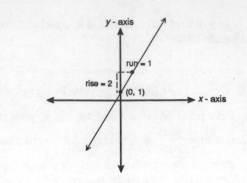

c) Start at (–1, 2).

$$m = -\frac{1}{3}$$

Given slope.

$$= \frac{-1}{3}$$

Rewrite the negative fraction with the negative in the numerator.

$$\frac{-1}{3} = \frac{\text{rise}}{\text{run}}$$

Fall (go down) 1 unit, run 3 units to the right.

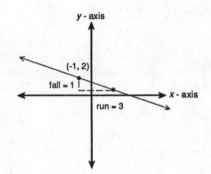

Note in c) that $-\frac{1}{3} = \frac{-1}{3} = \frac{1}{-3}$ so you can rise 1 unit, run to the *left* 3 units, and draw the line!

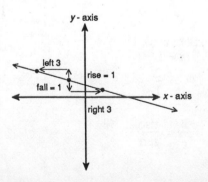

6.4 FINDING THE EQUATION OF A LINE

**Equations
of lines**

In this section we will find equations of lines, given various pieces of information. The table below will help you decide when to use each form of a linear equation. You *must* memorize these forms!

Given This Data	Use This Form	Name of the Form
Slope m and y-intercept b	$y = mx + b$	Slope–intercept
Point (x_1, y_1) and slope m	$y - y_1 = m(x - x_1)$	Point–slope
Two points (x_1, y_1) and (x_2, y_2)	First find $m = \dfrac{y_2 - y_1}{x_2 - x_1}$ then use: $y - y_1 = m(x - x_1)$	Slope of a line Point–slope
Horizontal line through (x_1, y_1)	$y = y_1$	
Vertical line through (x_1, y_1)	$x = x_1$	

Example 11 Write an equation of the line using the given information.

a) $m = 2$, *y-intercept* $= 1$

b) $m = \dfrac{3}{2}$, containing the point $(-1, -2)$

c) containing the points $(-1, 2)$ and $(2, 1)$

d) a horizontal line passing through $(3, 4)$

e) a vertical line passing through $(3, 4)$

Solution 11

a) $m = 2$, $b = 1$
$$y = mx + b$$
$$y = 2x + 1$$

Given slope and *y-intercept*.
Slope–intercept form.
Substitute $m = 2$ and $b = 1$ into the slope–intercept form of a line.

b) $m = \dfrac{3}{2}$, $(-1, -2)$

$$y - y_1 = m(x - x_1)$$

$$y - (-2) = \frac{3}{2}(x - (-1))$$

$$y + 2 = \frac{3}{2}(x + 1)$$

Given slope and a point.
Point–slope form.

Substitute $m = \dfrac{3}{2}$, $x_1 = -1$, $y_1 = -2$

Equation of the line.

c) (x_1, y_1) (x_2, y_2) **Given two points.**
   $(-1, 2)$ and $(2, 1)$

$$m = \frac{y_2 - y_1}{x_2 - x_1} = \frac{1 - 2}{2 - (-1)}$$ **First find the slope.**

$$m = -\frac{1}{3}$$

$$y - y_1 = m(x - x_1)$$ **Now use the point–slope form of a line.**

$$y - 2 = -\frac{1}{3}(x - (-1))$$

    Substitute $y_1 = 2$, $m = -\frac{1}{3}$, **and** $x_1 = -1$.

$$y - 2 = -\frac{1}{3}(x + 1)$$ **Equation of the line.**

If you had labeled your points (x_1, y_1) (x_2, y_2)

                            $(2, 1)$ $(-1, 2)$

your work would look like:

$$m = \frac{y_2 - y_1}{x_2 - x_1} = \frac{2 - 1}{(-1) - 2}$$ **First find the slope.**

$$m = \frac{1}{-3} = -\frac{1}{3}$$

$$y - y_1 = m(x - x_1)$$ **Now use the point–slope form of a line.**

$$y - 1 = -\frac{1}{3}(x - 2)$$

    Substitute $y_1 = 1$, $m = -\frac{1}{3}$, **and**

    $x_1 = 2$.

$$y - 1 = -\frac{1}{3}(x - 2)$$ **Equation of the line.**

Both of these answers are correct. In the next example, we will show that $y - 2 = -\frac{1}{3}(x + 1)$ and $y - 1 = -\frac{1}{3}(x - 2)$ are equivalent equations. Thus, you may label the points either way and get the correct answer.

d) Horizontal line through $(3, 4)$
    (x_1, y_1)
    $y = 4$ **Equation of line.**

e) Vertical line through $(3, 4)$
    $x = 3$ **Equation of line.**

Forms of linear equations

All the answers given in Example 12 *are* linear equations in two variables. You may need to write your answers in slope–intercept or standard form. *After* you have found the equation, use the Addition and Multiplication Properties of Equality to rewrite the equation in the desired form.

Forms of Linear Equations

$Ax + By = C$ Standard form
$y = mx + b$ Slope–intercept form

Example 12   Rewrite each equation in the required form.

a) $y = 2x + 1$ in standard form

b) $y + 2 = \dfrac{3}{2}(x + 1)$ in slope–intercept form

c) $y - 2 = -\dfrac{1}{3}(x + 1)$ in standard form

d) $y - 1 = -\dfrac{1}{3}(x - 2)$ in standard form

Solution 12

a) $y = 2x + 1$

$$\dfrac{-2x \qquad -2x}{-2x + y = 1}$$

or

$2x - y = -1$

We need $Ax + By = C$.
Get x and y on one side.

Multiply both sides by -1.

b) $y + 2 = \dfrac{3}{2}(x + 1)$

$y + 2 = \dfrac{3}{2}x + \dfrac{3}{2}$

$$\dfrac{-2 \qquad\qquad -2}{y = \dfrac{3}{2}x - \dfrac{1}{2}}$$

We need $y = mx + b$.

Distribute $\dfrac{3}{2}$.

Subtract 2 from both sides.

$y = mx + b$ form.

c) $y - 2 = -\dfrac{1}{3}(x + 1)$

$3(y - 2) = 3[-\dfrac{1}{3}(x + 1)]$

$3y - 6 = -1(x + 1)$
$3y - 6 = -x - 1$

$$\dfrac{+x + 6 = +x + 6}{x + 3y = 5}$$

We need $Ax + By = C$.

Multiply by the LCD, 3, to clear fractions.
Multiply by 3.

Distribute.
Get x and y on one side.
$Ax + By = C$ form.

d) $y - 1 = -\dfrac{1}{3}(x - 2)$

$3(y - 1) = 3[-\dfrac{1}{3}(x - 2)]$ We need $Ax + By = C$.

Multiply by the LCD, 3, to clear
fractions.

$3y - 3 = -1(x - 2)$ Multiply by 3.

$3y - 3 = -1x + 2$ Distribute the -1.
$\underline{+x + 3 = +x + 3}$ Add x and 3 to both sides.

$x + 3y = 5$

Compare this answer to the answer for c). Note that when the two equations

$y - 2 = -\dfrac{1}{3}(x + 1)$ and $y - 1 = -\dfrac{1}{3}(x - 2)$ are put in standard form, they are the same

equation.

Using slope–intercept to graph linear equations

We can now use the slope–intercept form of a line to graph lines since this form gives us a point $(0, b)$ and the slope m. Remember to solve for y first, if necessary.

Example 13   Graph each equation using the slope and *y-intercept*.
a) $-3x + y = 2$
b) $2x - 5y = 20$

Solution 13

a) $-3x + y = 2$
$\underline{+3x \quad +3x}$ Get y alone.
$y = 3x + 2$ Slope–intercept form: $y = mx + b$.

So $m = 3 = \dfrac{3}{1}$ and $b = 2$.

Start at $(0, 2)$.

$m = \dfrac{3}{1} = \dfrac{\text{rise}}{\text{run}}$.

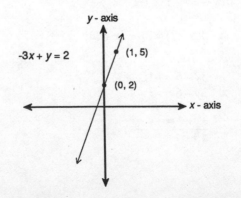

b) $2x - 5y = 20$

$$\underline{-2x \qquad\quad -2x}$$

$$-5y = -2x + 20$$

Add $-2x$ to both sides.

$$-\frac{1}{5}(-5y) = -\frac{1}{5}(-2x + 20)$$

Multiply both sides by $-\frac{1}{5}$.

$$y = \frac{2}{5}x - 4$$

Distribute $-\frac{1}{5}$.

Slope–intercept form: $y = mx + b$.

So $m = \frac{2}{5}$ and $b = -4$

Start at $(0, -4)$.

$$m = \frac{2}{5} = \frac{\text{rise}}{\text{run}}.$$

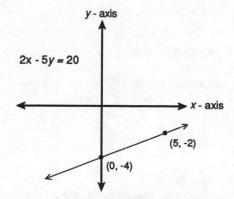

We can also use slope to determine whether lines are horizontal or vertical. If a line contains the point (x_1, y_1) and has $m = 0$, it must be a horizontal line with the equation $y = y_1$. If a line contains the point (x_1, y_1) and has undefined slope, it must be a vertical line with the equation $x = x_1$.

Example 14 Find the equation of a line with the given characteristics.

a) Contains the point $(-2, 5)$ and $m = 0$.
b) Contains the point $(-4, -1)$ and has undefined slope.

Solution 14

a) Since $m = 0$, this must be a horizontal line with equation $y = 5$.
b) Since the slope is undefined, this must be a vertical line with equation $x = -4$.

Parallel and perpendicular lines

Our last use of slope in this section involves parallel and perpendicular lines.

Parallel lines have equal slopes.
Perpendicular lines have slopes that are negative reciprocals of each other
(a and $-\dfrac{1}{a}$, for $a \neq 0$).

Example 15   Determine whether each pair of lines is parallel, perpendicular, or neither.

a) $y = 2x - 4$
   $-4x + 2y = 12$
b) $x - 2y = 10$
   $y = -2x + 3$
c) $y = 3x + 1$
   $3x + y = -4$

Solution 15   First find the slopes by writing each equation in $y = mx + b$ form.

a) Equation 1: $y = 2x - 4$ Already in $y = mx + b$ form.
                                                    $m = 2$.

   Equation 2: $-4x + 2y = 12$ Get y alone on one side.
                 $\underline{+4x \qquad\quad +4x}$ Add $4x$ to both sides.
                 $2y = 4x + 12$

   $\dfrac{1}{2}(2y) = \dfrac{1}{2}(4x + 12)$ Multiply both sides by $\dfrac{1}{2}$.

   $y = 2x + 6$ $m = 2$.

The lines have equal slopes of 2, so the lines are parallel.

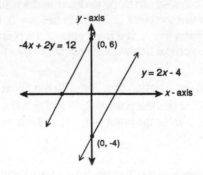

b) Equation 1:
   $x - 2y = 10$ Get y alone on one side.
   $\underline{-x \qquad\quad -x}$ Subtract x from both sides.
   $-2y = -x + 10$

   $-\dfrac{1}{2}(-2y) = -\dfrac{1}{2}(-x + 10)$ Multiply both sides by $-\dfrac{1}{2}$.

$$y = \frac{1}{2}x - 5$$

$$m = \frac{1}{2}.$$

Equation 2: $y = -2x + 3$

Already in $y = mx + b$ form.
$m = -2.$

The slopes of the lines are negative reciprocals and so the lines are perpendicular.

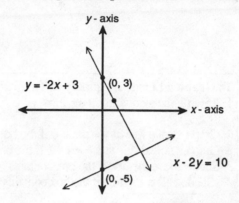

c) Equation 1: $y = 3x + 1$

Already in $y = mx + b$ form.
$m = 3.$

Equation 2: $3x + y = -4$
$\quad\quad\quad -3x \quad\quad -3x$
$\quad\quad\quad \overline{y = -3x - 4}$

Get y alone on one side.
Subtract $3x$ from both sides.
$m = -3.$

The slopes are *not* equal, so the lines are *not* parallel.
The slopes are *not* negative reciprocals, so the lines are *not* perpendicular.

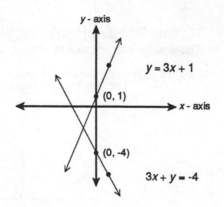

6.5 GRAPHING LINEAR INEQUALITIES

Recall that we graphed linear inequalities in one variable in Chapter 2, and that these graphs involved shading a part of the number line. In this section, we will graph linear inequalities in two variables, and these graphs will involve shading a part of the rectangular coordinate system.

Graphing linear inequalities in two variables

> **To Graph a Linear Inequality in Two Variables:**
> 1. Rewrite the inequality in the form $yx \;\square\; mx + b$, where the box contains $<, >, \leq,$ or $\geq$.
> 2. Graph a solid line at $y = mx + b$ if the box contains $\leq$ or $\geq$.
>   Graph a dotted line at $y = mx + b$ if the box contains $<$ or $>$.
> 3. Shade above the line if the box contains $>$ or $\geq$.
>   sShade below the line if the box contains $<$ or $\leq$.

Example 16 Graph each inequality.

a) $y < \dfrac{1}{2}x - 3$

b) $y \geq -2x + 1$

c) $2x - y < 4$

d) $y \leq 3x$

Solution 16

a) $y < \dfrac{1}{2}x - 3$ 　　　　　　　　　　　　Already in $yx \;\square\; mx + b$ form.

The line will be dotted because the inequality symbol is $<$.
The shading will be below the line because the inequality symbol is $<$.

Graph a dotted line with $m = \dfrac{1}{2}$ and $b = -3$.

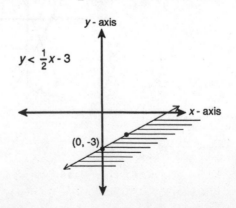

b) $y \geq -2x + 1$ Already in $yx \;\square\; mx + b$ form.
The line will be solid because the inequality symbol is $\geq$.
The shading will be above the line because the inequality symbol is $\geq$.

Graph a solid line with $m = -\dfrac{2}{1}$ and $b = 1$.

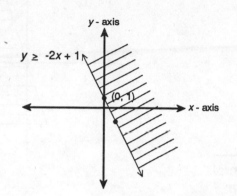

c) $2x - y < 4$ Rewrite in $yx \;\square\; mx + b$ form.
   $\underline{-2x \qquad -2x}$

   $-y < -2x + 4$
   $-1(-y) > -1(-2x + 4)$ Reverse the inequality symbol
                              when multiplying by a negative!
   $y > 2x - 4$

The line will be dotted because the inequality symbol is $>$.
The shading will be above the line because the inequality symbol is $>$.

Graph a dotted line with $m = \dfrac{2}{1}$ and $b = -4$.

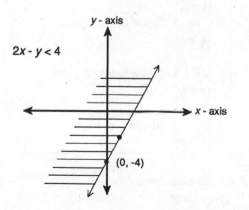

d) $y \leq 3x$
   $y \leq 3x + 0$ Write in $yx \;\square\; mx + b$ form.
The line will be solid because the inequality symbol is $\leq$.
The shading will be below the line because the inequality symbol is $\leq$.

Graph a solid line with $m = \dfrac{3}{1}$ and $b = 0$.

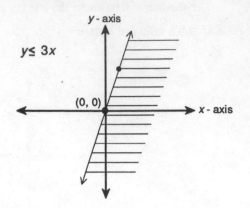

$y \leq 3x$

Graphing horizontal and vertical linear inequalities

To Graph Horizontal and Vertical Linear Inequalities:

1. Rewrite the inequality in the form $x \; \Box \; a$ or $y \; \Box \; b$ where $\Box$ contains $<, >, \leq$ or $\geq$.
2. Graph a solid line at $x = a$ or $y = b$ if the box contains $\leq$ or $\geq$.
   Graph a dotted line at $x = a$ or $y = b$ if the box contains $<$ or $>$.
3. Shade as follows:

$\left.\begin{array}{l} x < a \\ \text{or} \\ x \leq a \end{array}\right\}$ Shade to the left of the line.

$\left.\begin{array}{l} x > a \\ \text{or} \\ x \geq a \end{array}\right\}$ Shade to the right of the line.

$\left.\begin{array}{l} y < b \\ \text{or} \\ y \leq b \end{array}\right\}$ Shade below the line.

$\left.\begin{array}{l} y > b \\ \text{or} \\ y \geq b \end{array}\right\}$ Shade above the line.

Example 17 Graph each inequality.

    a) $x < -2$
    b) $x - 3 \geq 1$
    c) $y < 1$
    d) $y \geq -3$

Solution 17

a) $x < -2$

Dotted line at $x = -2$.
Shade to the left of the line.

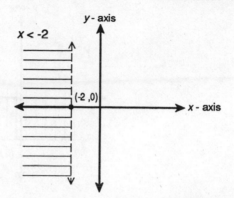

b) $x - 3 \geq 1$
$$\frac{+3 + \ 3}{x \geq 4}$$

Solid line at $x = 4$.

Shade to the right of the line.

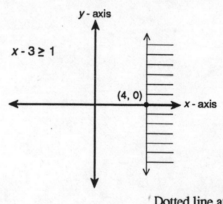

c) $y < 1$

Dotted line at $y = 1$.
Shade below the line.

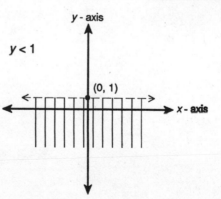

d) $y \geq -3$ Solid line at $y = -3$.
                                                   Shade above the line.

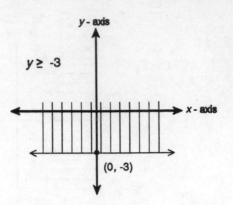

Practice Exercises

1. Determine whether the given ordered pair is a solution of the given equation.
   (a) $4x - 3y = 10$; $(1, -2)$
   (b) $3a - 2b = 17$; $(3, 4)$
   (c) $4x - 10y = -4$; $(\frac{1}{2}, \frac{1}{5})$
   (d) $2x + 3y = -4$; $(-5, 2)$

2. Complete the given ordered pairs for the equations.
   (a) $3x - 5y = -25$; $(x, 2)$
   (b) $6x + 4y = -2$; $(-\frac{5}{3}, y)$
   (c) $12p - 3q = -4$; $(p, 4)$
   (d) $2x - y = 9$; $(3, y)$

3. Graph.
   (a) $2x + y = 4$
   (b) $x = 8$
   (c) $3x - y = -3$
   (d) $y = 4x$

4. Graph.
   (a) $4x - 2y = 6$
   (b) $x - y = -6$
   (c) $3x - y = 2$
   (d) $2x = y$

5. Find the slope of each of the following lines.
   (a) the line through $(5, 1)$ and $(2, -1)$
   (b) the line through $(2, -3)$ and $(3, 12)$
   (c) the line through $(-1, 4)$ and $(0, 4)$
   (d) the line through $(2, 6)$ and $(2, -3)$

6. Graph the line with the given slopes and containing the given points.
   (a) $m = \frac{1}{2}$; $(2, 4)$
   (b) $m = 3$; $(0, 1)$

   (c) $m = -\frac{2}{5}$; $(2, -3)$
   (d) $m = 0$; $(-1, -7)$

7. Write an equation of the line using the given information.
   (a) $Q(-2, 6)$; $m = -\frac{2}{5}$
   (b) $P(0, 0)$; $m = \frac{2}{3}$
   (c) through the points $A(1, 3)$ and $B(5, -3)$
   (d) through $A(-4, -1)$ and parallel to the graph of $3x + 4y = 12$
   (e) a horizontal line through $(4, -2)$

8. Determine if the pair of lines is parallel, perpendicular, or neither.
   (a) $2x - 4y = 6$
       $2x + y = 8$
   (b) $y = -\frac{2}{5}$
       $5x + 2y = 1$

9. Graph each inequality.
   (a) $2x - y \le 4$
   (b) $3x + 4y < 8$
   (c) $x + 3y \le 6$
   (d) $2x - y < 4$

10. Graph each inequality.
    (a) $x > 2$
    (b) $y \le 3$
    (c) $x > -4$
    (d) $y < 0$

Answers

1. (a) yes
    (b) no
    (c) no
    (d) yes

2. (a) $x = -5$
    (b) $y = 2$
    (c) $p = \dfrac{2}{3}$
    (d) $y = -3$

3. (a)

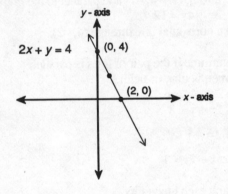

(b)

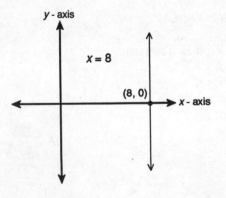

(c)

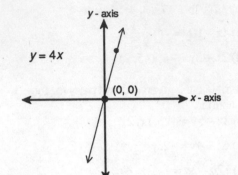

(d)

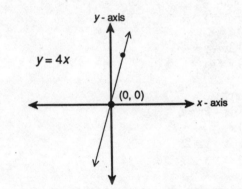

4. (a)

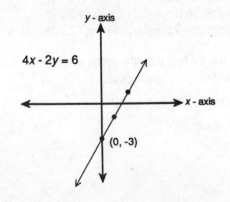

(b)

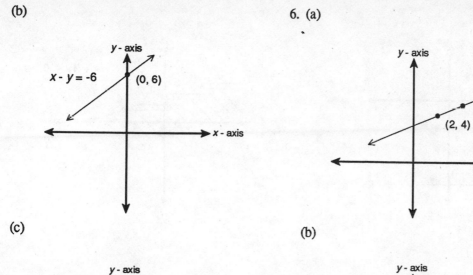

x - y = -6   (0, 6)

6. (a)

(c)

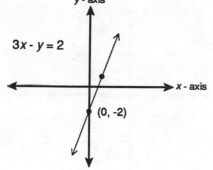

3x - y = 2

(0, -2)

(b)

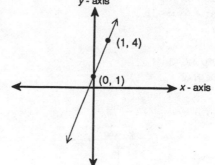

(1, 4)

(0, 1)

(d)

2x = y

(0, 0)

(c)

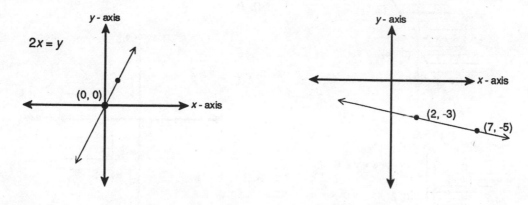

(2, -3)

(7, -5)

5. (a) $\frac{2}{3}$
   (b) 15
   (c) 0
   (d) undefined

(d)

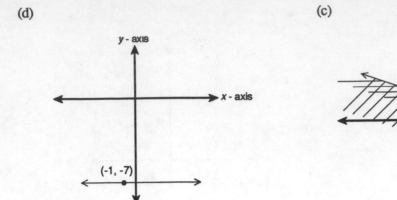

(c)

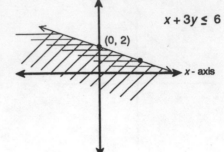

$x + 3y \leq 6$

7. (a) $2x + 5y = 26$
   (b) $2x - 3y = 0$
   (c) $3x + 2y = 9$
   (d) $3x + 4y = -16$
   (e) $y = -2$

8. (a) perpendicular
   (b) neither

9. (a)

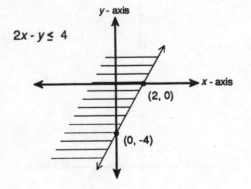

$2x - y \leq 4$

(d)

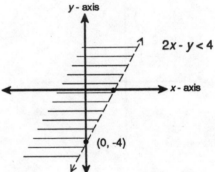

$2x - y < 4$

(b)

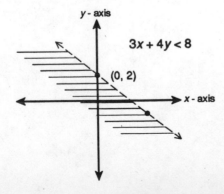

10. (a)

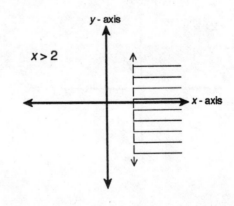

$x > 2$

(b)

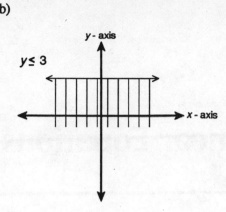

$y \leq 3$

(d)

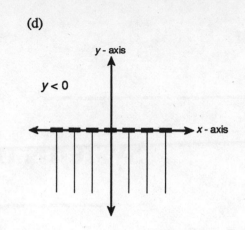

$y < 0$

(c)

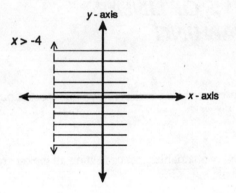

$x > -4$

7

Systems of Linear Equations

7.1 SOLVING SYSTEMS OF LINEAR EQUATIONS BY GRAPHING

Determining whether an ordered pair is a solution to a system of linear equations

A system of linear equations in two variables consists of two linear equations in two unknowns, such as

$$3x + 2y = 7$$
$$x - 2y = -11.$$

Solving a system of linear equations in two variables means finding all the ordered pairs that are solutions to *both* equations.

Example 1

a) Is (–1, 5) a solution to the following system?
   $$3x + 2y = 7$$
   $$x - 2y = -11$$
b) Is (2, 3) a solution to the following system?
   $$4x - 2y = 2$$
   $$2x + y = 5$$
c) Is (0, 6) a solution to the following system?
   $$5x + 2y = 12$$
   $$2x - 3y = 18$$

Solution 1

a) $3x + 2y = 7$
   $3(-1) + 2(5) = 7$ Substitute $x = -1, y = 5$.
   $-3 + 10 = 7$ True.
   $x - 2y = -11$
   $(-1) - 2(5) = -11$ Substitute $x = -1, y = 5$.
   $-1 - 10 = -11$ True.

Since $(-1, 5)$ is a solution to **both** equations, $(-1, 5)$ is a solution to the system.

b) $4x - 2y = 2$

$\quad 4(2) - 2(3) = 2$ — Substitute $x = 2, y = 3$.

$\quad 8 - 6 = 2$ — True.

$\quad 2x + y = 5$

$\quad 2(2) + 3 = 5$ — Substitute $x = 2, y = 3$.

$\quad 4 + 3 = 5$ — False.

Since $(2, 3)$ is not a solution to both equations, $(2, 3)$ is not a solution to the system.

c) $5x + 2y = 12$

$\quad 5(0) + 2(6) = 12$ — Substitute $x = 0, y = 6$.

$\quad 0 + 12 = 12$ — True.

$\quad 2x - 3y = 18$

$\quad 2(0) - 3(6) = 18$ — Substitute $x = 0, y = 6$.

$\quad 0 - 18 = 18$

$\quad -18 = 18$ — False.

Since $(0, 6)$ is not a solution to both equations, $(0, 6)$ is not a solution to the system.

Graphing systems of l inear equations

When two lines are graphed on the same set of axes, there are three possible types of solutions. Consider the following graphs of two lines:

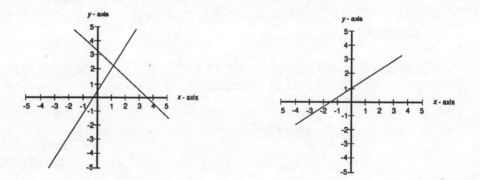

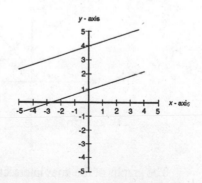

1 Solution	No Solutions	Infinite Number of Solutions
Consistent system	Inconsistent system	Consistent system
Independent equations	Independent equations	Dependent equations

> **To Find a Solution by Graphing:**
> 1. Write each equation in $y = mx + b$ form.
> 2. Graph both equations on the same set of x- and y-axes.
> 3. Look for the intersection point.
> 4. Check by substituting the ordered pair in each equation.

You must use a sharp pencil, graph paper, and a ruler to help you draw an accurate picture. Even with the best tools, your graph may be slightly off.

Example 2   Solve each system by graphing.

a) $x - y = -1$
   $x + y = 3$

b) $y = -\dfrac{3}{2}x$
   $x + 2y = 4$

c) $3x - y = 2$
   $3x - y = -1$

d) $x + 2y = 4$
   $2x + 4y = 8$

Solution 2

a)
$$
\begin{array}{ll}
x - y = -1 & x + y = 3 \\
\underline{-x \qquad -x} & \underline{-x \qquad -x} \\
-y = -x - 1 & y = -x + 3 \\
\\
y = x + 1 &
\end{array}
$$

Write equations in $y = mx + b$ form.

Graph each equation using the slope-intercept form.

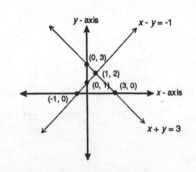

The graphs of the lines intersect at $(1, 2)$.

Check:

$$x - y = -1 \quad x + y = 3$$
$$1 - 2 = -1 \quad \text{True} \qquad 1 + 2 = 3 \quad \text{True}$$

Write the original equations.
Substitute $x = 1, y = 2$.

Since $(1, 2)$ is a solution to both equations, $(1, 2)$ is the solution to the system.

b) $y = -\dfrac{3}{2}x + 0 \; x + 2y = 4$

Write equations in $y = mx + b$ form.
Subtract x from both sides.

$$\underline{\quad -x \qquad -x \quad}$$
$$2y = -x + 4$$

$$\frac{1}{2}(2y) = \frac{1}{2}(-x + 4)$$

Multiply both sides by $\dfrac{1}{2}$.

$$y = -\frac{1}{2}x + 2$$

Graph each line using the slope-intercept form.

The graphs of the lines intersect at $(-2, 3)$.

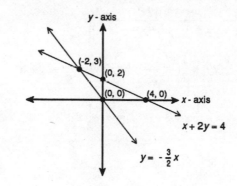

Check:

$$y = -\frac{3}{2}x \qquad\qquad x + 2y = 4$$

Write the original equations.

$$3 = -\frac{3}{2}(-2) \qquad (-2) + 2(3) = 4$$

Substitute $x = -2, y = 3$.

$$3 = 3 \quad \text{True} \qquad\qquad 4 = 4 \quad \text{True}$$

Since $(-2, 3)$ is a solution to both equations, $(-2, 3)$ is the solution to the system.

c) $3x - y = 2 \qquad 3x - y = -1$

Write equations in $y = mx + b$ form.

$$\underline{-3x \; -3x} \qquad \underline{-3x \qquad -3x}$$
$$-y = -3x + 2 \qquad -y = -3x - 1$$

$$-1(-y) = -1(-3x + 2) \quad -1(-y) = -1(-3x - 1)$$

Multiply by -1 to make the coefficient of y positive.

$$y = 3x - 2 \quad y = 3x + 1$$

Graph each line using the slope-intercept form.

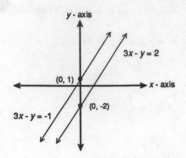

These are parallel lines. There are no solutions. This is called an inconsistent system.

d) $x + 2y = 4 \qquad 2x + 4y = 8$

$$\frac{-x \qquad\quad -x}{2y = -x + 4} \qquad \frac{-2x \qquad\quad -2x}{4y = -2x + 8}$$

Write equations in $y = mx + b$ form.

$$\frac{1}{2}(2y) = \frac{1}{2}(-x + 4) \qquad \frac{1}{4}(4y) = \frac{1}{4}(-2x + 8)$$

Multiply by the reciprocal of the coefficient of y.

$$y = -\frac{1}{2}x + 2 \qquad\qquad y = -\frac{1}{2}x + 2$$

Graph each line using the slope-intercept form.

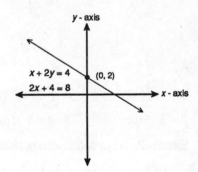

These are the same line. There are an infinite number of solutions. This is called a dependent system.

7.2 SOLVING SYSTEMS OF LINEAREQUATIONS BY ADDITION

The solutions we found by graphing in the previous section were integer solutions. It is more difficult to find a solution like $\left(\dfrac{1}{9}, \dfrac{2}{3}\right)$ by graphing! The next two sections present techniques for solving systems of linear equations without graphing.

Solving systems of linear equations by addition

To Solve a System by Addition:
1. Write both equations in the form $Ax + By = C$. Multiply by the LCD to eliminate any fractions.
2. If coefficients of either x or y are additive inverses (like 4 and –4), add the equations. If coefficients are not additive inverses, eliminate x's by multiplying each equation by the coefficient of x from the other equation. If the signs are the same, multiply one equation by –1.
3. Add the equations together.
4. Solve for y.
5. Substitute the value for y in either of the original equations to solve for x.
6. Check your answer.

Note: You may eliminate y's in the same manner, solve for x, substitute, and solve for y. Depending on the coefficients of x and y, it is sometimes easier to eliminate y. Study the examples below, keeping in mind that each could be solved by eliminating the other variable.

Example 3 Solve each system.

a) $x + y = -5$
   $2x - y = 2$

b) $2x + y = 13$
   $3x - 2y = 2$

c) $2x + 5y = 27$
   $4x - 3y = 15$

d) $\dfrac{1}{2}x - \dfrac{1}{3}y = \dfrac{8}{3}$

   $\dfrac{1}{4}x + \dfrac{2}{3}y = -\dfrac{17}{6}$

Solution 3

a) $x + y = -5$

   $2x - y = 2$

   Because the coefficients of y are additive inverses (1 and -1), add the equations.

   $x + y = -5$

   $\dfrac{2x - y = 2}{3x \quad\;\; = -3}$

   Solve for x.

   $x = -1$

   $x + y = -5$

   $(-1) + y = -5$

   $\dfrac{+1 \;+1}{y = -4}$

   Use either original equation.
   Substitute $x = -1$.

   $(-1, -4)$

   Proposed solution.

   Check: $x + y = -5$

   $(-1) + (-4) = -5$

   True.

   $2x - y = 2$

   $2(-1) - (-4) = 2$

   True.

b) $2x + y = 13$

   $3x - 2y = 2$

   Let's eliminate x.
   Multiply by coefficients of x.

   $3(2x + y = 13) \quad => 6x + 3y = 39$

   Since signs are the same, multiply one equation by -1.

   $2(3x - 2y = 2) \quad => 6x - 4y = 4$

   $-1(6x + 3y = 39) => -6x - 3y = -39$

   $6x - 4y = 4 \qquad => 6x - 4y = 4$

   $-6x - 3y = -39$

   $\dfrac{6x - 4y = 4}{-7y = -35}$

   Add the equations.

   Solve for y.

   $-\dfrac{1}{7}(-7y) = -\dfrac{1}{7}(-35)$

   $y = 5$

   $2x + y = 13$

   $2x + (5) = 13$

   $\dfrac{-5 \; -5}{2x = 8}$

   $x = 4$

   Use one of the original equations.
   Substitute $y = 5$.
   Solve for x.

   $(4, 5)$

   Proposed solution.

   Check: $2x + y = 13$

   $2(4) + 5 = 13$

   True.

$$3x - 2y = 2$$
$$3(4) - 2(5) = 2 \qquad\qquad \text{True.}$$

Note: We can combine two steps by multiplying by -3 and 2 or 3 and -2.
If you had decided to eliminate y, the work would look like:

$$2(2x + y = 13) \Rightarrow 4x + 2y = 26 \qquad \text{Multiply by the coefficients of } y.$$
$$1(3x - 2y = 2) \Rightarrow 3x - 2y = 2$$

$$4x + 2y = 26$$
$$\underline{3x - 2y = 2} \qquad\qquad \text{Add the equations.}$$
$$7x \quad\;\; = 28 \qquad\qquad \text{Solve for } x.$$

$$\frac{7x}{7} = \frac{28}{7} \qquad\qquad\qquad \text{Divide both sides by 7.}$$
$$x = 4$$
$$2x + y = 13 \qquad\qquad\quad \text{Use one of the original equations.}$$
$$\qquad\qquad\qquad\qquad\qquad\quad \text{Substitute } x = 4.$$

$$2(4) + y = 13$$
$$8 + y = 13 \qquad\qquad\quad \text{Solve for } y.$$
$$\underline{-8 - 8} \qquad\qquad\qquad\;\; \text{Subtract 8 from both sides.}$$
$$y = 5$$

(4, 5) is the same solution we obtained when we began by eliminating x. The check would be the same. Which way was easier?

c) $2x + 5y = 27$ Let's eliminate y.
     $4x - 3y = 15$
     $3(2x + 5y = 27) \Rightarrow 6x + 15y = 81$
     $5(4x - 3y = 15) \Rightarrow 20x - 15y = 75$

$$6x + 15y = 81$$
$$\underline{20x - 15y = 75} \qquad\quad \text{Add the equations.}$$
$$26x = 156 \qquad\qquad \text{Solve for } x.$$
$$x = 6$$

$$2x + 5y = 27 \qquad\qquad \text{Use one of the original equations.}$$

$$2(6) + 5y = 27 \qquad\qquad \text{Substitute } x = 6.$$
$$12 + 5y = 27 \qquad\qquad \text{Solve for } y.$$
$$\underline{12 - 12}$$
$$5y = 15$$
$$y = 3$$

(6, 3)   Proposed solution.

Check: $2x + 5y = 27$
$$2(6) + 5(3) = 27 \qquad\qquad \text{True.}$$

$$4x - 3y = 15$$
$$4(6) - 3(3) = 15 \qquad\qquad \text{True.}$$

d) $\frac{1}{2}x - \frac{1}{3}y = \frac{8}{3}$

$\frac{1}{4}x = \frac{2}{3}y = -\frac{17}{6}$

$6\left(\frac{1}{2}x + \frac{1}{3}y\right) = 6\left(\frac{8}{3}\right)$ Multiply by the LCD to eliminate fractions.

$12\left(\frac{1}{4}x + \frac{2}{3}y\right) = 12\left(-\frac{17}{6}\right) = 12(-\frac{17}{6})$

$3x - 2y = 16$
$3x + 8y = -34$
$-1(3x - 2y = 16) = -3x + 2y = -16$ Multiply by –1.
$3x + 8y = -34 = 3x + 8y = -34$

$-3x + 2y = -16$ Add the equations.
$\underline{3x + 8y = -34}$
$\quad\quad 10y = -50$ Solve for y.
$\quad\quad\quad y = -5$

Rather then substitute $y = -5$ into one of the original equations, it may be easier to eliminate y and solve for x!

$4(3x - 2y = 16)$ => $12x - 8y = 64$ Add the equations.
$3x + 8y = -34$ => $\underline{3x + 8y = -34}$
$\quad\quad\quad\quad\quad\quad\quad 15x \quad\quad = 30$ Solve for x by dividing both sides by 15.

$\quad\quad\quad\quad\quad\quad x = 2$

$(2, -5)$ Solution. It will check in both of the original equations.

Determining when a system is inconsistent or dependent

The graph of the solutions to the systems of parallel lines showed there were no solutions; similarly, the graph of a dependent system (coinciding lines) showed there were an infinite number of solutions. The following table will help you decide when a system is consistent and independent, inconsistent, or dependent when using the addition method.

Look For	Graph	Solution
Only one variable eliminated	Consistent and independent—two intersecting lines	One ordered-pair solution
Both variables eliminated and resulting statement is true	Dependent system—lines coincide	Infinite number of solutions
Both variables eliminated and resulting statement is false	Parallel lines	No solution

Example 4 Solve each system.

a) $2x - y = 6$
$4x - 2y = 12$

b) $2x - 3y = 12$
$2x - 3y = -3$

c) $x + 3y = 4$
$2x + 6y = 8$

d) $2x + 4y = 0$
$5x - 3y = 0$

Solution 4

a) $2x - y = 6$
$4x - 2y = 12$

$-2(2x - y = 6)$ $\Rightarrow$ $-4x + 2y = -12$
$4x - 2y = 12$ $\Rightarrow$ $4x - 2y = 12$ Eliminate y by multiplying the first equation by -2.

$\begin{array}{r} -4x + 2y = -12 \\ \underline{4x - 2y = 12} \\ 0 = 0 \end{array}$

Both variables eliminated. Resulting statement is true.
This is a dependent system. There are an infinite number of solutions.

b) $2x - 3y = 12$
$2x - 3y = -3$

Coefficients of y will be additive inverses if we multiply one equation by -1.

$-1(2x - 3y = 12)$ $\Rightarrow$ $-2x + 3y = -12$
$2x - 3y = -3$ $\Rightarrow$ $2x - 3y = -3$
$\begin{array}{r} -2x + 3y = -12 \\ \underline{2x - 3y = -3} \\ 0 = -15 \end{array}$

Both variables eliminated.
Resulting statement is false.

These are parallel lines. There are no solutions.

c) $x + 3y = 4$
$2x + 6y = 8$
$-2(x + 3y = 4)$ $\Rightarrow$ $-2x - 6y = -8$
$1(2x + 6y = 8)$ $\Rightarrow$ $2x + 6y = 8$ Eliminate x by multiplying the first equation by -2.

$\begin{array}{r} -2x - 6y = -8 \\ \underline{2x - 6y = 8} \\ 0 = 0 \end{array}$

Add the equations.
Both variables are eliminated, and the resulting statement is true.

This is a dependent system. There are an infinite number of solutions.

d) $2x + 4y = 0$
$5x - 3y = 0$
$3(2x + 4y = 0) => 6x + 12y = 0$
$4(5x - 3y = 0) => 20x - 12y = 0$ Eliminate y by multiplying the first equation by 3 and the second equation by 4.

$6x + 12y = 0$
$\underline{20x - 12y = 0}$ Add the equations.

$26x \qquad = 0$ Only one variable was eliminated.

$\dfrac{26x}{26} = \dfrac{0}{26}$ Solve for x by dividing both sides by 26.

$x = 0$
$2x + 4y = 0$ Use one of the original equations.
$2(0) + 4y = 0$ Substitute $x = 0$.
$0 + 4y = 0$ Solve for y.
$\dfrac{4y}{4} = \dfrac{0}{4}$ Divide both sides *by* 4.
$y = 0$

This is a consistent, independent system with one solution: $(0, 0)$.

7.3 SOLVING SYSTEMS OF LINEAR EQUATIONS BY SUBSTITUTION

Solving Systems by Substitution: If one of the equations is not in $Ax + By = C$ form, it is often more convenient to use the substitution method to solve a system.

> **To Solve a System by Substitution:**
> 1. Solve one equation for x or y, if necessary.
> 2. Substitute the expression from Step 1 into the other equation.
> 3. Solve the resulting equation.
> 4. Substitute the value from Step 3 into one of the original equations to find the other value.
> 5. Check, as necessary.

Example 5   Solve each system by substitution.
a) $2x + 3y = -12$
$y = 2x - 20$

b) $x + 3y = -14$
$\quad -4x + 5y = -12$

c) $2x + 3y = 1$
$\quad 4x + 5y = -1$

d) $x = \dfrac{1}{3}y + 1$
$\quad 3x - y = -5$

e) $4x - y = 0$
$\quad 8x - 2y = 0$

Solution 5

a) $2x + 3y = -12$
$\quad \mathbf{y = 2x - 20}$ .... This equation is solved for y.

$2x + 3(\mathbf{2x - 20}) = -12$ .... Substitute $(2x - 20)$ for y.

$2x + 6x - 60 = -12$ .... Solve for x.

$8x - 60 = -12$
$\underline{ +60 +60}$ .... Add 60 to both sides.
$ 8x = 48$ .... Divide both sides by 8.

$ x = 6$

Now solve for y:

$y = 2x - 20$
$y = 2(6) - 20$ .... It's easier to substitute into this equation since it is already solved for y.

$y = 12 - 20 = -8$

$(6, -8)$ .... Solution.

Check:

$2x + 3y = -12$	$y = 2x - 20$	Original equations.
$2(6) + 3(-8) = -12$	$-8 = 2(6) - 20$	Substitute $x = 6$, $y = -8$.
$12 - 24 = -12$	$-8 = 12 - 20$	Simplify each side.
$-12 = -12$	$-8 = -8$	Both statements are true, so $(6, -8)$ is the solution.

b) $x + 3y = -14$
$\quad -4x + 5y = -12$ .... This equation can easily be solved for x because it has a coefficient of 1.

$x + 3y = -14$ .... Solve for x.
$\underline{-3y -3y}$ .... Subtract $3y$ from both sides.
$ x = -3y - 14$

$$x = -3y - 14$$

Now use substitution into the other equation.

$$-4x + 5y = -12$$
$$-4(-3y - 14) + 5y = -12$$

Substitute $(-3y - 14)$ for x.

$$12y + 56 + 5y = -12$$

Solve for y.

$$17y + 56 = -12$$
$$\underline{-56 \quad -56}$$
$$17y = -68$$
$$y = -4$$

$$x + 3y = -14$$
$$x + 3(-4) = -14$$

Solve for x in the original equation.
Substitute $y = -4$.

$$x - 12 = -14$$
$$\underline{+12 +12}$$
$$x = -2$$

$$(-2, -4)$$

Solution.

Check: Try the check on your own. Remember to check in *both* of the original equations.

c) $2x + 3y = 1$
    $4x + 5y = -1$

To use substitution, one equation must be solved for x or y. Let's solve the first equation for x.

$$2x + 3y = 1$$
$$\underline{-3y -3y}$$
$$2x = -3y + 1$$

$$\frac{2x}{2} = \frac{-3y + 1}{2}$$

$$x = \frac{-3y + 1}{2}$$

Now substitute into the second equation.

$$4x + 5y = -1$$

$$4(\frac{-3y + 1}{2}) + 5y = -1$$

Substitute $x = \dfrac{-3y + 1}{2}$

$$2(-3y + 1) + 5y = -1$$

Solve for y.

$$-6y + 2 + 5y = -1$$

Combine similar terms.

$$-y + 2 = -1$$
$$\underline{-2 \quad -2}$$
$$y = -3$$

Subtract 2 from both sides.

$$-1(-y) = -1(-3)$$
$$y = 3$$

Multiply both sides by -1.

Since $x = \dfrac{-3y + 1}{2}$　　　　　　　　　　Now solve for x.

$x = \dfrac{-3(3) + 1}{2}$　　　　　　　　　　Substitute $y = 3$.

$x = \dfrac{-9 + 1}{2}$

$x = -4$

$(-4, 3)$　　　　　　　　　　Solution.

Check: Try the check on your own.

d) $x = \dfrac{1}{3}y + 1$

$3x - y = -5$　　　　　　　　　　This equation is already solved for x.

$3\left(\dfrac{1}{3} + 1\right) - y = -5$

　　　　　　　　　　Substitute $\dfrac{1}{3}y + 1$ for x.

$y + 3 - y = -5$　　　　　　　　　　Solve for y.

$3 = -5$　　　　　　　　　　False statement!

When both variables are eliminated and the resulting statement is false, there is *no solution* to the system.

e) $4x - y = 0$

　$8x - 2y = 0$

　$4x - y\ \ = 0$

　$\underline{-4x\ \ \ \ -4x}$

　　$-y\ \ = -4x$

　　　$y\ \ = 4x$　　　　　　　　　　This equation can easily be solved for y.

$8x - 2y = 0$　　　　　　　　　　Now use substitution.

$8x - 2(\mathbf{4x}) = 0$　　　　　　　　　　Substitute $4x$ for y.

$8x - 8x = 0$

$0 = 0$　　　　　　　　　　True statement!

When both variables are eliminated and the resulting statement is true, there are an *infinite number* of solutions.

Although these systems can be solved with either the addition method or the substitution method, there are some guidelines to help you decide which method to use. If one equation is already solved for one variable, or if one equation has a coefficient of 1, substitution works well. Otherwise, elimination is probably the better choice.

7.4 APPLICATIONS

The following steps will help you solve the problems in this section.

---

1. State what each variable you are using represents.
2. Translate the problem into a system of two equations.
3. Solve the system using addition or substitution.
4. Provide answers for the variable or variables as required.
5. Check your answer(s) in the original word problem.

Number applications

Some problems you have solved in the past using one variable can also be solved with two variables.

Example 6   One number is three times as large as a second number. The sum of the numbers is 28. Find the numbers.

Solution 6

Let x = one number	State what each variable represents.
y = other number	
$x = 3y$	Write a system of equations.
$x + y = 28$	This system can be solved easily using substitution.
$(3y) + y = 28$	Substitute $x = 3y$ into the second equation.
$4y = 28$	Solve for y.
$\dfrac{4y}{4} = \dfrac{28}{4}$	Divide both sides by 4.
$y = 7$	Then solve $x = 3y$:
$x = 3(7)$	Substitute $y = 7$.
$x = 21$	

The two numbers are 7 and 21.

Check: 21 is three times 7

    21 + 7 is 28

Money applications

An important concept used in both money and mixture applications involves finding the total value (in the money applications) and the total amount (in the mixture applications). If you purchase 10 stamps for 29¢ each, the total value of the stamps is found by multiplying the cost per stamp times the number of stamps:

$$\$0.29\,(10) = \$2.90.$$

Keep this idea in mind as the total value is found in the following examples.

Example 7

525 tickets to the outdoor concert were sold. Reserved seats sold for $10.00 and general admission tickets sold for $7.50. The total receipts were $4250.00. How many of each type of ticket were sold?

Solution 7

Let x = the number of $10.00 tickets sold
y = the number of $7.50 tickets sold

State what each variable represents.

$x + y = 525$
$10.00x + 7.50y = 4250.00$

Total number of tickets sold.
Total value.

$x = \mathbf{525 - y}$
$10.00(\mathbf{525 - y}) + 7.50y = 4250.00$

Solve first equation for x.
Substitute into second equation.

$5250.00 - 10.00y + 7.50y = 4250.00$
$\qquad\qquad\qquad -2.50y = -1000.00$
$\qquad\qquad\qquad\qquad\quad y = 400$

Solve for y.

$x + y = 525$
$x + 400 = 525$
$x = 125$

Solve for x.

125 tickets sold for $10.00 each
400 tickets sold for $7.50 each

Check: $x + y = 525$

Original equation.

$(125) + (400) = 525$
$525 = 525$
$10.00x + 7.50y = 4250.00$
$10.00(125) + 7.50(400) = 4250.00$
$1250.00 + 3000.00 = 4250.00$
$4250.00 = 4250.00$

Substitute $x = 125$, $y = 400$.
A true statement.
Original equation.
Substitute $x = 125$, $y = 400$.
Multiply before adding.
A true statement.

Mixture applications

Mixture applications will often contain percentages that need to be changed to decimals. Also, note that an 80% alcohol solution, for example, contains 80% alcohol and 20% water. If there are 40 liters of this 80% alcohol solution, this means there are:

$$40 \times 0.80 \text{ liters of alcohol} = 32 \text{ liters of alcohol}$$
$$\text{and}$$
$$40 \times 0.20 \text{ liters of water} = 8 \text{ liters of water.}$$

There could be many other solutions, such as antifreeze, potassium iodide, disinfectant, etc.

Example 8   A chemist needs 120 liters of 50% alcohol solution. The current stock contains two solutions: one is 80% alcohol, and the other is 30% alcohol. How many liters of each will be required to make the 120 liters of 50% alcohol solution?

Solution 8

Let x = the number of liters of 80% alcohol   State what each variable represents.
y = the number of liters of 30% alcohol

$x + y = 120$ Total number of liters.
$0.80x + 0.30y = 0.50(120)$ Total amount of alcohol.
$x = \mathbf{120 - y}$ Solve the first equation for x.
$0.80(\mathbf{120 - y}) + 0.30y = 0.50(120)$ Substitute $120 - y$ for x.
$96 - 0.80y + 0.30y = 60$ Solve for y.

$96 - 0.50y = 60$ Get y alone on one side.
$\underline{-96 \qquad\quad -96}$
$-0 \quad .50y = -36$ Divide both sides by -0.50.
$\qquad\quad y = 72$

$x + y = 120$ Solve for x.
$x + 72 = 120$ Substitute $y = 72$.
$x = 48$

48 liters of 80% alcohol must be mixed with 72 liters of 30% alcohol.

Check: $48 + 72 = 120$
$0.80(48) + 0.30(72) = 60$ Substitute $x = 48$ and $y = 72$ into the original equations.

Distance = rate × time applications

You may want to review the $D = R \cdot T$ examples in Chapter 5.

Example 9   A plane can travel 2660 miles into the wind in 7 hours and 2600 miles with the wind in 5 hours. Find the speed of the wind and the speed of the plane in still air.

Solution 9

Let x = speed of the plane in still air   State what each variable represents.
y = speed of the wind

Then $x + y$ = speed of the plane *with* the wind
$x - y$ = speed of the plane *into* the wind

	R	T	D
with the wind	$x + y$	5	2600
against the wind	$x - y$	7	2660

Since $R \cdot T = D$,
$$(x + y)5 = 2600$$
$$(x - y)7 = 2660$$

$$5x + 5y = 2600$$ Simplify the equations.
$$7x - 7y = 2660$$

Let's solve by addition.

$7(5x + 5y = 2600)$ => $35x + 35y = 18200$
$5(7x - 7y = 2660)$ => $35x - 35y = 13300$

$35x + 35y = 18200$ Add the equations.
$\underline{35x - 35y = 13300}$
$\ 70x = 31500$ Divide both sides by 70.
$x = 450$

$(x + y)5 = 2600$ Solve for y.
$(450 + y)5 = 2600$ Substitute $x = 450$.
$2250 + 5y = 2600$ Distribute.
$5y = 350$ Divide both sides by 5.
$y = 70$

The speed of the plane in still air is 450 mph.
The speed of the wind is 70 mph.

Check: $(x + y)5 = 2600$ Original equation.
$((450) + (70))5 = 2600$ Substitute $x = 450, y = 70$.
$(520)5 = 2600$ Work inside parentheses first.
$2600 = 2600$ True statement.
$(x - y)7 = 2660$ Original equation.
$((450) - (70))7 = 2660$ Substitute $x = 450, y = 70$.
$(380)7 = 2660$ Work inside parentheses first.
$2660 = 2660$ True statement.

7.5 SOLVING SYSTEMS OF LINEAR INEQUALITIES

Solving Systems of Linear Inequalities

You may want to review "Graphing Linear Inequalities" in Chapter 6.

To Solve a System of Linear Inequalities by Graphing:
1. Graph and shade each inequality on one set of axes. (Use a different type of shading or a different color for each inequality).
2. The solution to the system is where the shadings overlap.

Example 10   Graph the solution of each system.

a) $y \leq 2x + 1$
   $y \geq -2x + 5$

b) $x + 2y < -4$
   $y - 1 < x$

c) $x \geq 2$
   $y < -3$

Solution 10

a) $y \leq 2x + 1$ Both inequalities are in the form
   $y \geq -2x + 5$ $y \, \square \, mx + b$.
   $y \leq 2x + 1$ The line will be solid because the
                           inequality symbol is $\leq$. The
                           shading will be below the line.
                           Graph a solid line with slope $= 2 =$
                           $\dfrac{2}{1}$ and y–intercept $+1$.

   $y \geq -2x + 5$ The line will be solid because the
                           inequality symbol is $\geq$. The
                           shading will be above the line.
                           Graph a solid line with slope $= -2$
                           $= \dfrac{-2}{1}$ and y–intercept $+5$.

The solution to the system is where the shadings overlap.

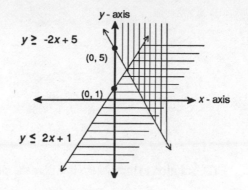

$y \geq -2x + 5$

(0, 5)

(0, 1)

y - axis

x - axis

$y \leq 2x + 1$

b) $x + 2y - 4$

$y - 1 < x$

First rewrite each inequality in $y \,\square\, mx + b$ form.

$x + 2y < -4$	$y - 1 < x$	Get y alone on one side.
$\dfrac{-x \qquad -x}{2y < -x - 4}$	$\dfrac{+1 +1}{y < x + 1}$	

$\dfrac{1}{2}(2y) < \dfrac{1}{2}(-x - 4)$

$y < -\dfrac{1}{2}x - 2$

$y < -\dfrac{1}{2}x - 2$ The line will be dotted because the inequality symbol is <. The shading will be below the line. Graph a dotted line with slope = $\dfrac{-1}{2}$ and y-intercept -2.

$y < x + 1$ The line will be dotted because the inequality symbol is <. The shading will be below the line. Graph a dotted line with slope = 1 $= \dfrac{1}{1}$ and y-intercept $+1$.

The solution to the system is where the shadings overlap.

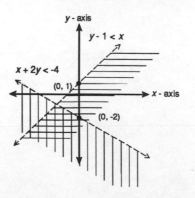

y - axis

$y - 1 < x$

$x + 2y < -4$

(0, 1)

x - axis

(0, -2)

c) $x \geq 2$
   $y < -3$

   $x \geq 2$

   The line is a vertical line at $x = 2$.
   The line will be solid because the inequality is $\geq$. Shade to the right of the line.

   $y < -3$

   The line is a horizontal line at $y = -3$. The line will be dotted because the inequality is $<$. Shade below the line.

The solution to the system is where the shadings overlap.

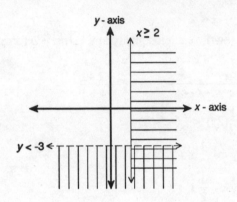

Practice Exercises

1. Determine whether the given ordered pair is a solution to the system.
   (a) $4x - 3y = 10$ $(1, -2)$
   $2x + y = 0$
   (b) $2x + y = 10$ $(3, 4)$
   $3x - 2y = 17$
   (c) $4x - 5y = -17$ $(-3, 1)$
   $3x - 2y = -11$

2. Solve each system by graphing.
   (a) $3x + y = 13$
   $x - 2y = -5$
   (b) $3x - y = -3$
   $x + 2y = -8$
   (c) $4x - 3y = 8$
   $8x - 6y = 16$
   (d) $2x + y = 6$
   $6x + 3y = 8$

3. Solve each system using the addition method.
   (a) $2x + y = 3$
   $x - y = 3$
   (b) $3x - y = 2$
   $6x + 2y = 20$
   (c) $3x - 4y = 17$
   $5x - 3y = 21$
   (d) $10x - 6y = -2$
   $15x + 9y = 9$

4. Solve each system.
   (a) $x - 5y = 3$
   $2x - 10y = 5$
   (b) $2x + y = 6$
   $4x + 2y = 12$
   (c) $5x - y = 6$
   $10x - 2y = 1$

5. Solve each system by substitution.
   (a) $6x - 3y = -12$
   $x = -2y - 7$
   (b) $6x - 3y = -15$
   $y = x + 4$
   (c) $18x - y = 14$
   $27x + 16y = -49$

(d) $3x + y = 4$
$6x + 2y = 8$

(e) $2x + y = 6$
$6x + 3y = 8$

6. Solve each problem.
   (a) One number is one more than twice the second number. The sum of the numbers is 10. Find the numbers.
   (b) The difference of two numbers is 8. The sum of the two numbers is 18. Find the numbers.
   (c) One number is four times as large as a second number. The sum of the numbers is 30. Find the numbers.

7. (a) There were 100 tickets sold to the puppet show. Children's tickets sold for $2.00, and adult tickets sold for $3.00. The total receipts were $265.00. How many of each type were sold?
   (b) There were 126 tickets sold for the comedy show. Tickets for dinner and the show sold for $25.00, and tickets for just the show sold for $15.00. The total receipts were $2790. How many of each type of ticket were sold?
   (c) There were 425 tickets sold for the talent show. Students with an I.D. card could purchase tickets for $1.00. Other tickets sold for $3.50. The total receipts were $550.00. How many of each type of ticket were sold?

8. Solve each problem.
   (a) A photographer needs 20 gallons of 25% acetic acid. She has 20% acetic acid and 40% acetic acid. How much of each will be needed?
   (b) The garage needs 100 gallons of 40% antifreeze. The owner has 30% antifreeze and 70% antifreeze in stock. How many gallons of each type should he use?
   (c) A piggy bank contained 113 coins in quarters and dimes for a total of $15.35. How many quarters and dimes were in the bank?

9. Solve each problem.
   (a) A plane travels 1000 miles with the wind for 5 hours, and 450 miles against the wind for 3 hours. Find the speed of the wind and the speed of the plane in still air.
   (b) A man can row a boat upstream for 5 hours and travel 10 miles. He can row downstream for 3 hours and travel 18 miles. Find the rate of the boat in still water and the speed of the water current.
   (c) A boat can travel upriver for 3 hours and travel 54 miles. It can travel downriver for 5 hours and travel 150 miles. Find the speed of the boat in still water and the speed of the current.

10. Graph the solutions of each system.
   (a) $y \geq \dfrac{1}{2}x - 2$
       $y < 3x + 1$
   (b) $x + 3y \leq 6$
       $y > x + 2$
   (c) $x < 4$
       $y \geq -2$

Answers

1. (a) yes
   (b) no
   (c) yes

2. (a) $(2, -1)$
   (b) $(2, 4)$
   (c) dependent system, same line
   (d) inconsistent system, parallel lines

3. (a) $(2, -1)$
   (b) $2, 4)$
   (c) $(3, -2)$
   (d) $\left(\dfrac{1}{5}, \dfrac{2}{3} \right)$

4. (a) no solutions, parallel lines
   (b) infinite number of solutions, same line
   (c) no solutions, parallel lines

5. (a) $(-3, -2)$
   (b) $(-1, 3)$
   (c) $\left(\dfrac{5}{9}, -4 \right)$
   (d) infinite number of solutions
   (e) no solutions

6. (a) 3 and 7
   (b) 5 and 13
   (c) 6 and 24

7. (a) 35 children, 65 adults
   (b) 90 dinner and show, 36 just show
   (c) 375 with I.D., 50 other

8. (a) 15 gal. @ 20%, 5 gal. @ 40%
   (b) 75 gal. @ 30%, 25 gal. @ 70%
   (c) 27 quarters, 86 dimes

9. (a) 25 mph, 175 mph
   (b) 4 mph in still water, 2 mph current
   (c) 24 mph in still water, 6 mph current

10. graphs
    a)

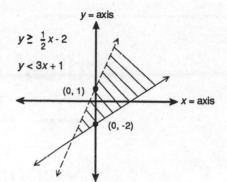

    b)

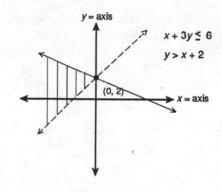

    c)

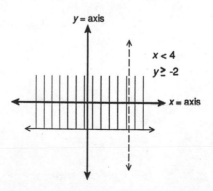

8

Radical Expressions

8.1 INTRODUCTION TO ROOTS AND RADICALS

We use exponents as shorthand for multiplication when we write $7^2 = 49$. We use a radical sign to reverse this process. You may want to review the exponent work covered in Chapter 3 before proceeding.

Basics

In the expression $\sqrt{49}$, read "the square root of 49," 49 is called the **radicand** and $\sqrt{}$ is called a **radical sign**. Since $7^2 = 49$ and $(-7)^2 = 49$, we use...

$\sqrt{49}$ to indicate that we want the positive square root of $49 = 7$
and
$-\sqrt{49}$ to indicate that we want the negative square root of $49 = -7$.

Example 1

Find each square root.

a) $\sqrt{36}$

b) $-\sqrt{36}$

c) $\sqrt{\dfrac{25}{49}}$

d) $\dfrac{-\sqrt{36}}{-\sqrt{64}}$

Solution 1

a) $\sqrt{36} = 6$

No sign in front of the radical means we want the positive square root of 36. $6^2 = 36$.

b) $-\sqrt{36} = -6$

The negative sign in front of the radical means we want the

negative square root of 36. $(-6)^2 =$ 36.

c) $\sqrt{\dfrac{25}{49}} = \dfrac{5}{7}$

No sign in front of the radical means we want the positive square root of $\dfrac{25}{49}$. $\left(\dfrac{5}{7}\right)^2 = \dfrac{25}{49}$.

d) $\dfrac{-\sqrt{36}}{-\sqrt{64}} = \dfrac{-6}{-8}$

$-\sqrt{36} = -\sqrt{64} = -8$.

$= \dfrac{3}{4}$

Reduce the fraction.

Rational versus irrational versus not real

The square root of a perfect square is a rational number. The square root of any other positive number is an irrational number. The square root of *any* negative number is *not* a real number (since there are no real numbers that multiply times themselves to equal a negative number). Study the following table.

Number	Rational or Irrational	Real or Not Real
$\sqrt{36}$	rational	real
$-\sqrt{36}$	rational	real
$\sqrt{11}$	irrational	real
$-\sqrt{11}$	irrational	real
$\sqrt{-4}$	neither	not real
$\sqrt{-13}$	neither	not real

Other roots

To write the reverse of $4^3 = 64$ and $5^4 = 625$ we write

$\sqrt[3]{64} = 4$, which is read "the cube root of 64 equals 4."

$\sqrt[4]{625} = 5$, which is read "the fourth root of 625 equals 5."

In the expression $\sqrt[3]{64}$, 3 is called the **index**, 64 is called the radicand, and $\sqrt{}$ is called a radical sign. When no index is written, it is understood to be a square root. The following table will help you recognize some square roots, cube roots, and fourth roots.

Square Roots	Cube Roots	Fourth Roots
$\sqrt{1} = 1$ $\quad$ $\sqrt{49} = 7$	$\sqrt[3]{1}$	$\sqrt[4]{1}$
$\sqrt{4} = 2$ $\quad$ $\sqrt{64} = 8$	$\sqrt[3]{8} = 2$	$\sqrt[4]{16} = 2$
$\sqrt{9} = 3$ $\quad$ $\sqrt{81} = 9$	$\sqrt[3]{27} = 3$	$\sqrt[4]{81} = 3$
$\sqrt{16} = 4$ $\quad$ $\sqrt{100} = 10$	$\sqrt[3]{64} = 4$	$\sqrt[4]{256} = 4$
$\sqrt{25} = 5$ $\quad$ $\sqrt{121} = 11$	$\sqrt[3]{125} = 5$	$\sqrt[4]{625} = 5$
$\sqrt{36} = 6$ $\quad$ $\sqrt{144} = 12$	$\sqrt[3]{216} = 6$	$\sqrt[4]{1296} = 6$

Example 2   Find each root if it exists.

a) $\sqrt[3]{64}$

b) $\sqrt[3]{-8}$

c) $-\sqrt[3]{1}$

d) $\sqrt[4]{\dfrac{16}{81}}$

e) $\sqrt[4]{-256}$

Solution 2

a) $\sqrt[3]{64} = 4$ $\hspace{3cm}$ since $4^3 = 64$

b) $\sqrt[3]{-8} = -2$ $\hspace{2.8cm}$ since $(-2)^3 = -8$

c) $-\sqrt[3]{1} = -1$ $\hspace{2.8cm}$ since
$$-\sqrt[3]{1} = -1(\sqrt[3]{1}) = -1(1) = -1$$

d) $\sqrt[4]{\dfrac{16}{18}} = \dfrac{2}{3}$

$\hspace{5cm}$ since $\left(\dfrac{2}{3}\right)^4 = \dfrac{16}{81}$

e) $\sqrt[4]{-256}$ $\hspace{3cm}$ does not exist. No real number multiplied times itself four times equals a negative number.

An even root (square root, fourth root, sixth root, etc.) of a negative number is *not a real number*.
An odd root (cube root, fifth root, seventh root, etc.) of a negative number *is* a real number.

8.2 SIMPLIFYING RADICAL EXPRESSIONS

To simplify radicals we use the following rules:

For x, y nonnegative real numbers,

$\sqrt[n]{xy} = \sqrt[n]{x}\ \sqrt[n]{y} =$ The nth root of a product is the product of the nth roots.

$\sqrt[n]{\dfrac{x}{y}} = \dfrac{\sqrt[n]{x}}{\sqrt[n]{y}}$ The nth root of a product is the product of the nth roots.

$\sqrt[4]{x^n} = x$ The nth root of xn is x.

A radical is in simplified form if
1. The index is greater than any exponent in the radicand.
2. There are no fractions under the radical.
3. There are no radicals in the denominator of a fraction. (See discussion in Section 8.5)

To simplify $\sqrt[n]{*}$
1. Prime factor the radicand.
2. Write each factor to the nth power whenever possible.
3. Use $\sqrt[n]{x^n} = x$ to bring perfect factors outside the radical. Any factor raised to a power less than n stays in the radicand.
Note: We will assume all variables represent nonnegative real numbers!

Example 3   Simplify.

    a) $\sqrt{48x^4}$

    b) $\sqrt[3]{48x^4}$

    c) $\sqrt[4]{48x^4}$

    d) $\sqrt[5]{48x^4}$

Solution 3

    a) $\sqrt{48x^4} = \sqrt{2^4 \cdot 3^1 \cdot x^4}$

            $= \sqrt{2^2}\ \sqrt{2^2}\ \sqrt{3^1}\ \sqrt{x^2}\ \sqrt{x^2}$ $\sqrt{x \cdot y} = \sqrt{x}\ \sqrt{y}$

$$= 2 \cdot 2 \cdot x \cdot x\sqrt{3}$$

Use $\sqrt[n]{x^n} = x = x$. Remember that no written index is an understood 2.

$$\sqrt[2]{2^2} = 2. \qquad \sqrt[2]{2^2} = x$$

$$= 4x^2 \sqrt{3}$$

Multiply $2 \cdot 2 \cdot x \cdot x = 4x^2$.

b) $\quad \sqrt[3]{48x^4} = \sqrt[3]{2^4 \cdot 3^1 \cdot x^4}$

Factor the radicals.

$$= \sqrt[3]{2^3\, 2^1\, 3^1\, x^3\, x^1}$$

Write each base using the index, 3, as exponent.

$$= \sqrt[3]{2^3}\ \sqrt[3]{2}\ \sqrt[3]{3}\ \sqrt[3]{x^3}\ \sqrt[3]{x}$$

$$\sqrt[3]{xy} = \sqrt[3]{x}\ \sqrt[3]{y}$$

$$= 2x\, \sqrt[3]{2\, 3\, x}$$

Use $\sqrt[n]{x^n} = x$.

$$\sqrt[3]{2^3} = 2. \quad \sqrt[3]{x^3} = x.$$

$$= 2x\, \sqrt[3]{6x}$$

Multiply.

c) $\quad \sqrt[4]{x^4} = \sqrt[4]{2^4 \cdot 3^1 \cdot x^4}$

Factor the radicand.

$$= \sqrt[4]{2^4}\ \sqrt[4]{3^4}\ \sqrt[4]{x^4}$$

$$\sqrt[4]{x \cdot y} = \sqrt[4]{x}\ \sqrt[4]{y}$$

$$= 2\ x\, \sqrt[4]{3}$$

Use $\sqrt[n]{x^n} = x$.

$$\sqrt[4]{2^4} = 2. \quad \sqrt[4]{x^4} = x.$$

$$= 2x\, \sqrt[4]{3}$$

Multiply.

d) $\quad \sqrt[5]{48x^4} = \sqrt[5]{2^4 \cdot 3^1 \cdot x^4}$

The index is greater than the exponents in the radicand.

$$= \sqrt[5]{48x^4}$$

This is already simplified.

Example 4   Simplify.
a) $\sqrt{75x^2y}$
b) $3a\sqrt{32a^3}$
c) $xy^3 \sqrt{8x^4y^3}$

Solution 4

a) $\sqrt{75x^2y} = \sqrt{5^2 \cdot 3 \cdot x^2 \cdot y}$

$= \sqrt{5^2}\sqrt{3}\sqrt{x^2}\sqrt{y}$
$= 5x\sqrt{3y}$

$\sqrt{5^2} = 5.\ \sqrt{x^2} = x.$

Factor the radicand: $75 = 25$
$3 = 5^2\ 3$
$\sqrt{xy} = \sqrt{x}\sqrt{y}$
Use $\sqrt[n]{x^n} = \text{r}\ (n, xn) = x.$

b) $3a\sqrt{32a^3} = 3a\sqrt{2^5 \cdot a^3}$
$= 3a\sqrt{2^2 \cdot 2^2 \cdot 2^1 \cdot a^2 \cdot a^1}$

$= 3a\sqrt{2^2}\sqrt{2^2}\sqrt{2}\sqrt{a^2}\sqrt{a}$
$= 3a \cdot 2 \cdot 2 \cdot a\sqrt{2a}$

$= 12a^2\sqrt{2a}$

Factor the radicand.

Write each base using 2 as the exponent.
$\sqrt{xy} = \sqrt{x}\sqrt{y}$

Use $\sqrt[n]{x^n} = x.$
$\sqrt{2^2} = 2.\ \sqrt{a^2} = a.$

Multiply. Be careful to write the exponent, 2, on a, and not as the index!

c) $xy\sqrt[3]{8x^4y^3} = xy\sqrt[3]{2^3\ x^3\ x^1\ y^3}$

$= xy \cdot 2 \cdot x \cdot y\sqrt[3]{x}$

$= 2x^2\ y^2\sqrt[3]{x}$

Factor the radicand and write each base using 3 as the exponent.

Use $\sqrt[n]{x^n} = x.$
$\sqrt[3]{2^3} = 2.\ \sqrt[3]{x^3} = x.$
$\sqrt[3]{y^3} = y.$

Multiply.

Fractions

If the radicand is a fraction, and can be factored so that its exponent equals the index, we can use $\sqrt[n]{x^n} = x$ to simplify.

Example 5 Simplify.

a) $\sqrt{\dfrac{4}{9}}$

b) $3\sqrt[9]{\dfrac{8x^3}{125y^6}}$

c) $\sqrt{\dfrac{8}{18}}$

Solution 5

a) $\sqrt{\dfrac{4}{9}} = \sqrt{\left(\dfrac{2}{3}\right)^2}$

Factor the radicand and write the base $\dfrac{2}{3}$ using 2 as the exponent.

$= \dfrac{2}{3}$

Use $\sqrt[n]{x^n} = x$.

b) $\sqrt[3]{\dfrac{8x^3}{125y^6}} = \sqrt[3]{\left(\dfrac{2x}{5y^2}\right)^3}$

Factor the radicand and write the base $\dfrac{2x}{5y^2}$ using 3 as the exponent.

Use $\sqrt[n]{x^n} = x$.

c) $\sqrt{\dfrac{8}{18}} = \sqrt{\dfrac{2 \cdot 4}{2 \cdot 9}}$

Reduce the fraction first.

$= \sqrt{\dfrac{4}{9}}$

Factor the radicand and write the base using 2 as the exponent.

$= \sqrt{\left(\dfrac{2}{3}\right)^2}$

Use $\sqrt[n]{x^n} = x$.

$= \dfrac{2}{3}$

Final answer.

We can also use the quotient rule for radicals $\sqrt{\dfrac{x}{y}} = \dfrac{\sqrt{x}}{\sqrt{y}}$ to simplify radicands that are fractions.

Example 6   Simplify.

a) $\sqrt{\dfrac{50x^3}{9}}$

b) $\sqrt{\dfrac{48}{16}}$

c) $\dfrac{4\sqrt{54a^3}}{\sqrt{25}}$

d) $\sqrt[3]{\dfrac{64x^5}{27}}$

e) $\sqrt{\dfrac{75p^4}{16m^2}}$

Solution 6

a) $\sqrt{\dfrac{50x^3}{9}} = \dfrac{\sqrt{50x^3}}{\sqrt{9}}$

$= \dfrac{\sqrt{5^2 \cdot 2 \cdot x^2 \cdot x}}{\sqrt{3^2}}$

$\sqrt{\dfrac{x}{y}} = \dfrac{\sqrt{x}}{\sqrt{y}}$

Factor the radicand in the numerator and in the denominator. Write each base using 2 as the exponent whenever possible.
$50 = 5 \cdot 10 = 5 \cdot 5 \cdot 2 = 5^2 \cdot 2$
$x^3 = x^2 x$

$= \dfrac{\sqrt{5^2}\ \sqrt{2}\ \sqrt{x^2}\ \sqrt{x}}{\sqrt{3^2}}$

$= \dfrac{5\ \sqrt{2x}\ \sqrt{x}}{3}$

$\sqrt{xy} = \sqrt{x}\ \sqrt{y}$

$= \dfrac{5x\ \sqrt{2}\ \sqrt{x}}{3}$

Use $\sqrt[n]{x^n} = x$.
$\sqrt{5^2} = 5. \quad \sqrt{x^2} = x \quad \sqrt{3^2} = 3.$

$= \dfrac{5x\sqrt{2x}}{3}$

Use the Commutative Property:
$\sqrt{2}x = x\sqrt{2}$

b) $\sqrt{\dfrac{48}{16}} = \dfrac{\sqrt{48}}{\sqrt{16}}$

Use $\sqrt{x}\sqrt{y} = \sqrt{xy}$:
$\sqrt{2}\sqrt{x} = \sqrt{2x}.$

$\sqrt{\dfrac{x}{y}} = \dfrac{\sqrt{x}}{\sqrt{y}}$

$= \dfrac{\sqrt{2^2 \cdot 2^2 \cdot 3}}{\sqrt{2^2 \cdot 2^2}}$

Factor the radicand in the numerator and in the denominator. Write each base using 2 as the exponent whenever possible.

$= \dfrac{\sqrt{2^2}\sqrt{2^2}\sqrt{3}}{\sqrt{2^2}\sqrt{2^2}}$

$= \dfrac{2 \cdot 2\sqrt{3}}{2 \cdot}$

$\sqrt{xy} = \sqrt{x}\sqrt{y}$

Use $\sqrt[n]{x^n} = x$.
$\sqrt{2^2} = 2.$

$= \dfrac{4\sqrt{3}}{4}$

$= \sqrt{3}$

Since $\dfrac{4}{4} = 1$, reduce.

Final answer.

or in this example, you could simplify the fraction first:

$$\sqrt{\frac{48}{16}} = \sqrt{3} \quad \text{since} \quad \frac{48}{16} = 3.$$

c) $\dfrac{4\sqrt{54a^3}}{\sqrt{25}} = \dfrac{4\sqrt{2 \cdot 3^3 \cdot a^3}}{\sqrt{5^2}}$

Factor the radicand in the numerator and in the denominator.
$54 = 6 \cdot 9 = 2 \cdot 3 \cdot 3 \cdot 3 = 2 \cdot 3^3$

$= \dfrac{4\sqrt{2 \cdot 3^2 \cdot 3 \cdot a^2 \cdot a}}{\sqrt{5^2}}$

Write each base using 2 as the exponent whenever possible.
$3^3 = 3^2 \cdot 3$
$a^3 = a^2 \cdot a$

$= \dfrac{4\sqrt{2}\sqrt{3^2}\sqrt{3}\sqrt{a^2}\sqrt{a}}{\sqrt{5^2}}$

Use $\sqrt{xy} = \sqrt{x}\sqrt{y}$

$= \dfrac{4\sqrt{2}\ 3\ \sqrt{3}\ a\ \sqrt{a}}{5}$

Use $\sqrt[n]{x^n} = x.$
$\sqrt{3^2} = 3.\ \sqrt{a^2} = a.\ \sqrt{5^2} = 5.$

$= \dfrac{4 \cdot 3 \cdot a\sqrt{2}\sqrt{3}\sqrt{a}}{5}$

Use the Commutative Property to change the order in the numerator.

$= \dfrac{4 \cdot 3 \cdot a\sqrt{6a}}{5}$

Use $\sqrt{x}\sqrt{y} = \sqrt{xy}$ to multiply:
$\sqrt{2}\sqrt{3}\sqrt{a} = \sqrt{6a}$

$= \dfrac{12a\sqrt{6a}}{5}$

Multiply $4 \cdot 3 \cdot a = 12a\ \ a = 12a.$

d) $\sqrt[3]{\dfrac{64x^5}{27}} = 3\dfrac{\sqrt[3]{64x^5}}{\sqrt[3]{27}} = \dfrac{\sqrt[3]{64x^5}}{\sqrt[3]{27}}$

Use $\dfrac{\sqrt[3]{x}}{y} = \dfrac{\sqrt[3]{x}}{\sqrt[3]{y}}$

$= \dfrac{\sqrt[3]{2^6 x^5}}{\sqrt[3]{3^3}}$

Factor the radicand in the numerator and in the denominator.

$= \dfrac{\sqrt[3]{2^3 \cdot 2^3 \cdot x^3 \cdot x^2}}{\sqrt[3]{3^3}}$

Write each base using 3 as the exponent whenever possible.

$$= \frac{\sqrt[3]{2^3}\ \sqrt[3]{2^3}\ \sqrt[3]{x^3}\ \sqrt[3]{x^2}}{\sqrt[3]{3^3}}$$

$$= \frac{2 \cdot 2 \cdot x\ \sqrt[3]{x^2}}{3}$$

$$= \frac{4x\sqrt[3]{x^2}}{3}$$

e) $\sqrt{\dfrac{75p^4}{16m^2}} = \dfrac{\sqrt{75p^4}}{\sqrt{16m^2}}$

$$= \frac{\sqrt{5^2 \cdot 3 \cdot p^4}}{\sqrt{2^4 \cdot m^2}}$$

$$= \frac{\sqrt{5^2 \cdot 3 \cdot p^2 \cdot p^2}}{\sqrt{2^4 \cdot 2^2 \cdot m^2}}$$

$$= \frac{\sqrt{5^2}\ \sqrt{3}\ \sqrt{p^2}\ \sqrt{p^2}}{\sqrt{2^4}\ \sqrt{2^2}\ \sqrt{m^2}}$$

$$= \frac{5\sqrt{3}\ p \cdot p}{2 \cdot 2 \cdot m}$$

$$= \frac{5p^2\sqrt{3}}{4m}$$

$2^6 = 2^3\ 2^3$. Remember exponents are added here. $x^5 = x^3\ x^2$.

Use $\sqrt[3]{xy} = \sqrt[3]{x}\ \sqrt[3]{y}$

Use $\sqrt[n]{x^n} = x.$

Multiply $2\ 2\ x = 4x.$

Use $\sqrt{\dfrac{x}{y}} = \dfrac{\sqrt{x}}{\sqrt{y}}$

Factor the radicand in the numerator and in the denominator.

Write each base using 2 as the exponent when possible.
$p^4 = p^2\ p^2$
$2^4 = 2^2\ 2^2$

Use $\sqrt{xy} = \sqrt{x}\sqrt{y}$

Use $\sqrt[n]{x^n} = x.$
$\sqrt{5^2} = 5.\ \sqrt{p^2} = p.\ \sqrt{2^2} = 2.$
$\sqrt{m^2} = m.$

Use the Commutative Property to reorder the factors in the numerator and multiply.

8.3 ADDING AND SUBTRACTING RADICAL EXPRESSIONS

Adding simplified radicals   Only radicals with the same index and the same radicand (called **similar radicals**) can be added or subtracted. We can use the Distributive Property to allow us to add or subtract the numbers in front of the radicals and keep the radicands the same. Note that this process is the same one used to add $4x + 7x = (4 + 7)x = 11x$.

Example 7   Combine terms, if possible.

a) $4\sqrt{7} - 6\sqrt{7}$

b) $\sqrt[3]{9} + 4\sqrt[3]{9}$

c) $3\sqrt{2} - 5\sqrt{2} + 8\sqrt{2}$

d) $3\sqrt{2} + 4\sqrt{5}$

e) $\sqrt[3]{5} + \sqrt{5}$

Solutions

a) $4\sqrt{7} - 6\sqrt{7} = (4 - 6)\sqrt{7}$ Use the Distributive Property.
     $= -2\sqrt{7}$ Simplify inside the parentheses: $4 - 6 = -2$.

b) $\sqrt[3]{9} + 4\sqrt[3]{9} = 1\sqrt[3]{9} + 4\sqrt[3]{9}$ There is an understood 1 in front of $\sqrt[3]{9}$.

     $= (1 + 4)\sqrt[3]{9}$ Use the Distributive Property.

     $= 5\sqrt[3]{9}$ Simplify inside the parentheses: $1 + 4 = 5$.

c) $3\sqrt{2} - 5\sqrt{2} + 8\sqrt{2}$ Use the Distributive Property.

     $= 6\sqrt{2}$ Simplify inside the parentheses: $3 - 5 + 8 = 6$.

d) $3\sqrt{2} + 4\sqrt{5}$ Cannot be combined. Both terms are square roots, but the radicands are not equal.

e) $\sqrt[3]{5} + \sqrt{5}$ Cannot be combined. The radicands are equal (5), but the indexes (3 and 2) are not equal.

Adding radicals that are not simplified   If the radicals are not already simplified, you may need to simplify before (or after) combining similar radicals.

Example 8   Combine terms, if possible.

a) $5\sqrt{2} + \sqrt{8}$

b) $3\sqrt{75} - 2\sqrt{3} + 2\sqrt{27}$

c) $2\sqrt{125} + \sqrt{20} - \sqrt{10}$

d) $\sqrt{12x^2} - 7x\sqrt{3}$

e) $4\sqrt[3]{16a^2} + \sqrt{54a^2}$

Solution 8

a) $5\sqrt{2} + \sqrt{8} = 5\sqrt{2} + \sqrt{2^2 \cdot 2}$ Simplify first.

$\quad = 5\sqrt{2} + 2\sqrt{2}$ $\sqrt{2^2 \cdot 2} = \sqrt{2^2}\sqrt{2} = 2\sqrt{2}$

$\quad = (5 + 2)\sqrt{2}$ Use the Distributive Property.

$\quad = 7\sqrt{2}$ Simplify inside the parentheses: $5 + 2 = 7$.

b) $3\sqrt{75} - 2\sqrt{3} + 2\sqrt{27} = 3\sqrt{5^2 \cdot 3} - 2\sqrt{3} + 2\sqrt{3^2 \cdot 3^1}$

$\qquad\qquad\qquad\qquad\qquad$ Factor each radicand.

$\quad = 3 \cdot 5\sqrt{3} - 2\sqrt{3} + 2 \cdot 3\sqrt{3^1}$ $\sqrt{5^2} = 5.\ \sqrt{3^2} = 3.$

$\quad = 15\sqrt{3} - 2\sqrt{3} + 6\sqrt{3}$ Multiply.

$\quad = (15 - 2 + 6)\sqrt{3}$ Use the Distributive Property.

$\quad = 19\sqrt{3}$ Simplify inside the parentheses: $15 - 2 + 6 = 19$.

c) $2\sqrt{125} + \sqrt{20} - \sqrt{10} = 2\sqrt{5^2 \cdot 5^1} + \sqrt{2^2 \cdot 5^1} - \sqrt{2 \cdot 5}$

$\qquad\qquad\qquad\qquad\qquad$ Factor each radicand.

$\quad = 2 \cdot 5\sqrt{5} + 2\sqrt{5} - \sqrt{10}$ $\sqrt{5^2} = 5.\ \sqrt{2^2} = 2.$

$\quad = 10\sqrt{5} + 2\sqrt{5} - \sqrt{10}$ Multiply.

$\quad = (10 + 2)\sqrt{5} - \sqrt{10}$ Use the Distributive Property.

$\quad = 12\sqrt{5} - \sqrt{10}$ Stop here since the radicands (5 and 10) are not equal!

d) $\sqrt{12x^2} - 7x\sqrt{3} = \sqrt{2^2\ 3\ x^2} - 7x\sqrt{3}$ Factor each radicand.

$\quad = 2x\sqrt{3} - 7x\sqrt{3}$ $\sqrt{2^2} = 2.\ \sqrt{x^2} = x.$

$\quad = (2x - 7x)\sqrt{3}$ Use the Distributive Property.

$\quad = -5x\sqrt{3}$ Simplify inside the parentheses: $2x - 7x = -5x$.

e) $4\sqrt[3]{16a^2} + \sqrt{54a^2} = 4\sqrt[3]{2^3 \cdot 2 \cdot a^2} + \sqrt[3]{3^3 \cdot 2 \cdot a^2})$

$\qquad\qquad\qquad\qquad\qquad$ Factor each radicand.

$\quad = 4\ 2\sqrt[3]{2a^2} + 3\sqrt[3]{2a^2}$

$$= 8 \sqrt[3]{2a^2} + 3 \sqrt[3]{2a^2}$$

$$= (8+3) \sqrt[3]{2a^2}$$

$$= 11 \sqrt[3]{2a^2}$$

$$\sqrt[3]{2^3} = 2. \quad \sqrt[3]{3^3} = 3.$$

Multiply.

Use the Distributive Property.

Simplify inside the parentheses: $8 + 3 = 11$

8.4 MULTIPLYING RADICAL EXPRESSIONS

Previously we used the rule $\sqrt[n]{x \cdot y} = \sqrt[n]{x}\sqrt[n]{y}$ to simplify radicals. We can use the same rule now to multiply radicals.

Multiplying radicals

To Multiply $(a\sqrt[n]{x})(b\sqrt[n]{y})$:
1. Multiply $a \cdot b\sqrt[n]{x \cdot y}$. Keep the index the same.
2. Simplify $\sqrt[n]{xy}$, if possible.

Example 9   Multiply.
a) $(2\sqrt{5})(-3\sqrt{6})$
b) $3\sqrt{2}(\sqrt{8} + 4\sqrt{10})$
c) $(\sqrt{3} + 4)(\sqrt{3} + 2)$
d) $(2\sqrt{x} - 3)(4\sqrt{x} + 1)$

Solution 9

a) $(2\sqrt{5})(-3\sqrt{6}) = (2 \cdot -3)\sqrt{5 \cdot 6}$

$$= -6\sqrt{30}$$

$(a\sqrt[n]{x})(b\sqrt[n]{y}) = a \cdot b\sqrt[n]{x \cdot y}$
Stop here since $\sqrt{30} = \sqrt{2 \cdot 3 \cdot 5}$.

b) $3\sqrt{2}(\sqrt{8} + 4\sqrt{10}) = (3\sqrt{2})(\sqrt{8}) + (3\sqrt{2})(4\sqrt{10})$

Use the Distributive Property.
$\sqrt{8} = 1\sqrt{8}$

$$= (3\sqrt{2})(1\sqrt{8}) + (3\sqrt{2})(4\sqrt{10})$$
$$= (3 \cdot 1\sqrt{2 \cdot 8}) + (3 \cdot 4\sqrt{2 \cdot 10})$$
$$= 3\sqrt{16} + 12\sqrt{20}$$

$(a\sqrt[n]{x})(b\sqrt[n]{y}) = a\,b\sqrt[n]{x\,y}$

$= 3\sqrt{2^2 \cdot 2^2} + 12\sqrt{2^2 \cdot 5}$

$= 3 \cdot 2 \cdot 2 \cdot + 12 \ 2\sqrt{5}$

Multiply.

Factor each radicand.

Use $\sqrt[n]{x^n} = x$.

$\sqrt{2^2} = 2$

$\sqrt{2^2 \cdot 5} = \sqrt{2^2}\sqrt{5} = 2\sqrt{5}$

Multiply before adding.

Stop here! Only similar radicals can be added!

$= 12 + 24\sqrt{5}$

$= 12 + 24\sqrt{5}$

You could simplify $\sqrt{8} = 2\sqrt{2}$ first and arrive at the same answer:

$3\sqrt{2}(\sqrt{8} + 4\sqrt{10}) = 3\sqrt{2}(2\sqrt{2} + 4\sqrt{10})$

Simplify $\sqrt{8} = 2\sqrt{2}$

$= (3\sqrt{2})(2\sqrt{2}) + (3\sqrt{2})(4\sqrt{10})$

Use the Distributive Property.

$= (3 \cdot 2\sqrt{2 \cdot 2}) + (3 \cdot 4\sqrt{2 \cdot 10})$

$(a\sqrt[n]{x})(b\sqrt[n]{y}) = a \cdot b \sqrt[n]{x \cdot y}$

Multiply.

$= 6\sqrt{4} + 12\sqrt{20}$

$= 6\sqrt{2^2} + 12\sqrt{2^2 \ 5}$

$= 6 \cdot 2 + 12 \cdot 2\sqrt{5}$

Factor each radicand.

Use $\sqrt[n]{x^n} = x$.

$\sqrt{2^2} = 2$

$\sqrt{2^2 \cdot 5} = \sqrt{2^2}\sqrt{5} = 2\sqrt{5}$

Multiply before adding.

Stop here! Only similar radicals can be added!

$= 12 + 24\sqrt{5}$

$= 12 + 24\sqrt{5}$

c) $(\sqrt{3} + 4)(\sqrt{3} + 2)$

Use **FOIL.**

F: $\sqrt{3}\sqrt{3} = \sqrt{9} = 3$

O: $\sqrt{3} \cdot 2 = 2\sqrt{3}$

I: $4 \cdot \sqrt{3} = 4\sqrt{3}$

L: $4 \ 2 = 8$

Multiply the first two terms.

Multiply the outer two terms.

Multiply the inner two terms.

Multiply the last two terms.

$= 3 + 2\sqrt{3} + 4\sqrt{3} + 8$

Add similar radicals:

$2\sqrt{3} + 4\sqrt{3} = (2 + 4)\sqrt{3} = 6\sqrt{3}$

Add similar terms:

$3 + 8 = 11$.

$= 11 + 6\sqrt{3}$

d) $(2\sqrt{x} - 3)(4\sqrt{x} + 1)$

Use FOIL.

F: $(2\sqrt{x})(4\sqrt{x})$

$= (2 \cdot 4\sqrt{x \cdot x})$

Multiply the first two terms.

$(a\sqrt[n]{x})(b\sqrt[n]{y}) = a \ b \sqrt[n]{x \cdot y}$

Multiply.

$= 8\sqrt{x^2}$

$= 8x$

$$\sqrt{x^2} = x$$

O: $(2\sqrt{x})(1)$

$= 2\sqrt{x}$

Multiply the outer two terms.
Identity property of 1.

I: $(-3)(4\sqrt{x})$

$= (-3 \cdot 4\ \sqrt{x})$

$= -12\sqrt{x}$

Multiply the inner two terms.

$(a\ \sqrt[n]{x})(b\ \sqrt[n]{y}) = a\ b\ \sqrt[n]{x\ y}$

Multiply.

L: $(-3)(+1)$

$= -3$

$= 8x + 2\sqrt{x} - 12\sqrt{x} - 3$

Multiply the last two terms.

Add similar radicals:
$2\sqrt{x} - 12\sqrt{x} = (2 - 12)\sqrt{x} = -10\sqrt{x}$

$= 8x - 10\sqrt{x} - 3$

Stop here! There are no other
similar terms to be added.

Special products

Recall from Chapter 3 that FOIL can be used to demonstrate the following rules:

$$(a + b)^2 = a^2 + 2ab + b^2$$
$$(a - b)^2 = a^2 - 2ab + b^2$$
$$(a + b)(a - b) = a^2 - b^2$$

When a and b are replaced with radicals, these rules still hold true.

Example 10   Multiply.

a) $(\sqrt{2} + 6)^2$

b) $(5\sqrt{2} - \sqrt{3})^2$

c) $(4 + \sqrt{3})(4 - \sqrt{3})$

d) $(\sqrt{x} + 7)^2$

e) $(\sqrt{y} - 4)^2$

f) $(3 + \sqrt{m})(3 - \sqrt{m})$

Solution 10

a) $(\sqrt{2} + 6)^2 = (\sqrt{2})^2 + 2(\sqrt{2})(6) + (6)^2$

$(a + b)^2 = a^2 + 2ab + b^2$
$a = \sqrt{2}$ and $b = 6$.

$= 2 + 12\sqrt{2} + 36$

$= 38 + 12\sqrt{2}$

$(\sqrt{2})^2 = \sqrt{2}\ \sqrt{2} = \sqrt{2^2} = 2$
Combine similar terms:
$2 + 36 = 38$.

b) $(5\sqrt{2} - \sqrt{3})^2 = (5\sqrt{2})^2 - 2(5\sqrt{2})(\sqrt{3}) + (\sqrt{3})^2$

$$(a - b)^2 = a^2 - 2ab + b^2$$
$$a = 5\sqrt{2} \text{ and } b = \sqrt{3}.$$

$$= (5\sqrt{2})(5\sqrt{2}) - 2(5\sqrt{2})(1\sqrt{3}) + (1\sqrt{3})(1\sqrt{3})$$

Use $x^2 = x \cdot x$ to rewrite the terms with exponents.

$$= (5 \cdot 5\sqrt{2 \cdot 2} - 2(5 \cdot \sqrt{2 \cdot 3}) + (1 \cdot 1\sqrt{3 \cdot 3})$$

$$(a\sqrt[n]{x})(b\sqrt[n]{y}) = a \cdot b \sqrt[n]{x \cdot y}$$

$$= 25\sqrt{2^2} - 2(5\sqrt{6}) + 1\sqrt{3^2}$$

Multiply.

$$= 25 \cdot 2 - 10\sqrt{6} + 1 \cdot 3$$

$$\sqrt{2^2} \cdot \sqrt{3^2} = 3.$$

$$= 50 - 10\sqrt{6} + 3$$

Multiply.

$$= 53 - 10\sqrt{6}$$

Combine similar terms:
$50 + 3 = 53.$
Stop here! Only similar radicals can be added.

c) $(4 + \sqrt{3})(4 - \sqrt{3}) = (4)^2 - (\sqrt{3})^2$

$(a + b)(a - b) = a^2 - b^2$;
$a = 4$ and $b = \sqrt{3}$.
$(\sqrt{3})^2 = (1\sqrt{3})(1\sqrt{3})$
$= 1\sqrt{3^2} = 1 \cdot 3 = 3.$

$$= 16 - 3$$

$$= 13$$

d) $(\sqrt{x} + 7)^2 = (\sqrt{x})^2 + 2\sqrt{x}(7) + (7)^2$

$(a + b)^2 = a^2 + 2ab + b^2$;
$a = \sqrt{x}$ and $b = 7$.
$(\sqrt{x})^2 = \sqrt{x}\sqrt{x} = \sqrt{x^2} = x$
Stop here! There are no similar radicals or similar terms to combine.

$$= x + 14\sqrt{x} + 49$$

e) $(\sqrt{y} - 4)^2 = (\sqrt{y})^2 + 2(\sqrt{y})(4) + (4)^2$

$(a - b)^2 = a^2 - 2ab + b^2$;
$a = r(y)$ and $b = 4$.
$(\sqrt{y})^2 = \sqrt{y}\sqrt{y} = \sqrt{y^2} = y.$
Stop here! There are no similar radicals or similar terms to combine.

$$= y - 8\sqrt{y} + 16$$

f) $(3 + \sqrt{m})(3 - \sqrt{m}) = (3)^2 - \sqrt{m^2}$

$(a + b)(a - b) = a^2 - b^2$;
$a = 3$ and $b = r(m)$.
$(\sqrt{m})^2 = (1\sqrt{m})(1\sqrt{m}) =$
$(1 \cdot 1r(m^2)) = 1 \cdot m = m.$

$$= 9 - m$$

Multiplying conjugates

The conjugate of a binomial $a - b$ is $a + b$, and the conjugate of $a + b$ is $a - b$. That is, you can find the conjugate of a binomial by changing the sign between the two terms.

Example 11 Find the conjugate of each of the following.
a) $5 + \sqrt{3}$
b) $3 - \sqrt{3}$
c) $\sqrt{7} + \sqrt{2}$
d) $2\sqrt{3} - 4\sqrt{11}$

Solution 11

a) The conjugate of $5 + \sqrt{3}$ is $5 - \sqrt{3}$.   Change the sign between the two terms.

b) The conjugate of $3 - \sqrt{3}$ is $3 + \sqrt{3}$.   Change the sign between the two terms.

c) The conjugate of $\sqrt{7} + \sqrt{2}$ is $- \sqrt{2}$.   Change the sign between the two terms.

d) The conjugate of $2\sqrt{3} - 4\sqrt{11}$ is $2\sqrt{3} + 4\sqrt{11}$ Change the sign between the two terms.

The product of conjugates can be found using the special product formula
$(a + b)(a - b) = a^2 - b^2$.

Example 12 Find the product of the following conjugates:
a) $(5 + \sqrt{3})(5 - \sqrt{3})$
b) $(3 - \sqrt{3})(3 + \sqrt{3})$
c) $(\sqrt{7} + \sqrt{2})(\sqrt{7} - \sqrt{2})$
d) $(2\sqrt{3} - 4\sqrt{11})(2\sqrt{3} + 4\sqrt{11})$

Solution 12

a) $(5 + \sqrt{3})(5 - \sqrt{3}) = (5)^2 - (\sqrt{3})^2$ Use $(a + b)(a - b) = a^2 - b^2$.
$a = 5$ and $b = \sqrt{3}$.

$= 25 - 3$ Square both terms.
$= 22$ Combine similar terms.

b) $(3 - \sqrt{3})(3 + \sqrt{3}) = (3)^2 - (\sqrt{3})2$ Use $(a + b)(a - b) = a^2 - b^2$.
$a = 3$ and $b = \sqrt{3}$.

$= 9 - 3$ Square both terms.
$= 6$ Combine similar terms.

c) $(\sqrt{7} + \sqrt{2})(\sqrt{7} - \sqrt{2}) = (\sqrt{7})^2 - (\sqrt{2})^2$ Use $(a + b)(a - b) = a^2 - b^2$.

$a = \sqrt{7}$ and $b = \sqrt{2}$.

$= 7 - 2$ Square both terms.
$= 5$ Combine similar terms.

d) $(2\sqrt{3} - 4\sqrt{11})(2\sqrt{3} + 4\sqrt{11}) \ (2\sqrt{3})^2 - (4\sqrt{11})^2$
Use $(a + b)(a - b) = a^2 - b^2$.
$a = 2\sqrt{3}$ and $b = 4\sqrt{11}$.

$$= (2\sqrt{3})(2\sqrt{3}) - (4\sqrt{11})(4\sqrt{11})$$
$$= (2 \cdot 2\sqrt{3 \cdot 3}) - (4 \cdot 4\sqrt{11 \cdot 11})$$
$$= 4\sqrt{3^2} - 16\sqrt{11^2}$$
$$= 4 \cdot 3 - 16 \cdot 11$$
$$= 12 - 176$$
$$= -164$$

Square both terms.
$$(a \sqrt[n]{x})(b \sqrt[n]{y}) = a\, b \sqrt[n]{x}\, y$$
Multiply.
$\sqrt{3^2} = 3;\ \sqrt{11^2} = 11.$
Multiply before subtracting.
Combine similar terms.

Look back at these products of conjugates. Notice that each conjugate involved one or two radicals. However, *none* of the products contained radicals! We will make use of this concept in the next section.

8.5 DIVIDING RADICAL EXPRESSIONS

We have already looked at division problems like $\sqrt{\dfrac{16}{25}} = \dfrac{4}{5}$ and

$\dfrac{\sqrt{72x^3}}{\sqrt{49}} = \dfrac{6x\sqrt{x}}{7}$ where the denominators became rational numbers. Other division problems may require the technique called "rationalizing the denominator" outlined below.

Division with Radicals:

1. Reduce, if possible, using $\dfrac{\sqrt{a}}{\sqrt{b}} = \sqrt{\dfrac{a}{b}}$.

2. If the denominator is a monomial, multiply by $\dfrac{\sqrt{b}}{\sqrt{b}}$.

3. If the denominator is a binomial, multiply the numerator and denominator by the conjugate of the denominator.
4. Reduce, if possible.

Rationalizing monomial denominators

Example 13 Simplify.

a) $\sqrt{\dfrac{1}{5}}$

b) $\sqrt{\dfrac{20}{7}}$

c) $\dfrac{10\sqrt{12}}{2\sqrt{6}}$

d) $\sqrt[3]{\dfrac{1}{2}}$

e) $\sqrt[3]{\dfrac{2}{25}}$

Solution 13

a) $\sqrt{\dfrac{1}{5}} = \dfrac{\sqrt{1}}{\sqrt{5}}$

The fraction will not reduce. Rewrite the fraction using $\sqrt{\dfrac{a}{b}} = \dfrac{\sqrt{a}}{\sqrt{b}}$.

$= \dfrac{\sqrt{1}}{\sqrt{5}} \cdot \dfrac{\sqrt{5}}{\sqrt{5}}$

Multiply by $\dfrac{\sqrt{5}}{\sqrt{5}}$ to make the denominator a rational number.

$(a \sqrt[n]{x})(b \sqrt[n]{y}) = a \cdot b \sqrt[n]{x \cdot y}$

$= \dfrac{\sqrt{5}}{\sqrt{5}}$

Use the rule for multiplying radicals:

$= \dfrac{\sqrt{5}}{5}$

Simplify the denominator: $\sqrt{5^2} = 5$.

b) $\sqrt{\dfrac{20}{7}} = \dfrac{\sqrt{20}}{\sqrt{7}}$

The fraction will not reduce. Rewrite the fraction using $\sqrt{\dfrac{a}{b}} = \dfrac{\sqrt{a}}{\sqrt{b}}$.

$= \dfrac{\sqrt{20}}{\sqrt{7}} \dfrac{\sqrt{7}}{\sqrt{7}}$

Multiply by $\dfrac{\sqrt{7}}{\sqrt{7}}$ to make the denominator a rational number.

$= \dfrac{\sqrt{140}}{\sqrt{7^2}}$

Use the rule for multiplying radicals:

$(a \sqrt[n]{x})(b \sqrt[n]{y}) = a \cdot b \sqrt[n]{x \cdot y}$.

$= \dfrac{\sqrt{140}}{\sqrt{7}}$

Simplify the numerator and the denominator.

$$\sqrt{140} = \sqrt{2^2 \cdot 5 \cdot 7} = 2\sqrt{35}$$

$$= \frac{2\sqrt{35}}{7}$$

Final answer.

c) $\dfrac{10\sqrt{12}}{2\sqrt{6}} = \dfrac{10}{2}\sqrt{\dfrac{12}{6}}$

Use $\dfrac{\sqrt{a}}{\sqrt{b}} = \sqrt{\dfrac{a}{b}}$.

$$= 5\sqrt{2}$$

Reduce.

There is no radical in the denominator, so we are finished.

d) $\sqrt[3]{\dfrac{1}{2}} = \dfrac{\sqrt[3]{1}}{\sqrt[3]{2}}$

The fraction will not reduce.

$$\sqrt[3]{\dfrac{a}{b}} = \dfrac{\sqrt[3]{a}}{\sqrt[3]{b}}$$

Rewrite the fraction using .

$$= \dfrac{\sqrt[3]{1}}{\sqrt[3]{2}} \cdot \dfrac{\sqrt[3]{2^2}}{\sqrt[3]{2^2}}$$

This is not a square root. You must multiply by $\sqrt[3]{2^2}$ to produce a rational denominator.

$$= \dfrac{\sqrt[3]{4}}{\sqrt[3]{2^3}}$$

Use the rule for multiplying radicals:

$$(a\ \sqrt[n]{x})(b\ \sqrt[n]{y}) = a \cdot b\ \sqrt[n]{x} \cdot y.$$

$$= \dfrac{\sqrt[3]{4}}{2}$$

Simplify the denominator:

$$\sqrt[3]{2^2} = 2.$$

e) $\dfrac{\sqrt[3]{2}}{25} = \dfrac{\sqrt[3]{2}}{\sqrt[3]{5^2}}$

The fraction will not reduce. Rewrite the fraction using $\dfrac{\sqrt{a}}{\sqrt{b}} = \sqrt{\dfrac{a}{b}}$.

$$= \dfrac{\sqrt[3]{2}}{\sqrt[3]{5^2}} \cdot \dfrac{\sqrt[3]{5^1}}{\sqrt[3]{5^1}}$$

$$\sqrt[3]{5^2} \cdot \sqrt[3]{5^1} = \sqrt[3]{5^3} = 5$$

$$= \frac{\sqrt[3]{2 \cdot 5}}{\sqrt[3]{5^3}}$$

Multiply the numerators; multiply the denominators.

$$= \frac{\sqrt[3]{10}}{5}$$

Simplify the denominator:
$\sqrt[3]{5^3} = 5 = 5$.

Rationalizing binomial denominators

Example 14 Rationalize the denominator by multiplying by the conjugate in each of the following:

a) $\dfrac{\sqrt{2}}{5 + \sqrt{3}}$

b) $\dfrac{12}{3 - \sqrt{3}}$

c) $\dfrac{2 - \sqrt{5}}{\sqrt{7} + \sqrt{2}}$

Solution 14

a) $\dfrac{\sqrt{2}}{5 + \sqrt{3}} = \dfrac{\sqrt{2}}{5 + \sqrt{3}} \cdot \dfrac{(5 - \sqrt{3})}{(5 - \sqrt{3})}$

Conjugate of $5 + \sqrt{3}$ is $5 - \sqrt{3}$.

$$= \frac{5\sqrt{2} - \sqrt{6}}{(5)^2 - (\sqrt{3})^2}$$

Use the Distributive Property to multiply the numerator. Use $(a + b)(a - b) = a^2 - b^2$ to multiply the conjugates in the denominator.

$$= \frac{5\sqrt{2} - \sqrt{6}}{25 - 3}$$

Square both terms in the denominator.

$$= \frac{5\sqrt{2} - \sqrt{6}}{22}$$

Combine similar terms in the denominator.

b) $\dfrac{12}{3 - \sqrt{3}} = \dfrac{12}{3 - \sqrt{3}} \cdot \dfrac{(3 + \sqrt{3})}{(3 + \sqrt{3})}$

Conjugate of $3 - \sqrt{3}$ is $3 + \sqrt{3}$.

$$= \frac{12(3 + \sqrt{3})}{(3)^2 - (\sqrt{3})^2}$$

$$= \frac{12(3 + \sqrt{3})}{9 - 3}$$

Use $(a + b)(a - b) = a^2 - b^2$ to multiply the conjugates in the denominator.

$$= \frac{12(3 + \sqrt{3})}{6}$$

Square both terms in the denominator.

$$= 2(3 + \sqrt{3})$$

Reduce $\frac{12}{6} = 2$.

Sometimes leaving the numerator factored can make reducing easier. If we had multiplied $12(3 + \sqrt{3}) = 36 + 12\sqrt{3})$, we would have had to factor before reducing!

c) $\dfrac{2 - \sqrt{5}}{\sqrt{7} + \sqrt{2}} = \dfrac{2 - \sqrt{5}}{\sqrt{7} + \sqrt{2}} \quad \dfrac{(\sqrt{7} - \sqrt{2})}{(\sqrt{7} - \sqrt{2})}$

Conjugate of $\sqrt{7} + \sqrt{2}$ is $\sqrt{7} - \sqrt{2}$.

$$= \frac{2\sqrt{7} - 2\sqrt{2} - \sqrt{5}\sqrt{7} + \sqrt{5}\sqrt{2}}{(\sqrt{7})^2 - (\sqrt{2})^2}$$

Use FOIL to multiply the numerators.
Use $(a + b)(a - b) = a^2 - b^2$ to multiply the conjugates in the denominator.

$$= \frac{2\sqrt{7} - 2\sqrt{2} - \sqrt{35} + \sqrt{10}}{7 - 2}$$

Square both terms in the denominator.

$$= \frac{2\sqrt{7} - 2\sqrt{2} - \sqrt{35} + \sqrt{10}}{5}$$

There are no common factors in the numerator and denominator, so the fraction does not reduce.

8.6 SOLVING EQUATIONS CONTAINING RADICAL EXPRESSIONS

Solving equations containing radicals makes use of the technique of squaring both sides of an equation. This technique can produce extraneous solutions—that is, solutions that will not check in the original equation. You *must* check every solution!

Steps for solving equations

> **To Solve an Equation Containing Radicals:**
> 1. Isolate one radical on one side of the equation.
> 2. Square both sides of the equation. Remember that $(a + b)^2 = a^2 + 2ab + b^2$.
> 3. Combine similar terms.
> 4. If there is still a radical in the equation, go back to Step 1.
> 5. Solve the resulting equation. If the resulting equation is linear, isolate the variable. If the resulting equation is a quadratic equation, get 0 on one side and factor.
> 6. Check all proposed solutions in the original equation.

Example 15   Solve.

a) $\sqrt{x - 2} = 5$

b) $\sqrt{a + 2} = -3$

c) $\sqrt{2p - 3} + 4 = 6$

d) $\sqrt{3x + 1} = x - 3$

e) $\sqrt{32 + x} - \sqrt{x} = 4$

Solution 15

a) $\sqrt{x - 2} = 5$

$(\sqrt{x - 2})^2 = (5)^2$ Square both sides.

$x - 2 = 25$ $(\sqrt{x - 2})^2 = (\sqrt{x - 2})^2 = x - 2.$

$\dfrac{+2 \ +2}{x = 27}$ Proposed solution.

Check:
$\sqrt{27 - 2} = 5$

$\sqrt{25} = 5$ True, so $x = 27$ is the solution.

b) $\sqrt{a + 2} = -3$

$(\sqrt{a + 2})^2 = (-3)^2$ Square both sides.
This is a linear equation. Isolate the variable.

$a + 2 = 9$
$\dfrac{-2 \ -2}{a = 7}$ Proposed solution.

Check:
$$\sqrt{7} + 2 = -3$$
$$\sqrt{9} = -3$$

False, so there is no solution. Remember that if there is no sign in front of the radical, we are asking for the positive square root of the radicand. Thus, $\sqrt{9} \neq -3$.

c) $\sqrt{2p - 3} + 4 = 6$ Isolate the radical.
          $\underline{-4 \quad -4}$

      $\sqrt{2p - 3} = 2$
      $(\sqrt{2p - 3}) = (2)^2$ Square both sides.

      $2p - 3 = 4$ This is a linear equation. Isolate the
      $\underline{+3 + 3}$

      $2p = 7$ variable.

      $p = \dfrac{7}{2}$ Proposed solution.

Check:
$$\sqrt{2\left(\dfrac{7}{2}\right) - 3} + 4 = 6$$
$$\sqrt{7 - 3} + 4 = 6$$
$$\sqrt{4} + 4 = 6$$ True, so $p = \dfrac{7}{2}$ is the solution.

d) $\sqrt{3x + 1} = x - 3$
      $(\sqrt{3x + 1})^2 = (x - 3)^2$ Square both sides.
      $3x + 1 = x^2 - 6x + 9$ $(x - 3)^2 = (x)^2 - 2(x)(3) + (3)^2.$
      $\underline{-3x - 1 \qquad -3x - 1}$
      $0 = x^2 - 9x + 8$ This is a quadratic equation. Get 0
                                            alone on one side.
      $(x - 8)(x - 1) = 0$ Factor.
           $x = 8$ or $x = 1$ Proposed solutions.

Check:
If $x = 8$:   If $x = 1$:
$$\sqrt{3(8) + 1} = \sqrt{3(1) + 1} = 1 - 3$$

$$\sqrt{25} = 5 \text{ True.}$$

                                True. $\sqrt{4} = -2$
                                False. $\sqrt{4}$ means the positive square
                                root of 4, which is 2.
                                Only $x = 8$ is a solution.

e) $\sqrt{32 + x} - \sqrt{x} = 4$ Isolate one radical.
                                                                  $+\sqrt{x} \ \underline{+\sqrt{x}}$

$$\sqrt{32 + x} = \sqrt{x} + 4$$
$$(\sqrt{32 + x})^2 = (\sqrt{x} + 4)^2 + 4$$ Square both sides.

$$32 + x = x + 8\sqrt{x} + 16$$ $(\sqrt{x} + 4)^2 = (\sqrt{x})^2 + 2\sqrt{x}(4) + (4)^2$
$$\underline{-16 - x = -x \qquad -16}$$
$$16 = 8\sqrt{x}$$ There is still a radical in the
                                                                  equation. Isolate the radical.

$$\frac{1}{8}(16) = \frac{1}{8}(8\sqrt{x})$$
$$(2)^2 = (\sqrt{x})^2$$ Square both sides.
$$4 = x$$ Proposed solution.

Check:
$$\sqrt{32 + 4} - \sqrt{4} = 4$$
$$\sqrt{36} - \sqrt{4} = 4$$
$$6 - 2 = 4$$ True, so $x = 4$ is the solution.

Practice Exercises

1. Find each square root.
   - (a) $\sqrt{64}$
   - (b) $-\sqrt{81}$
   - (c) $\sqrt{\dfrac{9}{4}}$
   - (d) $\dfrac{-\sqrt{49}}{-\sqrt{4}}$

2. Find each root, if it exists.
   - (a) $\sqrt[3]{-27}$
   - (b) $\sqrt{1}$
   - (c) $\sqrt[3]{343}$
   - (d) $\sqrt[3]{-16}$

3. Simplify.
   - (a) $\sqrt{147x^3y^2}$
   - (b) $5a\sqrt{50a^2b}$
   - (c) $p^2q\sqrt[3]{64p^4q^5}$

4. Simplify.
   - (a) $\sqrt{\dfrac{9}{100}}$
   - (b) $\sqrt[3]{\dfrac{216x^6}{343y^3}}$
   - (c) $\sqrt{\dfrac{32}{50}}$

5. Simplify.
   - (a) $\sqrt{\dfrac{98x}{25}}$
   - (b) $\sqrt{\dfrac{360}{10}}$
   - (c) $\dfrac{\sqrt[3]{125x^2}}{8}$

6. Perform the indicated operations.
   - (a) $\sqrt{13} + 4\sqrt{13}$
   - (b) $5\sqrt{72} + \sqrt{8}$
   - (c) $\sqrt{200t} - \sqrt{128t} + 6\sqrt{2t}$
   - (d) $4\sqrt{147} - \sqrt{27}$

7. Multiply.
   - (a) $(4\sqrt{3})(-5\sqrt{7})$
   - (b) $\sqrt{10}(3 - 4\sqrt{6})$
   - (c) $(3 - 2\sqrt{5})(4 - 6\sqrt{5})$
   - (d) $(3\sqrt{x} + 1)(2\sqrt{x} - 4)$

8. Multiply.
   - (a) $(3 + \sqrt{5})^2$
   - (b) $(2\sqrt{3} - 4)^2$
   - (c) $(5 - \sqrt{2})(5 + \sqrt{2})$
   - (d) $(\sqrt{a} + 4)^2$

9. Simplify.
   - (a) $\sqrt{\dfrac{11}{3}}$
   - (b) $\sqrt{\dfrac{27}{7}}$
   - (c) $\dfrac{8\sqrt{16}}{2\sqrt{8}}$
   - (d) $\sqrt[3]{\dfrac{1}{3}}$

10. Rationalize each denominator.
   - (a) $\dfrac{5}{2 + \sqrt{3}}$
   - (b) $\dfrac{\sqrt{6}}{3 - \sqrt{5}}$
   - (c) $\dfrac{4 + \sqrt{3}}{\sqrt{2} + \sqrt{3}}$

11. Solve.

(a) $\sqrt{3x + 1} = 4$

(b) $\sqrt{x - 4} = -2$

(c) $\sqrt{4a + 1} - 3 = 2$

(d) $\sqrt{x + 3} = x - 3$

(e) $4 - \sqrt{x} = \sqrt{x + 8}$

Answers

1. (a) 8
   (b) -9
   (c) $\dfrac{3}{2}$
   (d) $\dfrac{7}{2}$

2. (a) -3
   (b) 1
   (c) 7
   (d) does not exist

3. (a) $7xy\sqrt{3x}$
   (b) $25a^2\sqrt{2b}$
   (c) $4p^3 q^2 \sqrt[3]{pq^2}$

4. (a) $\dfrac{3}{10}$
   (b) $\dfrac{6x^2}{7y}$
   (c) $\dfrac{4}{5}$

5. (a) $\dfrac{7\sqrt{2x}}{5}$
   (b) 6
   (c) $\dfrac{5x^2 \sqrt[3]{x}}{2}$

6. (a) $5\sqrt{13}$
   (b) $32\sqrt{2}$
   (c) $8\sqrt{2t}$
   (d) $25\sqrt{3}$

7. (a) $-20\sqrt{21}$
   (b) $3\sqrt{10} - 8\sqrt{15}$
   (c) $72 - 26\sqrt{5}$
   (d) $6x - 10\sqrt{x} - 4$

8. (a) $14 + 6\sqrt{5}$
   (b) $28 - 16\sqrt{3}$
   (c) 23
   (d) $a + 8\sqrt{a} + 16$

9. (a) $\dfrac{\sqrt{33}}{3}$
   (b) $\dfrac{3\sqrt{21}}{7}$
   (c) $4\sqrt{2}$
   (d) $\dfrac{\sqrt[3]{9}}{3}$

10. (a) $10 - 5\sqrt{3}$
    (b) $\dfrac{3\sqrt{6} + \sqrt{30}}{4}$
    (c) $-4\sqrt{2} + 4\sqrt{3} - \sqrt{6} + 3$

11. (a) 5
    (b) no solution
    (c) 6
    (d) 6
    (e) 1

9

Quadratic Equations

9.1 SOLVING QUADRATIC EQUATIONS USING THE SQUARE ROOT METHOD

The square root property

A quadratic equation can be written as
$$ax^2 + bx + c = 0,$$

where a, b, and c are real numbers and $a \neq 0$. A quadratic equation like $x^2 = 16$ can be solved in your head to give solutions of $x = 4$ or $x = -4$. In so doing, you are making use of the following property:

The Square Root Property:
If $a^2 = b$, then $a = \sqrt{b}$ or $a = \sqrt{b}$.

Note: If $b \geq 0$, the solutions are real numbers. If $b < 0$, the solutions are complex numbers (see Section 8.4 on complex numbers).

To Solve Using the Square Root Property:
1. Isolate the squared term (it may be x^2 or $(x + d)^2$ or $(x - d)^2$) on one side of the equation and the constant term on the other side of the equation.
2. Take the square root of both sides of the equation.
3. Use $+\sqrt{\text{constant}}$ and $-\sqrt{\text{constant}}$, which is usually written $\pm\sqrt{\text{constant}}$.
4. Simplify the radicals.
5. Solve for x, if necessary.
6. Check the answers.

Example 1   Solve.

a) $x^2 = 25$
b) $y^2 = 6$
c) $(x - 2)^2 = 16$
d) $(x + 1)^2 = 8$
e) $2m^2 - 7 = 47$
f) $(x - 3)^2 = -4$

Solution 1

a) $x^2 = 25$

$\sqrt{x^2} = \pm\sqrt{25}$ Take the square root of both sides, using on the right.

$x = \pm 5$ Simplify the radicals.

This means $x = 5$ or $x = -5$.

b) $y^2 = 6$

$\sqrt{y^2} = \pm\sqrt{6}$ Take the square root of both sides, using on the right.

$y = \pm\sqrt{6}$ Simplify the radicals.

c) $(x - 2)^2 = 16$

$\sqrt{(x - 2)^2}$ Take the square root of both sides, using on the right.

$x - 2 = 4$ Simplify the radicals.

$\underline{+2 = +2}$

$x = 2 + 4$ Solve for x by adding 2 to both sides.

Since 2 can be combined with 4, we separate the two possible solutions to solve for x as follows:

$x - 2 = 4$	or	$x - 2 = -4$
$\underline{+2 + 2}$		$\underline{+2 + 2}$
$x = 6$		$x = -2$

Solve for x.

Check: $(x - 2)^2 = 16$ Original equation.

$((6) - 2)^2 \overset{?}{=} 16$ Substitute $x = 6$ into the original equation.

$4^2 \overset{?}{=} 16$ Simplify inside parentheses.

$16 = 16$ A true statement, so 6 is a solution.

$((-2) - 2)^2 \overset{?}{=} 16$ Substitute $x = -2$ into the original equation.

$(-4)^2 \overset{?}{=} 16$ Simplify inside parentheses.

$$16 = 16$$

A true statement, so -2 is a solution.

d) $(x+1)^2 = 8$

$\sqrt{(x+1)^2}$

Take the square root of both sides, using $\pm$ on the right
Simplify the radicals.

$x + 1 = \pm 2\sqrt{2}$

$\underline{-1\ -1}$

$x = -1 \pm 2\sqrt{2}$

Solve for x. Subtract 1 from both sides of the equation.

Since -1 cannot be combined with $\pm 2\sqrt{2}$, we do not need to separate the two solutions to solve for x.

Check: $(x+1)^2 = 8$

$((-1 + 2\sqrt{2}) + 1)^2 \overset{?}{=} 8$

$(2\sqrt{2})^2 \overset{?}{=} 8$

$8 = 8$

Original equation.
Substitute $x = -1 + 2\sqrt{2}$ into the original equation.
Simplify inside parentheses.
A true statement, so $-1 + 2\sqrt{2}$ is a solution.

$((-1 - 2\sqrt{2}) + 1)^2 \overset{?}{=} 8$

$(-2\sqrt{2})^2 \overset{?}{=} 8$

$8 = 8$

Substitue $x = -1 - 2\sqrt{2}$ into the original equation.
Simplify inside parentheses.

A true statement, so $-1 - 2\sqrt{2}$ is a solution.

$((-1 + 2\sqrt{2}) + 1)^2 \overset{?}{=} 8$

$(2\sqrt{2})^2 \overset{?}{=} 8$

$8 = 8$

Substitute $x = -1 + 2\sqrt{2}$ into the original equation.
Simplify inside parentheses.
A true statement, so $-1 + 2\sqrt{2}$ is a solution.

$((-1 - 2\sqrt{2}) + 1)^2 \overset{?}{=} 8$

$(-2\sqrt{2})^2 \overset{?}{=} 8$

$8 = 8$

Substitue $x = -1 - 2\sqrt{2}$ into the original equation.
Simplify inside parentheses.

A true statement, so -1 - $2\sqrt{2}$ is a solution.

e) $2m^2 - 7 = 47$

$\underline{+7\ \ +7}$

$2m^2 = 54$

Isolate the squared term first.

$\dfrac{2m^2}{2} = \dfrac{54}{2}$

$m^2 = 27 =$

Divide both sides by 2.

$$\sqrt{m^2} \pm \sqrt{27}$$

Take the square root of both sides, using $\pm$ on the right.

$$m = \pm 3\sqrt{3}$$

Simplify the radicals.

Check: $2m^2 - 7 = 47$

Original equation.

$$2(3\sqrt{3})^2 - 7 \overset{?}{=} 47$$

Substitute $x = 3\sqrt{3}$ into the original equation.

$$2(27) - 7 \overset{?}{=} 47$$

Simplify exponents before multiplying.

$$54 - 7 = 47$$

A true statement, so $3\sqrt{3}$ is a solution.

$$2(-3\sqrt{3})2 - 7 \overset{?}{=} 47$$

Substitute $x = -3\sqrt{3}$ into the original equation. $(-3\sqrt{3})2 = (-3\sqrt{3})(-3\sqrt{3}) = 9\sqrt{3}^2 = 27$.

$$2(27) - 7 \overset{?}{=} 47$$

$$54 - 7 = 47$$

A true statement, so $-3\sqrt{3}$ is a solution.

f) $(x - 3)^2 = -4$

$$\sqrt{(x - 3)^2}$$

These will *not* be real solutions since the square root of a negative number is not a real number.

No real number solutions.

9.2 SOLVING QUADRATIC EQUATIONS USING COMPLETING THE SQUARE

We will use the technique of completing the square in this section to solve quadratic equations; if you continue your study of mathematics, you will also use this process to find such things as the center of a circle and the vertex of a parabola.

**Completing
the square**

> **To Solve a Quadratic Equation by Completing the Square:**
> 1. Isolate the x^2 and x term on one side of the equation so the equation has the form $ax^2 + bx = c$. 2. If $a \neq 1$, divide every term by a, the coefficient of x^2. Equation should now have the form $x^2 + \dfrac{b}{a}x = \dfrac{c}{a}$
> 3. Add $\left(\dfrac{1}{2}\right)$ times the coefficient of x to both sides of the equation.
>
> 4. Simplify the right side of the equation.
> 5. Write the left side as a perfect square trinomial.
> 6. Solve using the Square Root Property.
> 7. Check the answers in the original equation.

Example 2   Solve by completing the square.
a) $x^2 + 6x - 7 = 0$
b) $x^2 - 5x + 4 = 0$
c) $x^2 + 4x + 1 = 0$

Solution 2

a) $x^2 + 6x - 7 = 0$ Isolate $x^2 + 6x$.

$$\underline{\quad +7 \quad +7 \quad}$$

$x^2 + 6x = 7$ Coefficient of $x^2 = 1$.

$x^2 + 6x + 9 = 7 + 9$ $\left(\dfrac{1}{2} \cdot 6\right)^2 = (3)^2 = 9$

$(x + 3)^2 = 16$ Factor.

$\sqrt{(x + 3)^2} = \pm\sqrt{16}$ Take the square root of both sides.

$x + 3 = \pm 4$ Simplify the radicals.

$x + 3 = 4$ or $x + 3 = -4$ Solve for x.
$\underline{\;-3\; -3\;}$ $\underline{\;-3\; -3\;}$
$x = 1$ or $x = -7$

Check: $x^2 + 6x - 7 = 0$ Original equation.

$(1)2 + 6(1) - 7 \stackrel{?}{=} 0$ Substitute $x = 1$ into the original equation.

$1 + 6 - 7 \stackrel{?}{=} 0$ Simplify.

$0 = 0$ A true statement, so $x = 1$ is a solution.

$$(-7)^2 + 6(-7) - 7 \stackrel{?}{=} 0$$

Substitute $x = -7$ into the original equation.

$$49 - 42 - 7 \stackrel{?}{=} 0$$

Simplify.

$$0 = 0$$

A true statement, so $x = -7$ is a solution.

b) $x^2 - 5x + 4 = 0$

Isolate $x^2 - 5x$.

$$\frac{-4 \quad -4}{x^2 - 5x \quad = -4}$$

Coefficient of x^2 is 1.

$$x^2 - 5x + \frac{25}{4} = -4 + \frac{25}{4}$$

$$\left(\frac{1}{2} \cdot -5\right)^2 = \left(-\frac{5}{2}\right)^2 \frac{25}{4}$$

$$x^2 - 5x + \frac{25}{4} = \frac{9}{4}$$

$$-\frac{4}{1} + \frac{25}{4} = -\frac{16}{4} + \frac{25}{4} = \frac{9}{4}$$

$$\left(x - \frac{5}{2}\right)^2 = \frac{9}{4}$$

Factor $x^2 - 5x + \frac{25}{4}$.

$$\sqrt{\left(x - \frac{5}{2}\right)^2} = \pm\sqrt{\frac{9}{4}}$$

Take the square root of both sides.

$$x - \frac{5}{2} = \pm\frac{3}{2}$$

Simplify the radicals.

$$x - \frac{5}{2} = \frac{3}{2} \qquad \text{or} \qquad x - \frac{5}{2} = \frac{3}{2}$$

Solve for x.

$$\frac{+\frac{5}{2} + \frac{5}{2}}{x = \frac{8}{2}} \qquad\qquad \frac{+\frac{5}{2} + \frac{5}{2}}{x = \frac{2}{2}}$$

$$x = 4 \qquad \text{or} \qquad x = 1$$

Check: Try the check on your own.

c) $x^2 + 4x + 5 = 0$

Isolate $x^2 + 4x$.

$$\frac{5 \quad -5}{x^2 + 4x \quad = -1}$$

Coefficient of x^2 is 1.

$$x^2 + 4x + 4 = -5 + 4$$

$$\left(\frac{1}{2} \cdot 4\right)^2 = (2)^2 = 4$$

$$x^2 + 4x + 4 = 9$$

Simplify right side.

$$(x+2)^2 = 9$$

Factor $x^2 + 4x + 4$.

$$\sqrt{(x+2)^2} = \pm\sqrt{9}$$

Take the square root of both sides.

$$x + 2 = \pm\sqrt{3}$$

Simplify the radicals.

$$\underline{-2\quad -2}$$
$$x = -2\ \sqrt{3}\quad x = -5 \text{ or } x = -2 -3 \text{ or}$$

Solve for x.

Solving quadratic equations by completing the square when $a \neq 1$

Example 3   Solve by completing the square.
a) $2x^2 - 4x - 6 = 0$
b) $2x^2 - 10x + 12 = 0$
c) $4x^2 + 9x + 3 = 0$
d) $3x^2 + 5x + 3 = 0$

Solution 3

a) $2x^2 - 4x - 6 = 0$

Isolate $2x^2 - 4x$.

$$\underline{+6\qquad +6}$$
$$2x^2 - 4x \quad = 6$$

$$\frac{2x^2}{2} - \frac{4x}{2} = \frac{6}{2}$$

Divide every term by 2 to make the coefficient of $x^2 = 1$.

$$x^2 - 2x = 3$$

$$x^2 - 2x + 1 = 3 + 1$$

$$\left(\frac{1}{2}\cdot -2\right)2 = (-1)^2 = 1$$

$$x^2 - 2x + 1 = 4$$

Simplify the right side.

$$(x-1)^2 = 4$$

Factor $x^2 - 2x + 1$.

$$\sqrt{(x-1)^2} = \pm\sqrt{4}$$

Take the square root of both sides.

$$x - 1 = \pm 2$$

Solve for x.

$$\underline{+1\qquad +1}$$
$$x \quad = 1 \pm 2$$

Separate into two equations to solve for x.

$$x = 1 + 2 \qquad\qquad x = 1 - 2$$
$$x = 3 \qquad\qquad\quad x = -1$$

Check: $2x^2 - 4x - 6 = 0$

Original equation.

$2(3)^2 - 4(3) - 6 \overset{?}{=} 0$

Substitute $x = 3$ into the original equation.

$2(9) - 4(3) - 6 \overset{?}{=} 0$

Simplify exponents before multiplying.

$18 - 12 - 6 \overset{?}{=} 0$

Multiply before subtracting.

$0 = 0$

A true statement, so $x = 3$ is a solution.

$2(-1)2 - 4(-1) - 6 \overset{?}{=} 0$

Substitute $x = -1$ into the original equation.

$2(1) - 4(-1) - 6 \overset{?}{=} 0$

Simplify exponents before multiplying.

$2 + 4 - 6 \overset{?}{=} 0$

Multiply before adding and subtracting.

$0 = 0$

A true statement, so $x = -1$ is a solution.

b) $2x^2 - 10x + 12 = 0$

Isolate $2x^2 - 10x$.

$$\underline{\quad\quad - 12\, -12\quad\quad}$$

$2x^2 - 10x = -12$

$\dfrac{2x^2}{2} - \dfrac{10x}{2} = \dfrac{-12}{2}$

Divide every term by 2 to make the coefficient of $x^2 = 1$.

$x^2 - 5x = -6$

$x^2 - 5x + \dfrac{25}{4} = -6 + \dfrac{25}{4}$

$\left(\dfrac{1}{2} \cdot -5\right)^2 = \dfrac{25}{4}$

$x^2 - 5x + \dfrac{25}{4} = \dfrac{1}{4}$

Factor.

$\sqrt{\left(x - \dfrac{5}{2}\right)^2} = \pm\sqrt{\dfrac{1}{4}}$

Take the square root of both sides.

$x - \dfrac{5}{2} = \pm\dfrac{1}{2}$

Simplify the radicals.

$$x - \frac{5}{2} = \frac{1}{2} \qquad \text{or} \qquad x - \frac{5}{2} = -\frac{1}{2}$$

$$+\frac{5}{2} \quad +\frac{5}{2} \qquad\qquad\qquad +\frac{5}{2} \quad +\frac{5}{2}$$

$$x \quad = \frac{6}{2} \qquad\qquad\qquad\qquad x \quad = \frac{4}{2}$$

$$x = 3 \text{ or } x = 2$$

Check: Try the check on your own.

c) $4x^2 + 9x + 3 = 0$ Isolate $4x^2 + 9x$.

$$\underline{-3 \;\; -3}$$

$$4x^2 + 9x = -3$$

$$\frac{4x^2}{4} + \frac{9x}{4} = -\frac{3}{4} \qquad\qquad \text{Divide every term by 4.}$$

$$x^2 + \frac{9}{4}x = -\frac{3}{4}$$

$$x^2 + \frac{9}{4}x + \frac{81}{64} = -\frac{3}{4} + \frac{81}{64} \qquad \left(\frac{1}{2} \cdot \frac{9}{4}\right)^2 = \left(\frac{9}{8}\right)^2 = \frac{81}{64}$$

$$x^2 + \frac{9}{4}x + \frac{81}{64} = \frac{33}{64} \qquad \left(-\frac{3}{4} \cdot \frac{16}{16}\right) + \frac{81}{64} =$$

$$-\frac{48}{64} = -\frac{48}{64} + \frac{81}{64} = \frac{33}{64}$$

$$\left(x + \frac{9}{8}\right)^2 = \frac{33}{64}$$

$$\sqrt{\left(x + \frac{9}{8}\right)^2} = \pm\sqrt{\frac{33}{64}} \qquad \text{Take the square root of both sides.}$$

$$x + \frac{9}{8} = \pm\frac{\sqrt{33}}{8} \qquad\qquad \text{Simplify the radicals.}$$

$$\underline{-\frac{9}{8} \qquad -\frac{9}{8}}$$

$$x = -\frac{9}{8} \pm \frac{\sqrt{33}}{8} \qquad\qquad \text{Solve for } x.$$

d) $3x^2 + 5x + 3 = 0$ Isolate $3x^2 + 5x$.

$$\underline{ -3 \;\; -3}$$

$$3x^2 + 5x = -3$$

$$\frac{3x^2}{3} + \frac{5x}{3} = -\frac{3}{3}$$ Divide every term by 3.

$$x^2 + \frac{5}{3}x = -1$$

$$x^2 + \frac{5}{3}x + \frac{25}{36} = -1 + \frac{25}{36}$$ $\left(\frac{1}{2} \cdot \frac{5}{3}\right)^2 = \left(\frac{5}{6}\right)^2 = \frac{25}{36}$

$$x^2 + \frac{5}{3}x + \frac{25}{36} = -$$ $-1 + \frac{25}{36} = -\frac{36}{36} + \frac{25}{36} = -\frac{11}{36}$

$$\left(x + \frac{5}{6}\right)^2 = -\frac{11}{36}$$

Stop here! There are no real number solutions because no real number squared can equal $-\frac{11}{36}$.

9.3 Solving Quadratic Equations Using the Quadratic Formula

Although completing the square can be used to solve any quadratic equation, it can be a long process. The quadratic formula can also be used to solve any quadratic equation, but you must memorize the formula to use it!

The quadratic formula

The Quadratic Formula:

The solutions to $ax^2 + bx + c = 0$, $a \neq 0$, are

$$x = \frac{-b \pm \sqrt{b^2 - 4ac}}{2a}$$

Solving quadratic equations using the quadratic formula

> **To Solve a Quadratic Equation Using the Formula:**
> 1. Put the equation in standard form: $ax^2 + bx + c = 0$. Multiply both sides by the LCD to clear fractions, if necessary.
> 2. Write down the values for a, b, and c.
> 3. Substitute the values for a, b, and c into the Quadratic Formula.
> 4. Simplify under the radical.
> 5. Simplify the radical, if possible.
> 6. Factor the numerator to reduce, if possible.
> 7. Check the answers.

Example 4   Solve using the Quadratic Formula.

a) $x^2 - 5x + 4 = 0$

b) $x^2 + 4x = -1$

c) $4x^2 = -12x - 9$

d) $\frac{1}{6}x^2 + x = -\frac{5}{12}$

Solution 4

a) $x^2 - 5x + 4 = 0$ Already in standard form.

$a = 1, b = -5, c = 4.$ Identify the values for a, b, and c.

$x = \dfrac{-b \pm \sqrt{b^2 - 4ac}}{2a}$

Write the formula

$x = \dfrac{-(-5) \pm \sqrt{(-5)^2 - 4(1)(4)}}{2(1)}$

Substitute the values for a, b, and c.

$x = \dfrac{5 \pm \sqrt{9}}{2}$

$(-5)^2 - 4(1)(4) = 25 - 16 = 9$

$x = \dfrac{5 \pm 3}{2}$

Simplify the radical.

$x = \dfrac{5 + 3}{2}$ or $x = \dfrac{5 - 3}{2}$

Solve for x.

$x = \dfrac{8}{2} = 4$ or $x = \dfrac{2}{2} = 1$

Check: $x^2 - 5x + 4 = 0$ Original equation.

$(4)^2 - 5(4) + 4 \overset{?}{=} 0$ Substitute $x = 4$ into the original
                                              equation.

$16 - 20 + 4 \overset{?}{=} 0$ Simplify.

$0 = 0$ A true statement, so $x = 4$ is a
                                              solution.

$(1)^2 - 5(1) + 4 \overset{?}{=} =$ Substitute $x = 1$ into the original
                                              equation.

$1 - 5 + 4 \overset{?}{=} 0$ Simplify.

$0 = 0$ A true statement, so $x = 1$ is a
                                              solution.

b) $x^2 + 4x = -1$

$\underline{+1 \quad +1}$ Put in standard form:
                                              $ax^2 + bx + c = 0$.

$x^2 + 4x + 1 = 0$

$a = 1, b = 4, c = 1$ Identify the values for a, b, and c.

$x = \dfrac{-b \pm \sqrt{b^2 - 4ac}}{2a}$ Write the formula.

$x = \dfrac{-(4) \pm \sqrt{(4)^2 - 4(1)(1)}}{2(1)}$ Substitute the values for a, b, and c.

$x = \dfrac{-4 \pm \sqrt{12}}{2}$ $(4)2 - 4(1)(1) = 16 - 4 + 12$

$x = \dfrac{-4 \pm 2\sqrt{3}}{2}$ Simplify the radical

$x = \dfrac{2(-2 \pm 1\sqrt{3})}{2}$ Factor the numerator.

$x = -2 \pm 1\sqrt{3}$ Reduce the fraction.

$x = -2 \pm \sqrt{3}$

c) $4x^2 \quad = -12x - 9$ Put in standard form.
   $\underline{2x + 9 \quad + \quad 12x + 9}$

         $4x^2 + 12x + 9 = 0$ $a = 4, b = 12, c = 9$

$x = \dfrac{-b \pm \sqrt{b^2 - 4ac}}{2a}$ Write the fomula

$$x = -12 \pm \frac{\sqrt{(12)^2 - 4(4)(9)}}{2(4)}$$

Substitute the values for a, b, and c.

$$x = \frac{-12 \pm \sqrt{0}}{8}$$

$(12)^2 - 4(4)(9) = 144 - 144 = 0$

$$x = \frac{-12 \pm 0}{8}$$

Simplify the radical.

$$x = -\frac{12}{8} = -\frac{3}{2}$$

Simplify the fraction.

Check: Try the check on your own.

d) $\frac{1}{6}x^2 + x = -\frac{5}{12}$

Put in standard form.

$$+\frac{5}{12} \quad +\frac{5}{12}$$

$$\frac{1}{6}x^2 + x + \frac{5}{12} = 0$$

$$12\left(\frac{1}{6}x^2 + x + \frac{5}{12}\right) = 12(0)$$

Multiply by 12 to clear fractions.

$$2x^2 + 12x + 5 = 0$$

$a = 2, b = 12, c = 5$

$$x = \frac{-b \pm \sqrt{b^2 - 4ac}}{2a}$$

Write the formula

$$x = -12 \pm \frac{\sqrt{(12)^2 - 4(2)(5)}}{2(4)}$$

$(12)^2 - 4(2)(5) = 144 - 40 = 104$

$$x = \frac{-12 =- 2\sqrt{26}}{4}$$

$\sqrt{104} = \sqrt{2^2 \cdot 26} = 2\sqrt{26}$

$$x = \frac{-6 =- 2\sqrt{26}}{4}$$

Factor the numerator

$$x = \frac{2(-6 \pm 1\sqrt{26})}{4}$$

Reduce the fraction

Stop here! You cannot reduce $-\frac{6}{2}$ because -6 is a term, not a factor!

Choosing methods to solve quadratic equations

So far you have seen several techniques for solving quadratic equations. When you are given a choice in the method used to solve a quadratic equation, you might consider the following pluses and minuses.

Method	Pluses	Minuses
Factoring	Usually fast.	Doesn't always work.
Completing the Square	Always works. Don't have to memorize a formula.	Many steps.
Quadratic Formula	Always works. Many calculators have the formula in memory.	Must memorize formula.

If you like to factor, try factoring first.
If you are good at memorizing formulas, use the Quadratic Formula.
If you took the time to understand completing the square, go for it!

9.4 COMPLEX NUMBERS

Previously we stated that the square root of a negative number is *not* a real number. Now we'll expand the set of real numbers using i.

Imaginary numbers

Definition: $i = \sqrt{-1}$ and $i^2 = -1$.

Square roots with negative radicands can be simplified using -1 as a factor. Numbers that are multiples of i are called imaginary numbers.

Example 5   Simplify.
a) $\sqrt{-7}$
b) $\sqrt{-4}$
c) $\sqrt{-18}$

Solution 5

a) $\sqrt{-7} = \sqrt{-1 \cdot 7}$ Factor.

$= i\sqrt{7}$ $\sqrt{-1} = i$

b) $\sqrt{-4} = \sqrt{-1 \cdot 2^2}$c)

    $= i \cdot 2$

    $= 2i$

Factor.

$\sqrt{-1} = i$ $\sqrt{2^2} = 2$

c) $\sqrt{-18} = \sqrt{-1 \cdot 2 \cdot 3^2}$

    $= i \cdot$

    $= 3i\sqrt{2}$

Factor

$\sqrt{-1} = i$ $\sqrt{3^2} = 3$

Complex numbers

Our new set of numbers, the complex numbers, contains all the real numbers and the imaginary numbers.

A complex number is in standard form when it is written as $a + bi$, where a and b are real numbers.

Treat i like any other variable, except that i^2 can be simplified to -1.

Adding and subtracting complex numbers

Example 6

Add or subtract, as indicated.
a) $(4 + 2i) + (6 - 7i)$
b) $(3 - 5i) - (2 - 9i)$
c) $(5 - 2i) - (4 - i) - (1 + 3i)$

Solution 6

a) $(4 + 2i) + (6 - 7i)$ $= (4 + 6) + (2 - 7)i$ Combine similar terms. Treat i like a variable.

                               $= 10 - 5i$

b) $(3 - 5i) - (2 - 9i)$ $= (3 - 2) + (-5 + 9)i$ Combine similar terms.

                               $= 1 + 4i$

c) $(5 - 2i) - (4 - i) - (1 + 3i)$

                     $= (5 - 4 - 1) + (-2 + 1 - 3)i$ Combine similar terms.

                     $= 0 + -4i = 4i$

Multiplying complex numbers

Example 7

Multiply.
a) $2i(4 - 3i)$
b) $(2 - 6i)(3 + 5i)$

Solution 7

a) $2i(4-3i)$ $= 8i - 6i^2$ Use the Distributive Property:
$2i(4) - 2i(3i)$

$= 8i - 6(-)$ Use $i^2 = -1$.
$= 8i + 6$

b) $(2-6i)(3+5i)$
$= 2(3) + 2(5i) + (-6i)(3) + (-6i)(5i)$ Use FOIL.
$= 6 + 10i - 18i - 30i^2$ Combine similiar terms:
$(10-18)i = -8i$.

$= 6 - 8i - 30i^2$
$= 6 - 8i - 30(-1)$ Use $i^2 = -1$.
$= 6 - 8i + 30$
$= 36 - 8i$ Add similar terms.

Dividing complex numbers

If a complex number is written as a fraction with i in the denominator, we use a process similar to rationalizing the denominator for radicals to write that complex number in standard form.

> **To Write Complex Number Quotients in Standard Form:**
>
> 1. If the denominator is a monomial involving i, multiply by $\frac{i}{i}$ and simplify. Write the answer in the form $a + bi$.
>
> 2. If the denominator is a binomial involving i, multiply the numerator and denominator by the conjugate of the denominator. Write the answer as $a + bi$.

Recall that the conjugate of $a + b$ is $a - b$, and the conjugate of $a - b$ is $a + b$.

Example 8 Write each quotient in standard form.

a) $\dfrac{2 + 3i}{4i}$

b) $\dfrac{2 - 3i}{1 + 4i}$

c) $\dfrac{6}{2 - 3i}$

Solution 8

a) $\dfrac{2 + 3i}{4i}$ $= \dfrac{2 + 3i}{4i} \cdot \dfrac{i}{i}$ Monomial denominator.

$= \dfrac{2 + 3i^2}{4i^2}$ Distribute i.

$= \dfrac{2i + 3(-1)}{4(-1)}$ $i^2 = -1$.

$$= \frac{2i - 3}{-4}$$

Simplify the numerator. Simplify the denominator.

$$= \frac{2i - 3}{-4} \cdot \frac{-1}{-1}$$

Multiply by $\frac{-1}{-1}$ to make the denominator positive.

$$= \frac{2i + 3}{-4}$$

$$= \frac{3}{4} - \frac{2}{4}i$$

Use $\frac{a+b}{c} = \frac{a}{c} + \frac{b}{c}$ to rewrite the fraction.

$$= \frac{3}{4} - \frac{1}{2}i$$

Write the answer in standard form.

b) $\dfrac{2 - 3i}{1 + 4i}$ $= \dfrac{2 - 3i}{1 + 4i} \cdot \dfrac{1 - 4i}{1 - 4i}$

Conjugate of $1 + 4i$ is $1 - 4i$.

$$= \frac{2 - 8i - 3i + 12i^2}{1 - 4i + 4i - 16i^2}$$

Use FOIL to multiply the numerators and the denominators.

$$= \frac{2 - 11i + 12(-1)}{1 - 16(-1)}$$

$i^2 = -1$.

$$= \frac{2 - 11i - 12}{1 + 16}$$

Combine similar terms in the numerator and denominator.

$$= \frac{-10 - 11i}{17}$$

Use $\dfrac{a+b}{c} = \dfrac{a}{c} + \dfrac{b}{c} =$ to rewrite the fraction.

$$= \frac{-10}{17} - \frac{11}{17}i$$

Write the answer in standard form.

c) $\dfrac{6}{2 - 3i} = \dfrac{6}{2 - 3i} \cdot \dfrac{2 + 3i}{2 + 3i}$

The conjugate of $2 - 3i$ is $2 + 3i$.

$$= \frac{12 + 18i}{4 + 6i - 6i - 9i^2}$$

Use the Distributive Property to multiply the numerators. Use FOIL to multiply the denominators.

$$= \frac{12 + 18i}{4 - 9(-1)}$$

Combine similar trms in the denomina–or: $+6i - 6i = 0$. Use i2 = –1.

$$= \frac{12 + 18i}{4 + 9}$$

Simplify the denominator.

$$= \frac{12 + 18i}{13}$$

Use $\frac{a+b}{c} = \frac{a}{c} + \frac{b}{c}$ to rewrite the fraction.

$$= \frac{12}{13} + \frac{18}{13}i$$

Write the answer in standard form.

Solving quadratic equations with complex solutions

We can now solve quadratic equations that have complex number solutions.

Example 9   Solve each quadratic equation.

a) $(x - 3)^2 = -16$

b) $t^2 - 6t + 10 = 0$

c) $\frac{2}{5}y^2 = -10\frac{1}{10}y - \frac{1}{2}$

Solution 9

a) $(x - 3)^2 = -16$

$\sqrt{(x-3)^2} = æ \sqrt{-16}$ Take the square root of both sides.

$x - 3 = \pm 4i$ $\sqrt{-16} = \sqrt{-1 \cdot 16} = 4i$

$\underline{+3 + 3}$

$x = 3 \pm 4i$ Solve for x.

b) $t^2 - 6t + 10 = 0$ $a = 1, b = -6, c = 10$

$t = \dfrac{-b \pm \sqrt{b^2 - 4ac}}{2a}$ The Quadratic Formula.

$t = \dfrac{-(6) \pm \sqrt{(-6)^2 - 4(1)(10)}}{2(1)}$ Substitute a, b, and c.

$t = \dfrac{6 \pm \sqrt{-4}}{2}$ $(-6)^2 - 4(1)(10) = 36 - 40 = -4$

$t = \dfrac{2(3 \pm 2i)}{2}$ Simplify the radical.

$$t = \frac{2(3 \pm 2i)}{2}$$

Factor the numerator.

$$t = 3 \pm i$$

Reduce the fraction.

c) $\frac{2}{5}y^2 = -10\frac{1}{10}y - \frac{1}{2}$

Write the equation in standard form.

$$+\frac{1}{10}y + \frac{1}{2} \quad +\frac{1}{10}y + \frac{1}{2}$$

$$\overline{\frac{2}{5}y^2 + \frac{1}{10}y + \frac{1}{2} = 0}$$

$$10\left(\frac{2}{5}y^2 + \frac{1}{10}y + \frac{1}{2}\right) = (10)0$$

Multiply by 10 to clear fractions.

$$4y^2 + y + 5 = 0$$

Identify $a = 4$, $b = 1$, and $c = 5$.

$$y = \frac{-b \pm \sqrt{b^2 - 4ac}}{2a}$$

Substitute a, b, and c.

$$y = \frac{-1 \pm \sqrt{-79}}{8}$$

$(1)^2 - 4(4)(5) = 1 - 80 = -79$

$$y = \frac{-1 \pm i\sqrt{79}}{8}$$

Simplify the radical.

9.5 GRAPHING QUADRATIC EQUATIONS

The graph of a linear equation in two variables is a straight line. The graph of a quadratic equation in the form $y = ax^2 + bx + c$ is a parabola.

Graphing $y = ax^2 + bx + c$

> **To Graph $y = ax^2 + bx + c$:**
> 1. Find the y-intercept by substituting $x = 0$ into the equation.
> 2. Find the x-intercepts (if possible) by substituting $y = 0$ into the equation.
> 3. Make a table of values, using enough x values to determine the shape of the parabola (usually 4 or 5 values).
> 4. The parabola opens up if $a > 0$.
>   The parabola opens down if $a < 0$.

Example 10   Graph.

a) $y = x^2$

b) $y = \frac{1}{4}x^2$

c) $y = -x^2 - 2x + 3$

Solution 10

a) $y = x^2$

If $x = 0$, $y = (0)^2$ Find the y-intercept.

         $y = 0$

If $y = 0$, $(0) = x^2$ Find the x-intercept.

         $\pm \sqrt{0} = \sqrt{x^2}$ Use the Square-Root Property to solve for x.

         $0 = x$

         $x = 0$

x	y
0	0
1	1
2	4
−1	1
2	4

Make a table of values. List the intercept in the table. Choose values for x, substitute each value into the original equation y = x 2, and solve for y.

If $x = 1$,	If $x = -1$,	If $x = 2$,	If $x = -2$,
$y = (1)^2$	$y = (-1)^2$	$y = (2)^2$	$y = (-2)^2$
$y = 1$	$y = 1$	$y = 4$	$y = 4$

To draw the graph, plot the points from your table:

Notice that the parabola $y = x^2$ opens up. When the coefficient of x^2 is positive, the parabola will open up. (Here the coefficient of $x^2 = 1x^2$ is 1.)

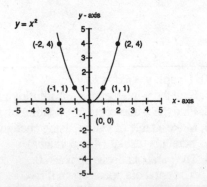

b) $y = \frac{1}{4}x^2$

If $x = 0$, $y = \frac{1}{4}(0)^2$ Find the y-intercept.

$y = 0$

If $y = 0$, $0 = \frac{1}{4}x^2$ Find the x-intercept(s).

$(0) = 4(\frac{1}{4}x^2)$ Multiply by 4 to clear fractions.

$0 = x^2$

$\pm\sqrt{0} = x$ Take the square root of both sides.

$0 = x$

x	y
0	0
–4	4
–2	1
–2	1
4	4

Make a table of values. List the intercept in the table.

If $x = -4$,   If $x = -2$,   If $x = 2$,   If $x = 4$,

$y = \frac{1}{4}(-4)^2$ $y = \frac{1}{4}(-2)^2$ $y = \frac{1}{4}(2)$ $2y = \frac{1}{4}(4)^2$

$y = \frac{1}{4}(16)$ $y = \frac{1}{4}(4)$ $y = \frac{1}{4}(4)$ $y = \frac{1}{4}(16)$

$y = 4$ $y = 1$ $y = 1$ $y = 4$

To draw the graph, plot the points from your table:

Notice that the parabola $y = \frac{1}{4}x^2$ opens up. When the coefficient of x^2 is

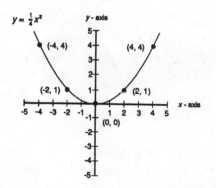

positive, the parabola will open up. (Here the coefficient of x2 is $\frac{1}{4}$.)

c) $y = -x^2 - 2x + 3$

If $x = 0$, $y = -0^2 - 2(0) + 3$ Find the y-intercept.
              $y = 3$

If $y = 0$, $0 = -x^2 - 2x + 3$ Find the x-intercepts.
              $1(0) = -1(-x^2 - 2x + 3)$ Multiply by –1 to make factoring
                                                    easier.

              $0 = x^2 + 2x - 3$ This is a quadratic equation that
                                                    factors.

              $0 = (x + 3)(x - 1)$ Factor.

$x + 3 = 0$ or $x - 1 = 0$
$\underline{-3 \; -3}$ $\underline{+1 \; +1}$ Set each factor equal to 0 and solve
$x = -3$ $x = 1$ for x.

x	y
0	3
–3	0
1	0
–1	4
–2	3

Make a table of the values. List the
intercepts in the table.

If $x = -1$,   If $x = -2$,
$y = -(-1)^2 - 2(-1) + 3$ $y = -(-2) - 2(-2) + 3$
$y = -1 + 2 + 3$ $y = -4 + 4 + 3$
$y = 4$ $y = 3$

To draw the graph, plot the points from your table:

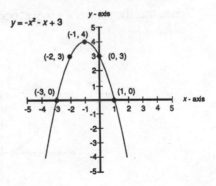

Notice that the parabola $y = -2x^2 - 2x + 3$ opens down. When the coefficient of x^2 is negative, the parabola will open down. (Here the coefficient of x^2 is –2).

Graphing $y = a(x - h)^2 + k$

If the equation of the parabola is written in the form $y = a(x - h)^2 + k$, you can use the vertex (the highest or lowest point) and the value of a to help you graph the equation.

> **Graphing Parabolas in the Form $y = a(x - h)^2 + k$:**
> 1. The vertex of the graph is the point (h, k).
> 2. If $a > 0$, the graph opens up from the vertex (h, k).
>   If $a < 0$, the graph opens down from the vertex (h, k).
> 3. If $0 < |a| < 1$, the graph is "fatter" than $y = x^2$.
>   If $|a| > 1$, the graph is "narrower" than $y = x^2$.
> 4. After you graph the vertex, select some values for x on both sides of the vertex to make a table of values.
> 5. Plot the points from your table and draw the parabola.

Example 11 Graph.

a) $y = (x - 1)^2 + 2$

b) $y = (x + 3)^2 - 1$

c) $y = -(x + 2)^2$

d) $y = x^2 - 3$

Solution 11

a) $y = (x - 1)^2 + 2$ Equation is in the form $y = a(x - h)^2 + k$, where $a = 1$, $h = 1$, and $k = 2$.

The vertex is $(1, 2)$.   Vertex is $(h, k) = (1, 2)$.

Graph opens up since $a = 1$.   Since $a > 0$, the parabola opens up.

The parabola will have the same basic shape as $y = x^2$ since $a = 1$.
Make a table of values using x values on both sides of the vertex.

x	y	
–1	6	
0	3	
1	2	Vertex
2	3	
3	6	

If $x = -1$,

$y = (x - 1)^2 + 2$

$y = ((-1) - 1)^2 + 2$

$y = (-2)^2 + 2$

$y = 4 + 2$

$y = 6$

If $x = 0$,

$y = (x - 1)^2 + 2$

$y = ((0) - 1)^2 + 2$

$y = (-1)^2 + 2$

$y = 1 + 2$

$y = 3$

If $x = 2$,

$y = (x - 1)^2 + 2$

$y = ((2) - 1)^2 + 2$

$y = (1)^2 + 2$

$y = 1 + 2$

$y = 3$

If $x = 3$,

$y = (x - 1)^2 + 2$

$y = ((3) - 1)^2 + 2$

$y = (2)^2 + 2$

$y = 4 + 2$

$y = 6$

Plot the points from your table and draw the parabola.

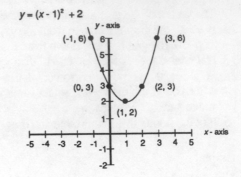

$$y = (x - 1)^2 + 2$$

b) $y = (x + 3)^2 - 1$

$y = (x + 3)^2 + (-1)$
$y = (x - (-3))^2 + (-1)$

$-1 = +(-1)$ $+3 = -(-3)$,
Rewrite in $y = a(x - h)^2 + k$ form. $a = 1$, $h = -3$, and $k = -1$.

Vertex is $(-3, -1)$.
Graph opens up since $a = 1$.

Vertex is $(h, k) = (-3, -1)$.
Since $a > 0$, the parabola opens up.

The parabola will have the same basic shape as $y = x^2$ since $a = 1$.

Make a table of values using x values on both sides of the vertex.

x	y	
-5	3	
-4	0	
-3	-1	Vertex
-2	0	
-1	3	

If $x = -5$,
$y = (x + 3)^2 - 1$
$y = ((-5) + 3)^2 - 1$
$y = (2)^2 - 1$
$y = 4 - 1$
$y = 3$

If $x = -4$,
$y = (x + 3)^2 - 1$
$y = ((-4) + 3)^2 - 1$
$y = (-1)^2 - 1$
$y = 1 - 1$
$y = 0$

If $x = -2$,
$y = (x + 3)^2 - 1$
$y = ((-2) + 3)^2 - 1$
$y = (1)^2 - 1$
$y = 1 - 1$
$y = 0$

If $x = -1$,
$y = (x + 3)^2 - 1$
$y = ((-1) + 3)^2 - 1$
$y = (2)^2 - 1$
$y = 4 - 1$
$y = 3$

Plot the points from your table and draw the parabola.

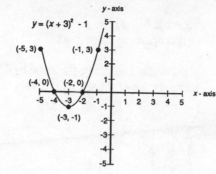

c) $y = -(x + 2)^2$
   $y = -1(x - (-2))^2 + 0$

Vertex is $(-2, 0)$.
Graph opens down since $a = -1$.

Rewrite in $y = a(x - h)^2 + k$ form.
$a = -1, h = -2, k = 0$.
Vertex is $(h, k) = (-2, 0)$.
Since $a < 0$, the parabola opens down.

The parabola will have the same basic shape as $y = x^2$ since $|a| = 1$.
Make a table of values using x values on both sides of the vertex.

x	y	
-4	-4	
-3	-1	
-2	0	Vertex
-1	-1	
0	-4	

If $x = -4$,
$y = -(x + 2)^2$
$y = -((-4) + 2)^2$
$y = -(-2)^2$
$y = -(4)$
$y = -4$

If $x = -3$,
$y = -(x + 2)^2$
$y = -((-3) + 2)^2$
$y = -(-1)^2$
$y = -(1)$
$y = -1$

If $x = -1$,
$y = -(x + 2)^2$
$y = -((-3) + 2)^2$
$y = -(1)^2$
$y = -(1)$
$y = -1$

If $x = 0$,
$y = -(x + 2)^2$
$y = -((0) + 2)^2$
$y = -(2)^2$
$y = -(4)$
$y = -4$

Plot the points from your table and draw the parabola.

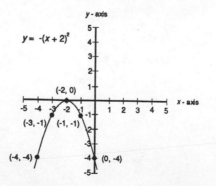

d) $y = x^2 - 3$

   $y = 1(x - 0)^2 + (-3)$ Rewrite in $y = a(x - h)^2 + k$ form.
                                      $a = 1$, $h = 0$, and $k = -3$.

   Vertex is $(0, -3)$.   Vertex is $(h, k) = (0, -3)$.
   Graph opens up since $a = 1$.   Since $a > 0$, the parabola opens up.

The parabola will have the same basic shape as $y = x^2$ since $a = 1$.
Make a table of values using x values on both sides of the vertex.

x	y	
-2	1	
-1	-2	
0	-3	Vertex
1	-2	
2	1	

If $x = -2$,   If $x = -1$,   If $x = 1$,   If $x = 2$
$y = x^2 - 3$ $y = x^2 - 3$ $y = x^2 - 3$ $y = x^2 - 3$
$y = (-2)^2 - 3$ $y = (-1)^2 - 3$ $y = (1)^2 - 3$ $y = (2)^2 - 3$
$y = 4 - 3$ $y = 1 - 3$ $y = 1 - 3$ $y = 4 - 3$
$y = 1$ $y = -2$ $y = -2$ $y = 1$

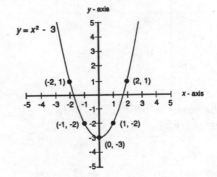

Plot the points from your table and draw the parabola.

Example 12   Graph.

   a) $y = \dfrac{1}{2}(x - 2)^2 + 3$

   b) $y = -4(x + 3)^2 + 1$

Solution 12

   a) $y = \dfrac{1}{2}(x - 2)^2 + 3$ Already in $y = a(x - h)^2 + k$ form.

                                                $a = \dfrac{1}{2}$, $h = 2$, and $k = 3$.

Vertex is (2,3).
The graph opens up.
The parabola will be fatter than $y = x^2$.

Vertex is $(h, k) = (2,3)$.
Since $a > 0$, the graph opens up.
Since $0 < |a| < 1$, the graph is fatter than $y = x^2$.

Make a table of values using x values on both sides of the vertex.

x	y	
0	5	
1	$3\frac{1}{2}$	
2	3	Vertex
3	$3\frac{1}{2}$	
4	5	

If $x = 0$,
$$y = \frac{1}{2}(x-2)^2 + 3$$
$$y = \frac{1}{2}((0)-2)^2 + 3$$
$$y = \frac{1}{2}(-2)^2 + 3$$
$$y = \frac{1}{2}(4) + 3$$
$$y = 2 + 3$$
$$y = 5$$

If $x = 1$,
$$y = \frac{1}{2}(x-2)^2 + 3$$
$$y = \frac{1}{2}((1)-2)^2 + 3$$
$$y = \frac{1}{2}(-1)^2 + 3$$
$$y = \frac{1}{2}(1) + 3$$
$$y = \frac{1}{2} + 3$$
$$y = 3\frac{1}{2}$$

If $x = 3$,
$$y = \frac{1}{2}(x-2)^2 + 3$$
$$y = \frac{1}{2}((3)-2)^2 + 3$$
$$y = \frac{1}{2}(1)^2 + 3$$
$$y = \frac{1}{2}(1) + 3$$
$$y = \frac{1}{2} + 3$$
$$y = 3\frac{1}{2}$$

If $x = 4$,
$$y = \frac{1}{2}(x-2)^2 + 3$$
$$y = \frac{1}{2}((4)-2)^2 + 3$$
$$y = \frac{1}{2}(2)^2 + 3$$
$$y = \frac{1}{2}(4) + 3$$
$$y = 2 + 3$$
$$y = 5$$

Plot the points from your table and draw the parabola.

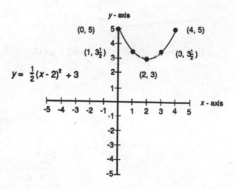

b) $y = -4(x + 3)^2 + 1$
   $y = -4(x - (-3))^2 + 1$

Write in $y = a(x - h)^2 + k$ form.
$a = -4$, $h = -3$, and $k = 1$.

Vertex is (–3, 1).
Graph opens down.

Vertex is $(h, k) = (-3, 1)$.
Since $a < 0$, the parabola opens down.

The graph is narrower than $y = x^2$.

Since $|a| > 1$, the graph is narrower than $y = x^2$

Make a table of values:

x	y	
–5	–15	
–4	–3	
–3	1	Vertex
–2	–3	
–1	–15	

If $x = -5$,
$y = -4(x + 3)^2 + 1$
$y = -4((-5) + 3)^2 + 1$

If $x = -4$,
$y = -4(x + 3)^2 + 1$
$y = -4((-4) + 3)^2 + 1$

Original equation.
Substitute x values into the original equation.

$y = -4(-2)^2 + 1$
$y = -4(4) + 1$
$y = -16 + 1$
$y = -15$

$y = -4(-1)^2 + 1$
$y = -4(1) + 1$
$y = -4 + 1$
$y = -3$

Simplify inside parentheses first.
Simplify exponents.
Multiply before adding.

If $x = -2$,
$y = -4(x + 3)^2 + 1$
$y = -4((-2) + 3)^2 + 1$

If $x = -1$,
$y = -4(x + 3)^2 + 1$
$y = -4((-1) + 3)^2 + 1$

Original equation.
Substitute x values into the original equation.

$y = -4(1)^2 + 1$
$y = -4(1) + 1$
$y = -4 + 1$
$y = -3$

$y = -4(2)^2 + 1$
$y = -4(4) + 1$
$y = -16 + 1$
$y = -15.$

Simplify inside parentheses first.
Simplify exponents.
Multiply before adding.

Plot the points from your table and draw the parabola.

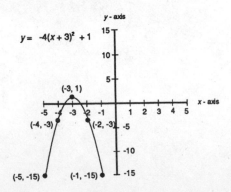

Writing an equation in $y = a(x - h)^2 + k$ form

You may need to use completing the square to write the equation in $y = a(x-h)^2 + k$ form. Study the following example.

Example 13 Find the vertex for the following.

a) $y = x^2 - 6x + 4$
b) $y = x^2 + 4x - 6$

Solution 13

a) $y = x^2 - 6x + 4$

$$y = x^2 - 6x + 4$$

Isolate $x^2 - 6x$.

$$\underline{-4 \qquad\quad -4}$$

$$y - 4 = x^2 - 6x$$

$$\left(\frac{1}{2} \cdot -6\right)^2 = (-3)^2 = 9$$

$$y - 4 + 9 = x^2 - 6x + 9$$
$$y + 5 = x^2 - 6x + 9$$

Add 9 to both sides.

Factor $x^2 - 6x + 9$.

$$y + 5 = (x - 3)^2$$

$$\underline{-5 \qquad\quad -5}$$

$$y = (x - 3)^2 - 5$$

Write in $y = a(x - h)^2 + k$ form.

$$y = (x - 3)^2 + (-5)$$

Vertex is $(3, -5)$.

Vertex is $(h,k) = (3, -5)$.

b) $y = x^2 + 4x - 6$

$$y = x^2 + 4x - 6$$

Isolate $x^2 + 4x$.

$$\underline{+6 \qquad\quad +6}$$

$$y + 6 = x^2 + 4x$$

$$\left(\frac{1}{2} \cdot 4\right)^2 = (2)^2 = 4$$

$$y + 6 + 4 = x^2 + 4x + 4$$
$$y + 10 = (x + 2)^2$$

Add 4 to both sides.
Factor $x^2 + 4x + 4$.

$$y + 10 = (x + 2)^2$$

$$-10 \qquad\quad -10$$

Write in $y = a(x - h)^2 + k$ form.

$$y = (x + 2)^2 - 10$$

$$y = (x - (-2))^2 + (-10)$$

Vertex is $(-2, -10)$.

Vertex is $(h, k) = (-2, -10)$.

Practice Exercises

1. Solve.
   (a) $x^2 = 100$
   (b) $(x+3)^2 = 36$
   (c) $25m^2 - 6 = 42$
   (d) $(x-2)^2 = -25$

2. Solve by completing the square.
   (a) $x^2 + 2x - 15 = 0$
   (b) $x2 + x - 12 = 0$
   (c) $x2 - 10x - 2 = 0$

3. Solve by completing the square.
   (a) $2x^2 + 12x - 22 = 0$
   (b) $3x^2 - 15x - 3 = 0$
   (c) $x^2 + 10x + 57 = 0$

4. Solve using the quadratic formula.
   (a) $x^2 + 4x - 12 = 0$
   (b) $x^2 - 8x - 12 = 0$
   (c) $x^2 = 3x + 9$
   (d) $\frac{1}{5}x^2 - x = 1$

5. Simplify.
   (a) $\sqrt{-11}$
   (b) $\sqrt{-128}$
   (c) $\sqrt{-49}$

6. Add or subtract, as indicated.
   (a) $(5 + 3i) + (2 - 11i)$
   (b) $(2 - 7i) - (8 - i)$
   (c) $(3 + 2i) - (4 - 5i) - (6 + i)$

7. Multiply.
   (a) $3i(2 + 5i)$
   (b) $(4 - 3i)(2 + 5i)$
   (c) $(3 - 2i)(3 + 2i)$

8. Write each quotient in standard form.
   (a) $\frac{5 + 2i}{3i}$
   (b) $\frac{1 - 4i}{3 - 2i}$
   (c) $\frac{4}{2 + i}$

9. Solve each quadratic equation.
   (a) $(x + 2)^2 = -25$
   (b) $x^2 - 8x + 43 = 0$
   (c) $\frac{1}{6}x^2 = x - \frac{25}{6})$

10. Graph.
    (a) $y = (x + 1)^2$
    (b) $y = (x - 2)^2 + 1$
    (c) $y = x^2 + 3$

Answers

1. (a) ± 10
   (b) $-9, 3$
   (c) $\pm \dfrac{4\sqrt{3}}{5}$
   (d) no real solutions

2. (a) $-5, 3$
   (b) $-4, 3$
   (c) $5 \pm 3\sqrt{3}$

3. (a) $-3 \pm 2\sqrt{5}$
   (b) $\dfrac{5 \pm \sqrt{29}}{2}$
   (c) no real solutions

4. (a) $-6, 2$
   (b) $4 \pm 2\sqrt{7}$
   (c) $\dfrac{3 \pm 3\sqrt{5}}{2}$
   (d) $\dfrac{5 \pm 3\sqrt{5}}{2}$

5. (a) $i\sqrt{11}$
   (b) $8i\sqrt{2}$
   (c) $7i$

6. (a) $7 - 8i$
   (b) $-6 - 6i$
   (c) $-7 + 6i$

7. (a) $-15 + 6i$
   (b) $23 + 14i$
   (c) 13

8. (a) $\dfrac{2}{3} - \dfrac{5}{3}i$
   (b) $\dfrac{11}{13} - \dfrac{10}{13}i$
   (c) $\dfrac{8}{5} - \dfrac{4}{5}i$

9. (a) $-2 \pm 5i$
   (b) $4 \pm 3i\sqrt{3}$
   (c) $3 \pm 4i$

10. (a)

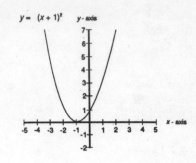

b)

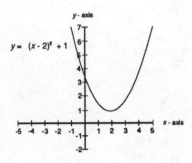

c)

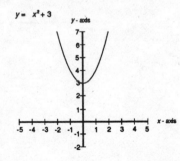

Index

N

Natural numbers, 4
Number(s)
  complex. *See* Complex numbers
  imaginary, 277–278
  irrational, 4, 239
  natural, 4
  rational. *See* Rational numbers
  real. *See* Real numbers
  signed. *See* Signed numbers
  systems of, 4–5
  whole, 4
  writing, in expanded form,
    84–85
  writing, in scientific notation,
    83–84
Number line, 5–6
Number problems, solving, 57–58,
  169–170, 227
Numerator, 4
Numerical coefficient, 41, 88

O

Operations, order of. *See* Order of
  operations
Order of operations, 10–11
  and division, 21–22
  and multiplication, 18
Ordered pairs, 178–179
  graphing, 182–183
  as solution to system of linear
    equations, 213–214
Origin, 182

P

Parabola, graphing, 282–291
Parallel lines, 201–202
Perfect square trinominal, 123
Perimeter of a square, 61
Perpendicular lines, 201–202
Polynomial(s), 88
  adding, 89–90
  dividing, 99–103
  factoring special, 123–132
  multiplying, 91–94
  subtracting, 90–91
  vocabulary for, 88–89
Positive integer exponents, 74–78
  exponent laws for, 75–78
Product, 4

Proportions, 162–164
Pythagorean theorem, 136

Q

Quadratic equations
  graphing, 282–292
  solving by completing the
    square, 267–273
  solving by quadratic formula,
    273–276
  solving, by square root method,
    264–267
  solving factorable, 132–134
  solving with complex solutions,
    281–282
Quadratic formula, 273
  solving quadratic equations by,
    273–276
Quotient, 4

R

Radical expressions
  adding, 247–249
  dividing, 255–259
  multiplying, 250–254
  roots and radicals in, 238–240
  simplifying, 241–247
  solving equations containing,
    259–261
  subtracting, 247–249
Radical sign, 238
Radicals, 238–240
Radicand, 238
Rational expressions
  adding, 152–156
  applications, 168–174
  dividing, 146–149
  multiplying, 146–149
  reducing, 142–146
  solving equations containing,
    164–168
  subtracting, 152–156
  writing, using the least common
    multiple, 149–152
Rational number(s), 4, 239
  least common denominator in,
    29–31
  operations using, 27–34
Rationalizing the denominator,
  255–259
Ratios, 161–162

Real numbers, 5, 23, 239
  adding, 12–14
  associative property of, 23–24
  combining two or more proper-
    ties, 26–27
  commutative property of, 23–24
  distributive property of, 25–26
  dividing, 19–22
  identity property of, 24–25
  inverse property of, 24–25
  multiplying, 17–18
  subtracting, 15–16
Reciprocal, 50
Rectangle, area of, 61, 136
Remainder, 4
Roots, 238–240

S

Scientific notation, 83
  using exponent laws with, 86–87
  writing numbers in, 83–84
Signed numbers, 5–6
  and grouping symbols, 14
  multiplication of, 17, 19
Similar radicals, 247
Similar terms, 41, 88
Simplifying, 3
  expressions, 43–44
  radical expressions, 241–247
Slope, 189–193
  graphing using, 193–195
  of parallel lines, 201–202
  of perpendicular lines, 201–202
Slope-intercept, 198
  using, to graph linear equations,
    199–201
Solution, 46
Special products, 252–253
Square, perimeter of, 61
Square root, 239, 240
Square root method, solving
  quadratic equations using,
    264–267
Square root property, 264
Squaring binomial, 96–97
Standard form, 198
Substitution, solving systems of
  linear equations by,
    223–226
Subtraction, 2
  of complex numbers, 278
  of fractions, 31–34